HANDBOOK OF AGRICULTURAL TECHNOLOGY

HANDBOOK OF AGRICULTURAL TECHNOLOGY

By

Dr. H. Shivanna

Professor & Head
Deptt. of Forest Biology & Tree Improvement
College of Forestry
SIRSI, Uttar Kannada
Karnataka (India)

DPH

DISCOVERY PUBLISHING HOUSE PVT. LTD.
NEW DELHI-110 002

Published by:
Tilak Wasan

DISCOVERY PUBLISHING HOUSE PVT. LTD.
4383/4A, Ansari Road, Darya Ganj
New Delhi-110 002 (India)
Phone : +91-11-23279245, 43596064-65
Fax : +91-11-23253475
E-mail : parul.wasan@gmail.com
discoverypublishinghouse@gmail.com
web : www.discoverypublishinggroup.com

***First Edition:* 2012**

ISBN: 978-93-5056-090-7

Handbook of Agricultural Technology

Printed at:
Shree Balaji Art Press
Delhi

Preface

Agriculture was developed at least 10,000 years ago, and it has undergone significant developments since the time of the earliest cultivation. Evidence points to the Fertile Crescent of the Middle East as the site of the earliest planned sowing and harvesting of plants that had previously been gathered in the wild. Independent development of agriculture is also believed to have occurred in northern and southern China, Africa's Sahel, New Guinea and several regions of the Americas. Agricultural practices such as irrigation, crop rotation, fertilizers, and pesticides were developed long ago but have made great strides in the past century. The Haber-Bosch method for synthesizing ammonium nitrate represented a major breakthrough and allowed crop yields to overcome previous constraints.

In the past century, agriculture has been characterized by enhanced productivity, the replacement of human labour by synthetic fertilizers and pesticides, selective breeding, and mechanization. The recent history of agriculture has been closely tied with a range of political issues including water pollution, biofuels, genetically modified organisms, tariffs, and farm subsidies. In recent years, there has been a backlash against the external environmental effects of mechanized agriculture, and increasing support for the organic movement and sustainable agriculture.

Scholars have proposed a number of theories to explain the historical development of farming. Most likely, there was a gradual transition from hunter-gatherer to agricultural societies after a lengthy period during which some crops were deliberately planted and other foods were gathered in the wild. Although localised climate change is the favoured explanation for the origins of agriculture in the Levant, the fact that farming was 'invented' at least three times elsewhere, suggests that social reasons may have been instrumental. When major climate change took place after the last ice age (c.11,000 BC), much of the earth became subject to long dry seasons. These conditions favoured annual plants which die off in the long dry season, leaving a dormant seed or tuber. These plants tended to put more energy into producing seeds than into woody growth. An abundance of readily storable wild grains and pulses enabled hunter-gatherers in some areas to form the first settled villages at this time.

The Oasis Theory was proposed by Raphael Pumpelly in 1908, and popularized by Vere Gordon Childe who summarized the theory in his book *'Man Makes Himself'*. This theory maintains that as the climate got drier, communities contracted to oases where they were forced into close association with animals which were then domesticated together with planting of seeds. The theory has little support from contemporary scholars, as the climate data for the time does not support the theory.

The Hilly Flanks hypothesis, proposed by Robert Braidwood in 1948, suggests that agriculture began in the hilly flanks of the Taurus and Zagros mountains, and that it developed from intensive focussed grain gathering in the region.

The Feasting model by Bryan Hayden suggests that agriculture was driven by ostentatious displays of power, such as throwing feasts to exert dominance. This required assembling large quantities of food which drove agricultural technology.

Author

Contents

1 Introduction

Agriculture was developed at least 10,000 years ago, and it has undergone significant developments since the time of the earliest cultivation. Evidence points to the Fertile Crescent of the Middle East as the site of the earliest planned sowing and harvesting of plants that had previously been gathered in the wild. Independent development of agriculture is also believed to have occurred in northern and southern China, Africa's Sahel, New Guinea and several regions of the Americas. Agricultural practices such as irrigation, crop rotation, fertilizers, and pesticides were developed long ago but have made great strides in the past century. The Haber-Bosch method for synthesizing ammonium nitrate represented a major breakthrough and allowed crop yields to overcome previous constraints.

In the past century, agriculture has been characterized by enhanced productivity, the replacement of human labour by synthetic fertilizers and pesticides, selective breeding, and mechanization. The recent history of agriculture has been closely tied with a range of political issues including water pollution, biofuels, genetically modified organisms, tariffs, and farm subsidies. In recent years, there has been a backlash against the external environmental effects of mechanized agriculture, and increasing support for the organic movement and sustainable agriculture.

Scholars have proposed a number of theories to explain the historical development of farming. Most likely, there was a gradual transition from hunter-gatherer to agricultural societies after a lengthy period during which some crops were deliberately planted and other foods were gathered in the wild. Although localised climate change is the favoured explanation for the origins of agriculture in the Levant, the fact that farming was 'invented' at least three times elsewhere, suggests that social reasons may have been instrumental. When major climate change took place after the last ice age (c.11,000 BC), much of the earth became subject to long dry seasons. These conditions favoured annual plants which die off in the long dry season, leaving a dormant seed or tuber. These plants tended to put more energy into producing seeds than into woody growth. An abundance of readily storable wild grains and pulses enabled hunter-gatherers in some areas to form the first settled villages at this time.

The Oasis Theory was proposed by Raphael Pumpelly in 1908, and popularized by Vere Gordon Childe who summarized the theory in his book. *'Man Makes Himself'*. This theory maintains that as the climate got drier, communities contracted to oases where they were forced into close association with animals which were then domesticated together with planting of seeds. The theory has little support from contemporary scholars, as the climate data for the time does not support the theory.

The Hilly Flanks hypothesis, proposed by Robert Braidwood in 1948, suggests that agriculture began in the hilly flanks of the Taurus and Zagros mountains, and that it developed from intensive focussed grain gathering in the region.

The Feasting model by Bryan Hayden suggests that agriculture was driven by ostentatious displays of power, such as throwing feasts to exert dominance. This required assembling large quantities of food which drove agricultural technology.

The Demographic theories were proposed by Carl Sauer and adapted by Lewis Binford and Kent Flannery. They describe an increasingly sedentary population, expanding up to the carrying capacity of the local environment, and requiring more food than can be gathered. Various social and economic factors help drive the need for food.

The evolutionary/intentionality theory, advanced by scholars including David Rindos, is the idea that agriculture is a co-evolutionary adaptation of plants and humans. Starting with domestication by protection of wild plants, followed specialization of location and then domestication.

Identifying the exact origin of agriculture remains problematic because the transition from hunter-gatherer societies began thousands of years before the invention of writing.

Anthropological and archaeological evidence from sites across Southwest Asia and North Africa indicate use of wild grain (e.g., from the ca. 20,000 BC site of Ohalo II in Israel, many Natufian sites in the Levant and from sites along the Nile in the 10th millennium BC). There is even evidence of planned cultivation and trait selection: grains of rye with domestic traits have been recovered from Epi-Palaeolithic contexts at Abu Hureyra in Syria, but this appears to be a localised phenomenon resulting from cultivation of stands of wild rye, rather than a definitive step towards domestication.

Previously, archaeobotanists/paleoethnobotanists had traced the selection and cultivation of specific food plant characteristics in search of the origins of agriculture. One notable example is the semi-tough rachis (and larger seeds) traced to just after the Younger Dryas (about 9500 BC) in the early Holocene in the Levant region of the Fertile Crescent. However, studies have demonstrated monophyletic characteristics attained without any sort human intervention, implying that what some may perceive as domestication among rachis could have occurred quite naturally. In fact, the timescale insisted upon for rachis domestication (approx. 3000 years) coincidentally has been demonstrated to directly coincide with the statistically generated timeframe numerically modeled that would be required for monophyly to be reached if a population were simply abandoned and left to only natural demands, implying that if any sort of human intervention had occurred at all then the timescale insisted upon should be considerably shorter (than 3000 years).

It was not until after 9500 BC that the eight so-called founder crops of agriculture appear: first emmer and einkorn wheat, then hulled barley, peas, lentils, bitter vetch, chick peas and flax. These eight crops occur more or less simultaneously on PPNB sites in the Levant, although the consensus is that wheat was the first to be grown and harvested on a significant scale.

At around the same time (9400 BC), another study argues, parthenocarpic fig trees appear to have been domesticated. The simplicity associated with cutting branches off fig trees and replanting them alongside wild cereals owes to the basis of this argument.

By 7000 BC, sowing and harvesting reached Mesopotamia, and there, in the fertile soil just north of the Persian Gulf, Sumerians systematized it and scaled it up. By 8000 BC farming was entrenched on the banks of the Nile River. About this time, agriculture was developed independently in the Far East, probably in China, with rice rather than wheat as the primary crop. Maize was first domesticated, probably from teosinte, in the Americas around 3000-2700 BC, though there is some archaeological evidence of a much older development. The potato, the tomato, the pepper, squash, several varieties of bean, and several other plants were also developed in the New World, as was quite extensive terracing of steep hillsides in much of Andean South America. Agriculture was also independently developed on the island of New Guinea.

In Europe, there is evidence of emmer and einkorn wheat, barley, sheep, goats and pigs that suggest a food producing economy in Greece and the Aegean by 7000 BC. Archaeological evidence from various sites on the Iberian peninsula suggest the domestication of plants and animals between 6000 and 4500 BC. Céide Fields in Ireland, consisting of extensive tracts of land enclosed by stone walls, date to 5500 BC and are the oldest known field systems in the world. The horse was domesticated in Ukraine around 4000 BC.

In China, rice and millet were domesticated by 8000 BC, followed by the beans mung, soy and azuki. In the Sahel region of Africa local rice and sorghum were domestic by 5000 BC. Local crops were domesticated independently in West Africa and possibly in New Guinea and Ethiopia. Evidence of the presence of wheat and some legumes in the 6th millennium BC have been found in the Indus Valley. Oranges were cultivated in the same millennium. The crops grown in the valley around 4000 BC were typically wheat, peas, sesame seed, barley, dates and mangoes. By 3500 BC cotton growing and cotton textiles were quite advanced in the valley. By 3000 BC farming of rice had started. Other monsoon crops of importance of the time was cane sugar. By 2500 BC, rice was an important component of the staple diet in Mohenjodaro near the Arabian Sea. By this time the Indians had large cities with well-stocked granaries. Three regions of the Americas independently domesticated corn, squashes, potato and sunflowers.

By the Bronze Age, wild food contributed a nutritionally insignificant component to the usual diet. If the operative definition of *agriculture* includes large scale intensive cultivation of land, mono-cropping, organized irrigation, and use of a specialized labour force, the title 'inventors of agriculture' would fall to the Sumerians, starting ca. 5,500 BC. Intensive farming allows a much greater density of population than can be supported by hunting and gathering, and allows for the accumulation of excess product for off-season use, or to sell/barter. The ability of farmers to feed large numbers of people whose activities have nothing to do with agriculture was the crucial factor in the rise of standing armies. Sumerian agriculture supported a substantial territorial expansion which along with internecine conflict between cities, made them the first empire builders. Not long after, the Egyptians, powered by farming in the fertile Nile valley, achieved a population density from which enough warriors could be drawn for a territorial expansion more than tripling the Sumerian empire in area.

In Sumer, barley was the primary crop; wheat, flax, dates, apples, plums, and grapes were grown as well. Mesopotamian agriculture was both supported and limited by flooding from the Tigris and Euphrates rivers, as floods came in late spring or early summer from snow melting from the Anatolian mountains. The timing of the flooding, along with salt deposits in the soil, made farming in Mesopotamia difficult. Sheep and goats were domesticated, kept mainly for meat and milk, butter and cheese being made from the latter. Ur, a large town that covered about 50 acres (20 hectares), had 10,000 animals kept in sheepfolds and stables and 3,000 slaughtered every year. The city's population of 6,000 included a labour force of 2,500, cultivated 3,000 acres (12 km^2) of land. The labour force contained storehouse recorders, work foremen, overseers, and harvest supervisors to supplement labourers. Agricultural produce was given to temple personnel, important people in the community, and small farmers.

The land was plowed by teams of oxen pulling light unwheeled plows and grain was harvested with sickles in the spring. Wagons had solid wheels covered by leather tires kept in position by copper nails and were drawn by oxen and the Syrian onager (now extinct). Animals were harnessed by collars, yokes, and headstalls. They were controlled by reins, and a ring through the nose or upper lip and a strap under the jaw. As many as four animals could pull a wagon at one time. The horse was domesticated in Ukraine around 4000 BC, and was in use by the Sumerians around 2000 BC.

Classical Antiquity

In classical antiquity, Roman agriculture built off techniques pioneered by the Sumerians, transmitted to them by subsequent cultures, with a specific emphasis on the cultivation of crops for trade and export. Romans laid the groundwork for the manorial economic system, involving serfdom, which flourished in the Middle Ages. The farm sizes in Rome can be divided into three categories. Small farms were from 18-88 iugera (one iugera is equal to about 0.65 acre). Medium-sized farms were from 80-500 iugera (singular iugerum). Large estates (called latifundia) were over 500 iugera.

The Romans had four systems of farm management: direct work by owner and his family; slaves doing work under supervision of slave managers; tenant farming or sharecropping in which the owner and a tenant divide up a farm's produce; and situations in which a farm was leased to a tenant. There was a great deal of commerce between the provinces of the empire, all the regions of the empire became interdependent with one another, some provinces specialized in the production of grain, others in wine and others in olive oil, depending on the soil type.

REGIONAL HISTORIES

Europe

European agriculture underwent a number of significant changes during the Middle Ages. Tools including the scythe and plow were improved from classical versions, a three field system of crop rotation was invented, and the moldboard plow and wheeled plow were increasingly used. Draft horses were bred and increasingly used as a working animal in many parts of Europe, while oxen continued to be used for this purpose. Metal horseshoes were widely adopted. Much of Europe had low population densities during this period, to which extensive farming was well-suited. In parts of Southern Europe, more intensive farming combined techniques continued from classical Roman agriculture and those transferred from Islamic regions. In the late Middle Ages, the use of manure as fertilizer increased, which in turn decreased the necessity of regular fallowing of fields.

China

Records from the Warring States (481 BC-221 BC), Qin Dynasty (221 BC-207 BC), and Han Dynasty (202 BC-220 AD) provide a picture of early Chinese agriculture which included a nation-wide granary system, and widespread use of sericulture. However, the oldest extant Chinese book on agriculture is the *Chimin Yaoshu* of 535 AD, written by Jia Sixia. Jia's writing style was straightforward and lucid relative to the elaborate and allusive writing typical of the time. Jia's book was also very long, with over one hundred thousand written Chinese characters, and it quoted 160 other Chinese books that were written previously (but no longer survive). The contents of Jia's 6th century book include sections on land preparation, seeding, cultivation, orchard management, forestry, and animal husbandry. The book also includes peripherally related content covering trade and culinary uses for crops. The work and the style in which it was written proved influential on later Chinese agronomists, such as Wang Zhen and his groundbreaking *Nong Shu* of 1313 AD.

For agricultural purposes, the Chinese had innovated the hydraulic-powered trip hammer by the 1st century BC. Although it found other purposes, its main function to pound, decorticate, and polish grain that otherwise would have been done manually. The Chinese also innovated the square-pallet chain pump by the 1st century AD, powered by a waterwheel or an oxen pulling a on a system of mechanical wheels. Although the chain pump found use in public works of providing water for urban and palatial pipe systems, it was used largely to lift water from a lower to higher elevation in filling irrigation canals and channels for farmland.

Papua

Ancient Papuans are thought to have begun practicing agriculture around 7000 BC. They began domesticating sugarcane and root crops. Pigs may also have been domesticated around this time. By 3000 BC, Papuan agriculture was characterized by water control for irrigation.

India

Wheat, barley, and jujube were domesticated in the Indian subcontinent by 9000 BCE; Domestication of sheep and goat soon followed. Barley and wheat cultivation—along with the domestication of cattle, primarily sheep and goat–continued in Mehrgarh culture by 8000-6000 BCE. This period also saw the first domestication of the elephant. Agro pastoralism in India included threshing, planting crops in rows—either of two or of six–and storing grain in granaries. By the 5th millennium BCE agricultural communities became widespread in Kashmir. Cotton was cultivated by the 5th millennium BCE-4th millennium BCE.

Archaeological evidence indicates that rice was a part of the Indian diet by 8000 BCE The Encyclopedia Britannica—on the subject of the first certain cultivated rice–holds that: A number of cultures have evidence of early rice cultivation, including China, India, and the civilizations of Southeast Asia.

Irrigation was developed in the Indus Valley Civilization by around 4500 BCE. The size and prosperity of the Indus civilization grew as a result of this innovation, which eventually led to more planned settlements making use of drainage and sewers. Archaeological evidence of an animal-drawn plough dates back to 2500 BC in the Indus Valley Civilization.

Mesoamerica

In Mesoamerica, wild teosinte was transformed through human selection into the ancestor of modern maize, more than 6000 years ago. It gradually spread across North America and was the major crop of Native Americans at the time of European exploration. Other Mesoamerican crops include hundreds of varieties of squash and beans. Cocoa was also a major crop in domesticated Mexico and Central America. The turkey, one of the most important meat birds, was probably domesticated in Mexico or the U.S. Southwest.

In Mesoamerica, the Aztecs were active farmers and had an agriculturally focused economy. The land around Lake Texcoco was fertile, but not large enough to produce the amount of food needed for the population of their expanding empire. The Aztecs developed irrigation systems, formed terraced hillsides, and fertilized their soil. However, their greatest agricultural technique was the chinampas, or artificial islands, also known as 'floating gardens'. These were used to make the swampy areas around the lake suitable for farming. To make chinampas, canals were dug through the marshy islands and shores, then mud was heaped on huge mats made of woven reeds. The mats were anchored by tying them to posts driven into the lake bed and then planting trees at their corners that took root and secured the artificial islands permanently. The Aztecs grew corn, squash, vegetables, and flowers on chinampas.

South America

In the Andes region of South America the major domesticated crop was potatoes, domesticated perhaps 5000 years ago. Large varieties of beans were domesticated, in South America, as well as animals, including llamas, alpacas, and guinea pigs. Coca, still a major crop, was also domesticated in the Andes.

The Andean civilizations were predominantly agricultural societies; the Incas took advantage of the ground, conquering the adversities like the Andean area and the inclemencies of the weather. The adaptation of agricultural technologies that already were used previously, allowed the Incas to organize the production a diversity of products of the coast, mountain and jungle, so them could be able to redistribute to villages that did not have access to other regions. The technological achievements reached to agricultural level, had not been possible without the workforce that was at the disposal of the Sapa Inca, as well as the road system that was allowing to store adequately the harvested resources and to distribute them for all the territory.

Eastern North America

The indigenous people of the Eastern U.S. appear to have domesticated numerous crops. Sunflowers, tobacco, varieties of squash and Chenopodium, as well as crops no longer grown, including marshelder and little barley, were domesticated. Other wild foods may have undergone some selective cultivation, including wild rice and maple sugar. The most common varieties of strawberry were domesticated from Eastern North America. Two major crops, pecans and Concord grapes, were utilized extensively in prehistoric times but do not appear to have been domesticated until the 19th century.

Islamic World

From the 8th century, the mediaeval Islamic world underwent a fundamental transformation in agricultural practice which has been described as the 'Arab Agricultural Revolution'. This transformation was driven by a number of factors including the diffusion of many crops and plants along Muslim trade routes, the spread of more advanced farming techniques, and an agricultural-economic system which promoted increased yields and efficiency. The shift in agricultural practice led to significant changes in economy, population distribution, vegetation cover, agricultural production, population levels, urban growth, the distribution of the labour force, linked industries, cooking and diet, clothing, and numerous other aspects of life in the Islamic world.

Muslim traders covered an expansive area of the Old World, and these trade routes enabled the diffusion of many crops, plants and farming techniques across the Islamic world, as well as the adaptation of crops, plants and techniques from beyond the Islamic world. Historian Andrew Watson has argued that this diffusion introduced a number of crops of major importance to Europe by way of Al-Andalus, along with the techniques for their cultivation. Important crops involved in this transfer included sugar cane, rice, and cotton. A number of additional fruit trees, nut trees, and vegetables were also transferred.

Agricultural technologies that were widely adopted during this period included intensive irrigation systems, crop rotation systems, and use of agricultural manuals. A sophisticated system of irrigation made use of norias, water mills, water raising machines, dams and reservoirs. Some irrigation infrastructure and technology was continued from Roman times, and some introduced by Muslims. In later centuries, Persian Muslims transmitted cultural elements, including advanced agricultural techniques, into Turkic lands and western India. These irrigation technologies made it possible to greatly expand the cultivatable land area. Application of a scientific approach and accumulated knowledge from other regions to farming lead to improved farming techniques. Farming manuals from this period detail where, when, and how to plant and grow various crops.

The economic system in place in Muslim areas incorporated reformed land ownership rules and labourers' rights, combining the recognition of private ownership and the rewarding of cultivators with a harvest share commensurate with their efforts also improved agricultural practices. The cities of the Near East, North Africa and Moorish Spain were supported by highly structured agricultural systems. Such regional systems were in many cases significantly more productive than the agricultural practices in most of Europe at the time which relied heavily on grazing animals and systems of fallowing.

Britain

Between the 16th century and the mid-19th century, Great Britain saw a massive increase in agricultural productivity and net output. New agricultural practices like enclosure, mechanization, four-field crop rotation and selective breeding enabled an unprecedented population growth, freeing up a significant percentage of the workforce, and thereby helped drive the Industrial Revolution. By the early 19th century, agricultural practices, particularly careful selection of hardy strains and cultivars, had so improved that yield per land unit was many times that seen in the Middle Ages and before.

The 18th and 19th centuries also saw the development of glasshouses, or greenhouses, initially for the protection and cultivation of exotic plants imported to Europe and North America from the tropics. Experiments on Plant Hybridization in the late 19th century yielded advances in the understanding of plant genetics, and subsequently, the development of hybrid crops. Increasing dependence upon monoculture crops lead to famines and food shortages, most notably the Irish Potato Famine (1845-1849). Storage silos and grain elevators appeared in the 19th century.

The history of agriculture in the Age of Discovery and Early modern era was closely tied to the processes of European exploration and colonization. After 1492 the world's agricultural patterns were shuffled in the widespread exchange of plants and animals known as the Columbian Exchange. Crops and animals that were previously only known in the Old World were now transplanted to the New and vice versa. Perhaps most notably, the tomato became a favourite in European cuisine, and maize and potatoes were widely adopted. Other transplanted crops include pineapple, cocoa, and tobacco. In the other direction, several wheat strains quickly took to western hemisphere soils and became a dietary staple even for native North, Central and South Americans. Agriculture was a key element in the Atlantic slave trade, Triangular trade, and the expansion by European powers into the Americas. In the expanding Plantation economy, large plantations producing crops including sugar, cotton, and indigo, were heavily dependent upon slave labour.

With the rapid rise of mechanization in the late 19th century and 20th century, particularly in the form of the tractor, and later the Combine harvester, farming tasks could be done with a speed and on a scale previously impossible. These advances, joined to science-driven innovations in methods and resources, have led to efficiencies enabling certain modern farms in the United States, Argentina, Israel, Germany and a few other nations to output volumes of high quality produce per land unit at what may be the practical limit. The development of rail and highway networks and the increasing use of container shipping and refrigeration in developed nations have also been essential to the growth of mechanized agriculture, allowing for the economical long distance shipping of produce.

While chemical fertilizer and pesticide have existed since the 19th century, their use grew significantly in the early 20th century. Until the development of chemical fertilizers, Guano was widely used as a fertilizer, though expensive. The Haber-Bosch method for synthesizing ammonium nitrate represented a major breakthrough and allowed crop yields to overcome previous constraints. It was first patented by German chemist Fritz Haber. In 1910 Carl Bosch, while working for German chemical company BASF, successfully commercialized the process and secured further patents. Norman Borlaug and other scientists began developing crops for increased yields in the 1940s in Mexico. Their work lead to the Green Revolution, which applied western advances in fertilizer and pesticide use to farms worldwide, with varying success. Other applications of scientific research since 1950 in agriculture include gene manipulation, Hydroponics, and the development of economically viable biofuels such as Ethanol.

Though the intensive farming practices pioneered and extended in recent history generally led to increased outputs, they have also led to the destruction of farmland, most notably in the dust bowl area of the United States following World War I. As global population increases, agriculture continues to replace natural ecosystems with monoculture crops. Since the 1970s, western farmers and consumers have become increasingly aware of, and in some cases critical of, widely used intensive agriculture practices. This growing awareness has led to increased interest in such areas of agriculture as organic farming, permaculture, Heirloom plants and biodiversity, the growth of the Slow Food movement, and an ongoing discussion surrounding the potential for sustainable agriculture.

2 Agricultural Techniques

Agriculture encompasses a wide variety of specialties and techniques, including ways to expand the lands suitable for plant raising, by digging water-channels and other forms of irrigation. Cultivation of crops on arable land and the pastoral herding of livestock on rangeland remain at the foundation of agriculture. In the past century there has been increasing concern to identify and quantify various forms of agriculture. In the developed world the range usually extends between sustainable agriculture (e.g. permaculture or organic agriculture) and intensive farming (e.g. industrial agriculture).

Modern agronomy, plant breeding, pesticides and fertilizers, and technological improvements have sharply increased yields from cultivation, but at the same time have caused widespread ecological damage and negative human health effects. Selective breeding and modern practices in animal husbandry such as intensive pig farming (and similar practices applied to the chicken) have similarly increased the output of meat, but have raised concerns about animal cruelty and the health effects of the antibiotics, growth hormones, and other chemicals commonly used in industrial meat production.

The major agricultural products can be broadly grouped into foods, fibers, fuels, and raw materials. In the 21st century, plants have been used to grow biofuels, biopharmaceuticals, bioplastics, and pharmaceuticals. Specific foods include cereals, vegetables, fruits, and meat. Fibres include cotton, wool, hemp, silk and flax. Raw materials include lumber and bamboo. Other useful materials are produced by plants, such as resins.

Biofuels include methane from biomass, ethanol, and biodiesel. Cut flowers, nursery plants, tropical fish and birds for the pet trade are some of the ornamental products.

In 2007, one third of the world's workers were employed in agriculture. The services sector has overtaken agriculture as the economic sector employing the most people worldwide. Despite the size of its workforce, agricultural production accounts for less than five per cent of the gross world product.

Agriculture has played a key role in the development of human civilization. Until the Industrial Revolution, the vast majority of the human population laboured in agriculture. Development of agricultural techniques has steadily increased agricultural productivity, and the widespread diffusion of these techniques during a time period is often called an agricultural revolution. A remarkable shift in agricultural practices has occurred over the past century in response to new technologies. In particular, the Haber-Bosch method for synthesizing ammonium nitrate made the traditional practice of recycling nutrients with crop rotation and animal manure less necessary.

Synthetic nitrogen, along with mined rock phosphate, pesticides and mechanization, have greatly increased crop yields in the early 20th century. Increased supply of grains has led to cheaper livestock as well. Further, global yield increases were experienced later in the 20th century when high-yield varieties of common staple grains such as rice, wheat, and corn (maize) were introduced as a part of the Green Revolution. The Green Revolution exported the technologies (including pesticides and synthetic nitrogen) of the developed world to the developing world. Thomas Malthus famously predicted that the Earth would not be able to support its growing population, but technologies such as the Green Revolution have allowed the world to produce a surplus of food.

Many governments have subsidized agriculture to ensure an adequate food supply. These agricultural subsidies are often linked to the production of certain commodities such as wheat, corn (maize), rice, soybeans, and milk. These subsidies, especially when instituted by developed countries have been noted as protectionist, inefficient, and environmentally damaging.

In the past century agriculture has been characterized by enhanced productivity, the use of synthetic fertilizers and pesticides, selective breeding, mechanization, water contamination, and farm subsidies. Proponents of organic farming such as Sir Albert Howard argued in the early 20th century that the overuse of pesticides and synthetic fertilizers damages the long-term fertility of the soil. While this feeling lay dormant for decades, as environmental awareness has increased in the 21st century there has been a movement towards sustainable agriculture by some farmers, consumers, and policymakers.

In recent years there has been a backlash against perceived external environmental effects of mainstream agriculture, particularly regarding water pollution, resulting in the organic movement. One of the major forces behind this movement has been the European Union, which first certified organic food in 1991 and began reform of its Common Agricultural Policy (CAP) in 2005 to phase out commodity-linked farm subsidies, also known as decoupling. The growth of organic farming has renewed research in alternative technologies such as integrated pest management and selective breeding. Recent mainstream technological developments include genetically modified food.

In late 2007, several factors pushed up the price of grains consumed by humans as well as used to feed poultry and dairy cows and other cattle, causing higher prices of wheat (up 58%), soybean (up 32%), and maize (up 11%) over the year. Food riots took place in several countries across the world. Contributing factors included drought in Australia and elsewhere, increasing demand for grain-fed animal products from the growing middle classes of countries such as China and India, diversion of foodgrain to biofuel production and trade restrictions imposed by several countries.

An epidemic of stem rust on wheat caused by race Ug99 is currently spreading across Africa and into Asia and is causing major concern. Approximately 40 per cent of the world's agricultural land is seriously degraded. In Africa, if current trends of soil degradation continue, the continent might be able to feed just 25 per cent of its population by 2025, according to UNU's Ghana-based Institute for Natural Resources in Africa.

Agricultural practices such as irrigation, crop rotation, fertilizers, and pesticides were developed long ago, but have made great strides in the past century. The history of agriculture has played a major role in human history, as agricultural progress has been a crucial factor in worldwide socio-economic change. Division of labour in agricultural societies made commonplace specializations rarely seen in hunter-gatherer cultures. So, too, are arts such as epic literature and monumental architecture, as well as codified legal systems. When farmers became capable of producing food beyond the needs of their own families, others in their society were freed to devote themselves to projects other than food acquisition. Historians and anthropologists have long argued that the development of agriculture made civilization possible.

The Fertile Crescent of Western Asia, Egypt, and India were sites of the earliest planned sowing and harvesting of plants that had previously been gathered in the wild. Independent development of agriculture occurred in northern and southern China, Africa's Sahel, New Guinea and several regions of the Americas. The eight so-called Neolithic founder crops of agriculture appear: first emmer wheat and einkorn wheat, then hulled barley, peas, lentils, bitter vetch, chick peas and flax.

By 7000 BC, small-scale agriculture reached Egypt. From at least 7000 BC the Indian subcontinent saw farming of wheat and barley, as attested by archaeological excavation at Mehrgarh in Balochistan in what is present day Pakistan. By 6000 BC, mid-scale farming was entrenched on the banks of the Nile. This, as irrigation had not yet matured sufficiently. About this time, agriculture was developed independently in the Far East, with rice, rather than wheat, as the primary crop. Chinese and Indonesian farmers went on to domesticate taro and beans including mung, soy and azuki. To complement these new sources of carbohydrates, highly organized net fishing of rivers, lakes and ocean shores in these areas brought in great volumes of essential protein. Collectively, these new methods of farming and fishing inaugurated a human population boom that dwarfed all previous expansions and continues today.

By 5000 BC, the Sumerians had developed core agricultural techniques including large-scale intensive cultivation of land, monocropping, organized irrigation, and the use of a specialized labor force, particularly along the waterway now known as the Shatt al-Arab, from its Persian Gulf delta to the confluence of the Tigris and Euphrates. Domestication of wild aurochs and mouflon into cattle and sheep, respectively, ushered in the large-scale use of animals for food/fiber and as beasts of burden. The shepherd joined the farmer as an essential provider for sedentary and seminomadic societies. Maize, manioc, and arrowroot were first domesticated in the Americas as far back as 5200 BC.

The potato, tomato, pepper, squash, several varieties of bean, tobacco, and several other plants were also developed in the Americas, as was extensive terracing of steep hillsides in much of Andean South America. The Greeks and Romans built on techniques pioneered by the Sumerians, but made few fundamentally new advances. Southern Greeks struggled with very poor soils, yet managed to become a dominant society for years. The Romans were noted for an emphasis on the cultivation of crops for trade.

In the same region, a parallel agricultural revolution occurred, resulting in some of the most important crops grown today. In Mesoamerica wild teosinte was transformed through human selection into the ancestor of modern maize, more than 6000 years ago. It gradually spread across North America and was the major crop of Native Americans at the time of European exploration. Other Mesoamerican crops include hundreds of varieties of squash and beans. Cocoa was also a major crop in domesticated Mexico and Central America. The turkey, one of the most important meat birds, was probably domesticated in Mexico or the U.S. Southwest. In the Andes region of South America the major domesticated crop was potatoes, domesticated perhaps 5000 years ago. Large varieties of beans were domesticated, in South America, as well as animals, including llamas, alpacas, and guinea pigs. Coca, still a major crop, was also domesticated in the Andes.

A minor centre of domestication, the indigenous people of the Eastern U.S. appear to have domesticated numerous crops. Sunflowers, tobacco, varieties of squash and Chenopodium, as well as crops no longer grown, including marshelder and little barley were domesticated. Other wild foods may have undergone some selective cultivation, including wild rice and maple sugar. The most common varieties of strawberry were domesticated from Eastern North America.

By 3500 BC, the simplest form of the plough was developed, called the ard. Before this period, simple digging sticks or hoes were used. These tools would have also been easier to transport, which was a benefit as people only stayed until the soil's nutrients were depleted. However, trough excavations in Mexico it has been found that the continuous cultivating of smaller pieces of land would also have been a sustaining practice. Additional research in central Europe later revealed that agriculture was indeed practiced at this method. For this method, ards were thus much more efficient than digging sticks.

Middle Ages

During the Middle Ages, farmers in North Africa, the Near East, and Europe began making use of agricultural technologies including irrigation systems based on hydraulic and hydrostatic principles, machines such as norias, water-raising machines, dams, and reservoirs. This combined with the invention of a three-field system of crop rotation and the moldboard plow greatly improved agricultural efficiency.

In the European mediaeval period, agriculture was considered part of the set of *seven mechanical arts.*

After 1492, a global exchange of previously local crops and livestock breeds occurred. Key crops involved in this exchange included the tomato, maize, potato, manioc, cocoa bean and tobacco going from the New World to the Old, and several varieties of wheat, spices, coffee, and sugar cane going from the Old World to the New. The most important animal exportation from the Old World to the New were those of the horse and dog (dogs were already present in the pre-Columbian Americas but not in the numbers and breeds suited to farm work). Although not usually food animals, the horse (including donkeys and ponies) and dog quickly filled essential production roles on western-hemisphere farms.

The potato became an important staple crop in northern Europe. Since being introduced by Portuguese in the 16th century, maize and manioc have replaced traditional African crops as the continent's most important staple food crops.

By the early 19th century, agricultural techniques, implements, seed stocks and cultivated plants selected and given a unique name because of its decorative or useful characteristics had so improved that yield per land unit was many times that seen in the Middle Ages. Although there is a vast and interesting history of crop cultivation before the dawn of the 20th century, there is little question that the work of Charles Darwin and Gregor Mendel created the scientific foundation for plant breeding that led to its explosive impact over the past 150 years.

With the rapid rise of mechanization in the late 19th century and the 20th century, particularly in the form of the tractor, farming tasks could be done with a speed and on a scale previously impossible. These advances have led to efficiencies enabling certain modern farms in the United States, Argentina, Israel, Germany, and a few other nations to output volumes of high-quality produce per land unit at what may be the practical limit.

The Haber-Bosch method for synthesizing ammonium nitrate represented a major breakthrough and allowed crop yields to overcome previous constraints. In the past century agriculture has been characterized by enhanced productivity, the substitution of labor for synthetic fertilizers and pesticides, water pollution, and farm subsidies. In recent years there has been a backlash against the external environmental effects of conventional agriculture, resulting in the organic movement.

The cereals rice, corn, and wheat provide 60 per cent of human food supply. Between 1700 and 1980, "the total area of cultivated land worldwide increased 466 per cent" and yields increased dramatically, particularly because of selectively bred high-yielding varieties, fertilizers, pesticides, irrigation, and machinery. For example, irrigation increased corn yields in eastern Colorado by 400 to 500 per cent from 1940 to 1997.

However, concerns have been raised over the sustainability of intensive agriculture. Intensive agriculture has become associated with decreased soil quality in India and Asia, and there has been increased concern over the effects of fertilizers and pesticides on the environment, particularly as population increases and food demand expands. The monocultures typically used in intensive agriculture increase the number of pests, which are controlled through pesticides. Integrated pest management (IPM), which "has been promoted for decades and has had some notable successes" has not significantly affected the use of pesticides because policies encourage the use of pesticides and IPM is knowledge-intensive.

Although the 'Green Revolution' significantly increased rice yields in Asia, yield increases have not occurred in the past 15-20 years. The genetic 'yield potential' has increased for wheat, but the yield potential for rice has not increased since 1966, and the yield potential for maize has 'barely increased in 35 years'. It takes a decade or two for herbicide-resistant weeds to emerge, and insects become resistant to insecticides within about a decade. Crop rotation helps to prevent resistances.

Agricultural exploration expeditions, since the late 19th century, have been mounted to find new species and new agricultural practices in different areas of the world. Two early examples of expeditions include Frank N. Meyer's fruit-and nut-collecting trip to China and Japan from 1916-1918 and the Dorsett-Morse Oriental Agricultural Exploration Expedition to China, Japan, and Korea from 1929-1931 to collect soybean germplasm to support the rise in soybean agriculture in the United States.

In 2009, the agricultural output of China was the largest in the world, followed by the European Union, India and the United States, according to the International Monetary Fund. Economists measure the total factor productivity of agriculture and by this measure agriculture in the United States is roughly 2.6 times more productive than it was in 1948.

Six countries — the US, Canada, France, Australia, Argentina and Thailand — supply 90 per cent of grain exports. The United States controls almost half of world grain exports. Water deficits, which are already spurring heavy grain imports in numerous middle-sized countries, including Algeria, Iran, Egypt, and Mexico, may soon do the same in larger countries, such as China or India.

Crop Production Systems

Cropping systems vary among farms depending on the available resources and constraints; geography and climate of the farm; government policy; economic, social and political pressures; and the philosophy and culture of the farmer. Shifting cultivation (or slash and burn) is a system in which forests are burnt, releasing nutrients to support cultivation of annual and then perennial crops for a period of several years.

Then the plot is left fallow to regrow forest, and the farmer moves to a new plot, returning after many more years (10-20). This fallow period is shortened if population density grows, requiring the input of nutrients (fertilizer or manure) and some manual pest control. Annual cultivation is the next phase of intensity in which there is no fallow period. This requires even greater nutrient and pest control inputs.

Further industrialization lead to the use of monocultures, when one cultivar is planted on a large acreage. Because of the low biodiversity, nutrient use is uniform and pests tend to build up, necessitating the greater use of pesticides and fertilizers. Multiple cropping, in which several crops are grown sequentially in one year, and intercropping, when several crops are grown at the same time are other kinds of annual cropping systems known as polycultures.

In tropical environments, all of these cropping systems are practiced. In subtropical and arid environments, the timing and extent of agriculture may be limited by rainfall, either not allowing multiple annual crops in a year, or requiring irrigation. In all of these environments perennial crops are grown (coffee, chocolate) and systems are practiced such as agroforestry. In temperate environments, where ecosystems were predominantly grassland or prairie, highly productive annual cropping is the dominant farming system.

The last century has seen the intensification, concentration and specialization of agriculture, relying upon new technologies of agricultural chemicals (fertilizers and pesticides), mechanization, and plant breeding (hybrids and GMO's). In the past few decades, a move towards sustainability in agriculture has also developed, integrating ideas of socio-economic justice and conservation of resources and the environment within a farming system. This has led to the development of many responses to the conventional agriculture approach, including organic agriculture, urban agriculture, community supported agriculture, ecological or biological agriculture, integrated farming and holistic management, as well as an increased trend towards agricultural diversification.

Livestock Production Systems

Animals, including horses, mules, oxen, camels, llamas, alpacas, and dogs, are often used to help cultivate fields, harvest crops, wrangle other animals, and transport farm products to buyers. Animal husbandry not only refers to the breeding and raising of animals for meat or to harvest animal products (like milk, eggs, or wool) on a continual basis, but also to the breeding and care of species for work and companionship. Livestock production systems can be defined based on feed source, as grassland - based, mixed, and landless.

Grassland based livestock production relies upon plant material such as shrubland, rangeland, and pastures for feeding ruminant animals. Outside nutrient inputs may be used, however manure is returned directly to the grassland as a major nutrient source. This system is particularly important in areas where crop production is not feasible because of climate or soil, representing 30-40 million pastoralists. Mixed production systems use grassland, fodder crops and grain feed crops as feed for ruminant and monogastic (one stomach; mainly chickens and pigs) livestock. Manure is typically recycled in mixed systems as a fertilizer for crops. Approximately 68 per cent of all agricultural land is permanent pastures used in the production of livestock.

Landless systems rely upon feed from outside the farm, representing the de-linking of crop and livestock production found more prevalently in OECD member countries. In the U.S., 70 per cent of the grain grown is fed to animals on feedlots. Synthetic fertilizers are more heavily relied upon for crop production and manure utilization becomes a challenge as well as a source for pollution.

Production Practices

Tillage is the practice of plowing soil to prepare for planting or for nutrient incorporation or for pest control. Tillage varies in intensity from conventional to no-till. It may improve productivity by warming the soil, incorporating fertilizer and controlling weeds, but also renders soil more prone to erosion, triggers the decomposition of organic matter releasing CO_2, and reduces the abundance and diversity of soil organisms.

Pest control includes the management of weeds, insects/mites, and diseases. Chemical (pesticides), biological (biocontrol), mechanical (tillage), and cultural practices are used. Cultural practices include crop rotation, culling, cover crops, intercropping, composting, avoidance, and resistance. Integrated pest management attempts to use all of these methods to keep pest populations below the number which would cause economic loss, and recommends pesticides as a last resort.

Nutrient management includes both the source of nutrient inputs for crop and livestock production, and the method of utilization of manure produced by livestock. Nutrient inputs can be chemical inorganic fertilizers, manure, green manure, compost and mined minerals. Crop nutrient use may also be managed using cultural techniques such as crop rotation or a fallow period. Manure is used either by holding livestock where the feed crop is growing, such as in managed intensive rotational grazing, or by spreading either dry or liquid formulations of manure on cropland or pastures.

Water management is where rainfall is insufficient or variable, which occurs to some degree in most regions of the world. Some farmers use irrigation to supplement rainfall. In other areas such as the Great Plains in the U.S. and Canada, farmers use a fallow year to conserve soil moisture to use for growing a crop in the following year. Agriculture represents 70 per cent of freshwater use worldwide.

Processing, Distribution, and Marketing

In the United States, food costs attributed to processing, distribution, and marketing have risen while the costs attributed to farming have declined. This is related to the greater efficiency of farming, combined with the increased level of value addition (e.g. more highly processed products) provided by the supply chain. From 1960 to 1980 the farm share was around 40 per cent, but by 1990 it had declined to 30 per cent and by 1998, 22.2 per cent. Market concentration has increased in the sector as well, with the top 20 food manufacturers accounting for half the food-processing value in 1995, over double that produced in 1954. As of 2000 the top six US supermarket groups had 50 per cent of sales compared to 32 per cent in 1992. Although the total effect of the increased market concentration is likely increased efficiency, the changes redistribute economic surplus from producers (farmers) and consumers, and may have negative implications for rural communities.

Crop Alteration and Biotechnology

Crop alteration has been practiced by humankind for thousands of years, since the beginning of civilization. Altering crops through breeding practices changes the genetic make-up of a plant to develop crops with more beneficial characteristics for humans, for example, larger fruits or seeds, drought-tolerance, or resistance to pests. Significant advances in plant breeding ensued after the work of geneticist Gregor Mendel. His work on dominant and recessive alleles gave plant breeders a better understanding of genetics and brought great insights to the techniques utilized by plant breeders. Crop breeding includes techniques such as plant selection with desirable traits, self-pollination and cross-pollination, and molecular techniques that genetically modify the organism.

Domestication of plants has, over the centuries increased yield, improved disease resistance and drought tolerance, eased harvest and improved the taste and nutritional value of crop plants. Careful selection and breeding have had enormous effects on the characteristics of crop plants. Plant selection and breeding in the 1920s and 1930s improved pasture (grasses and clover) in New Zealand. Extensive X-ray an ultraviolet induced mutagenesis efforts (i.e. primitive genetic engineering) during the 1950s produced the modern commercial varieties of grains such as wheat, corn (maize) and barley.

The green revolution popularized the use of conventional hybridization to increase yield many folds by creating "high-yielding varieties". For example, average yields of corn (maize) in the USA have increased from around 2.5 tons per hectare (t/ha) (40 bushels per acre) in 1900 to about 9.4 t/ha (150 bushels per acre) in 2001. Similarly, worldwide average wheat yields have increased from less than 1 t/ha in 1900 to more than 2.5 t/ha in 1990. South American average wheat yields are around 2 t/ha, African under 1 t/ha, Egypt and Arabia up to 3.5 to 4 t/ha with irrigation. In contrast, the average wheat yield in countries such as France is over 8 t/ha. Variations in yields are due mainly to variation in climate, genetics, and the level of intensive farming techniques.

Genetic Engineering

Genetically Modified Organisms (GMO) are organisms whose genetic material has been altered by genetic engineering techniques generally known as recombinant DNA technology. Genetic engineering has expanded the genes available to breeders to utilize in creating desired germlines for new crops. After mechanical tomato-harvesters were developed in the early 1960s, agricultural scientists genetically modified tomatoes to be more resistant to mechanical handling. More recently, genetic engineering is being employed in various parts of the world, to create crops with other beneficial traits.

Herbicide-tolerant GMO Crops

Roundup Ready seed has a herbicide resistant gene implanted into its genome that allows the plants to tolerate exposure to glyphosate. Roundup is a trade name for a glyphosate-based product, which is a systemic, non-selective herbicide used to kill weeds. Roundup Ready seeds allow the farmer to grow a crop that can be sprayed with glyphosate to control weeds without harming the resistant crop. Herbicide-tolerant crops are used by farmers worldwide. Today, 92 per cent of soybean acreage in the US is planted with genetically modified herbicide-tolerant plants.

With the increasing use of herbicide-tolerant crops, comes an increase in the use of glyphosate-based herbicide sprays. In some areas glyphosate resistant weeds have developed, causing farmers to switch to other herbicides. Some studies also link widespread glyphosate usage to iron deficiencies in some crops, which is both a crop production and a nutritional quality concern, with potential economic and health implications.

Insect-resistant GMO Crops

Other GMO crops used by growers include insect-resistant crops, which have a gene from the soil bacterium Bacillus thuringiensis (Bt), which produces a toxin specific to insects. These crops protect plants from damage by insects; one such crop is Starlink. Another is cotton, which accounts for 63 per cent of US cotton acreage.

Some believe that similar or better pest-resistance traits can be acquired through traditional breeding practices, and resistance to various pests can be gained through hybridization or cross-pollination with wild species. In some cases, wild species are the primary source of resistance traits; some tomato cultivars that have gained resistance to at least nineteen diseases did so through crossing with wild populations of tomatoes.

Costs and Benefits of GMOs

Genetic engineers may someday develop transgenic plants which would allow for irrigation, drainage, conservation, sanitary engineering, and maintaining or increasing yields while requiring fewer fossil fuel derived inputs than conventional crops. Such developments would be particularly important in areas which are normally arid and rely upon constant irrigation, and on large scale farms. However, genetic engineering of plants has proven to be controversial. Many issues surrounding food security and environmental impacts have risen regarding GMO practices. For example, GMOs are questioned by some ecologists and economists concerned with GMO practices such as terminator seeds, which is a genetic modification that creates sterile seeds. Terminator seeds are currently under strong international opposition and face continual efforts of global bans.

Another controversial issue is the patent protection given to companies that develop new types of seed using genetic engineering. Since companies have intellectual ownership of their seeds, they have the power to dictate terms and conditions of their patented product. Currently, ten seed companies control over two-thirds of the global seed sales. Vandana Shiva argues that these companies are guilty of biopiracy by patenting life and exploiting organisms for profit Farmers using patented seed are restricted from saving seed for subsequent plantings, which forces farmers to buy new seed every year. Since seed saving is a traditional practice for many farmers in both developing and developed countries, GMO seeds legally bind farmers to change their seed saving practices to buying new seed every year.

Locally adapted seeds are an essential heritage that has the potential to be lost with current hybridized crops and GMOs. Locally adapted seeds, also called land races or crop eco-types, are important because they have adapted over time to the specific microclimates, soils, other environmental conditions, field designs, and ethnic preference indigenous to the exact area of cultivation. Introducing GMOs and hybridized commercial seed to an area brings the risk of cross-pollination with local land races Therefore, GMOs pose a threat to the sustainability of land races and the ethnic heritage of cultures. Once seed contains transgenic material, it becomes subject to the conditions of the seed company that owns the patent of the transgenic material.

Modern Agriculture

Modern agriculture is a term used to describe the wide majority of production practices employed by America's farmers. The term depicts the push for innovation, stewardship and advancements continually made by growers to sustainably produce higher-quality products with a reduced environmental impact. Intensive scientific research and robust investment in modern agriculture during the past 50 years has helped farmers double food production while essentially freezing the footprint of total cultivated farmland.

Safety

The agriculture industry works with government agencies and other organizations to ensure that farmers have access to the technologies required to support modern agriculture practices. Farmers are supported by education and certification programmes that ensure they apply agricultural with care and only when required.

Sustainability

Technological advancements help provide farmers with tools and resources to help reduce their environmental footprint and to make farming more sustainable.

New technologies have given rise to innovations like conservation tillage, a farming process which helps prevent land loss to erosion, water pollution and enhances carbon sequestration.

The World Bank, the Bill and Melinda Gates Foundation and others have noted that integrated crop management is based on agro-ecological principles and can increase yields while reducing environmental damage.

Food Safety, Labelling and Regulation

Food security issues also coincide with food safety and food labelling concerns. Currently a global treaty, the BioSafety Protocol, regulates the trade of GMOs. The EU currently requires all GMO foods to be labelled, whereas the US does not require transparent labelling of GMO foods. Since there are still questions regarding the safety and risks associated with

GMO foods, some believe the public should have the freedom to choose and know what they are eating and require all GMO products to be labelled.

The Food and Agriculture Organization of the United Nations (FAO) leads international efforts to defeat hunger and provides a neutral forum where nations meet as equals to negotiate agreements and debate food policy and the regulation of agriculture. According to Dr. Samuel Jutzi, director of FAO's animal production and health division, lobbying by 'powerful' big food corporations has stopped reforms that would improve human health and the environment. The "real, true issues are not being addressed by the political process because of the influence of lobbyists, of the true powerful entities," he said, speaking at the Compassion in World Farming annual forum. For example, recent proposals for a voluntary code of conduct for the livestock industry that would have provided incentives for improving standards for health, and environmental regulations, such as the number of animals an area of land can support without long-term damage, were successfully defeated due to large food company pressure.

Environmental Impact

Agriculture imposes external costs upon society through pesticides, nutrient runoff, excessive water usage, and assorted other problems. A 2000 assessment of agriculture in the UK determined total external costs for 1996 of £2,343 million, or £208 per hectare. A 2005 analysis of these costs in the USA concluded that cropland imposes approximately $5 to 16 billion ($30 to $96 per hectare), while livestock production imposes $714 million. Both studies concluded that more should be done to internalize external costs, and neither included subsidies in their analysis, but noted that subsidies also influence the cost of agriculture to society. Both focussed on purely fiscal impacts. The 2000 review included reported pesticide poisonings but did not include speculative chronic effects of pesticides, and the 2004 review relied on a 1992 estimate of the total impact of pesticides.

A key player who is credited to saving billions of lives because of his revolutionary work in developing new agricultural techniques is Norman Borlaug. His transformative work brought high-yield crop varieties to developing countries and earned him an unofficial title as the father of the Green Revolution.

Livestock Issues

A senior UN official and co-author of a UN report detailing this problem, Henning Steinfeld, said "Livestock are one of the most significant contributors to today's most serious environmental problems". Livestock production occupies 70 per cent of all land used for agriculture, or 30 per cent of the land surface of the planet. It is one of the largest sources of greenhouse gases, responsible for 18 per cent of the world's greenhouse gas emissions as measured in CO_2 equivalents. By comparison, all transportation emits 13.5 per cent of the CO_2. It produces 65 per cent of human-related nitrous oxide (which has 296 times the global warming potential of CO_2) and 37 per cent of all human-induced methane (which is 23 times as warming as CO_2. It also generates 64 per cent of the ammonia, which contributes to acid rain and acidification of ecosystems. Livestock expansion is cited as a key factor driving deforestation, in the Amazon basin 70 per cent of previously forested area is now occupied by pastures and the remainder used for feedcrops. Through deforestation and land degradation, livestock is also driving reductions in biodiversity.

Land Transformation and Degradation

Land transformation, the use of land to yield goods and services, is the most substantial way humans alter the Earth's ecosystems, and is considered the driving force in the loss of biodiversity. Estimates of the amount of land transformed by humans vary from 39-50 per cent. Land degradation, the long-term decline in ecosystem function and productivity, is estimated to be occurring on 24 per cent of land worldwide, with cropland overrepresented. The UN-FAO report cites land management as the driving factor behind degradation and reports that 1.5 billion people rely upon the degrading land. Degradation can be deforestation, desertification, soil erosion, mineral depletion, or chemical degradation (acidification and salinization).

Eutrophication

Eutrophication, excessive nutrients in aquatic ecosystems resulting in algal blooms and anoxia, leads to fish kills, loss of biodiversity, and renders water unfit for drinking and other industrial uses. Excessive fertilization and manure application to cropland, as well as high livestock stocking densities cause nutrient (mainly nitrogen and phosphorus) runoff and leaching from agricultural land. These nutrients are major non-point pollutants contributing to eutrophication of aquatic ecosystems.

Pesticides

Pesticide use has increased since 1950 to 2.5 million tons annually worldwide, yet crop loss from pests has remained relatively constant. The World Health Organization estimated in 1992 that 3 million pesticide poisonings occur annually, causing 220,000 deaths. Pesticides select for pesticide resistance in the pest population, leading to a condition termed the 'pesticide treadmill' in which pest resistance warrants the development of a new pesticide.

An alternative argument is that the way to 'save the environment' and prevent famine is by using pesticides and intensive high yield farming, a view exemplified by a quote heading the Center for Global Food Issues website: 'Growing more per acre leaves more land for nature'. However, critics argue that a trade-off between the environment and a need for food is not inevitable, and that pesticides simply replace good agronomic practices such as crop rotation.

Climate Change

Climate change has the potential to affect agriculture through changes in temperature, rainfall (timing and quantity), CO_2, solar radiation and the interaction of these elements. Agriculture can both mitigate or worsen global warming. Some of the increase in CO_2 in the atmosphere comes from the decomposition of organic matter in the soil, and much of the methane emitted into the atmosphere is caused by the decomposition of organic matter in wet soils such as rice paddies. Further, wet or anaerobic soils also lose nitrogen through denitrification, releasing the greenhouse gas nitric oxide. Changes in management can reduce the release of these greenhouse gases, and soil can further be used to sequester some of the CO_2 in the atmosphere.

International Economics and Agriculture

Differences in economic development, population density and culture mean that the farmers of the world operate under very different conditions.

A US cotton farmer may receive US$230 in government subsidies per acre planted (in 2003), while farmers in Mali and other third-world countries do without. When prices decline, the heavily subsidized US farmer is not forced to reduce his output, making it difficult for cotton prices to rebound, but his Mali counterpart may go broke in the meantime.

A livestock farmer in South Korea can calculate with a (highly subsidized) sales price of US$1300 for a calf produced. A South American Mercosur country rancher calculates with a calf's sales price of US$120-200 (both 2008 figures). With the former, scarcity and high cost of land is compensated with public subsidies, the latter compensates absence of subsidies with economics of scale and low cost of land.

In the Peoples Republic of China, a rural household's productive asset may be one hectare of farmland. In Brazil, Paraguay and other countries where local legislature allows such purchases, international investors buy thousands of hectares of farmland or raw land at prices of a few hundred US$ per hectare.

Since the 1940s, agricultural productivity has increased dramatically, due largely to the increased use of energy-intensive mechanization, fertilizers and pesticides. The vast majority of this energy input comes from fossil fuel sources. Between 1950 and 1984, the Green Revolution transformed agriculture around the globe, with world grain production increasing by 250 per cent as world population doubled. Modern agriculture's heavy reliance on petrochemicals and mechanization has raised concerns that oil shortages could increase costs and reduce agricultural output, causing food shortages.

Agriculture and Food System Share (%) of Total Energy Consumption by Three Industrialized Nations

Modern or industrialized agriculture is dependent on fossil fuels in two fundamental ways: (1) direct consumption on the farm; and (2) indirect consumption to manufacture inputs used on the farm. Direct consumption includes the use of lubricants and fuels to operate farm vehicles and machinery; and use of gas, liquid propane, and electricity to power dryers, pumps, lights, heaters, and coolers. American farms directly consumed about 1.2 exajoules (1.1 quadrillion BTU) in 2002, or just over 1 per cent of the nation's total energy.

Indirect consumption is mainly oil and natural gas used to manufacture fertilizers and pesticides, which accounted for 0.6 exajoules (0.6 quadrillion BTU) in 2002. The energy used to manufacture farm machinery is also a form of indirect agricultural energy consumption, but it is not included in USDA estimates of U.S. agricultural energy use. Together, direct and indirect consumption by U.S. farms accounts for about 2 percent of the nation's energy use. Direct and indirect energy consumption by U.S. farms peaked in 1979, and has gradually declined over the past 30 years.

Food systems encompass not just agricultural production, but also off-farm processing, packaging, transporting, marketing, consumption, and disposal of food and food-related items. Agriculture accounts for less than one-fifth of food system energy use in the United States.

Oil shortages could impact this food supply. Some farmers using modern organic-farming methods have reported yields as high as those available from conventional farming without the use of synthetic fertilizers and pesticides. However, the reconditioning of soil to restore nutrients lost during the use of monoculture agriculture techniques made possible by petroleum-based technology takes time.

In 2007, higher incentives for farmers to grow non-food biofuel crops combined with other factors (such as over-development of former farm lands, rising transportation costs, climate change, growing consumer demand in China and India, and population growth) to cause food shortages in Asia, the Middle East, Africa, and Mexico, as well as rising food prices around the globe. As of December 2007, 37 countries faced food crises, and 20 had imposed some sort of food-price controls. Some of these shortages resulted in food riots and even deadly stampedes.

The biggest fossil fuel input to agriculture is the use of natural gas as a hydrogen source for the Haber-Bosch fertilizer-creation process. Natural gas is used because it is the cheapest currently available source of hydrogen. When oil production becomes so scarce that natural gas is used as a partial stopgap replacement, and hydrogen use in transportation increases, natural gas will become much more expensive. If the Haber Process is unable to be commercialized using renewable energy (such as by electrolysis) or if other sources of hydrogen are not available to replace the Haber Process, in amounts sufficient to supply transportation and agricultural needs, this major source of fertilizer would either become extremely expensive or unavailable. This would either cause food shortages or dramatic rises in food prices.

Mitigation of Effects of Petroleum Shortages

One effect oil shortages could have on agriculture is a full return to organic agriculture. In light of peak-oil concerns, organic methods are more sustainable than contemporary practices because they use no petroleum-based pesticides, herbicides, or fertilizers. Some farmers using modern organic-farming methods have reported yields as high as those available from conventional farming. Organic farming may however be more labour-intensive and would require a shift of the workforce from urban to rural areas.

It has been suggested that rural communities might obtain fuel from the biochar and synfuel process, which uses agricultural *waste* to provide charcoal fertilizer, some fuel *and* food, instead of the normal food *vs.* fuel debate. As the synfuel would be used on-site, the process would be more efficient and might just provide enough fuel for a new organic-agriculture fusion.

It has been suggested that some transgenic plants may some day be developed which would allow for maintaining or increasing yields while requiring fewer fossil-fuel-derived inputs than conventional crops. The possibility of success of these programmes is questioned by ecologists and economists concerned with unsustainable GMO practices such as terminator seeds, and a January 2008 report shows that GMO practices "fail to deliver environmental, social and economic benefits".

While there has been some research on sustainability using GMO crops, at least one hyped and prominent multi-year attempt by Monsanto

Company has been unsuccessful, though during the same period traditional breeding techniques yielded a more sustainable variety of the same crop. Additionally, a survey by the bio-tech industry of subsistence farmers in Africa to discover what GMO research would most benefit sustainable agriculture only identified non-transgenic issues as areas needing to be addressed. Nevertheless, some governments in Africa continue to view investments in new transgenic technologies as an essential component of efforts to improve sustainability.

3 Precision Farming Technology

'Precision Farming' or 'Precision Agriculture' aims at increasing productivity, decreasing production costs and minimizing the environmental impact of farming. In this context, the present study has been undertaken to understand the impact of precision farming on resource-poor regions and underprivileged farmers. Specifically, the study has looked into productivity, income, employment, and adoption behaviour of technology in agriculture. The study, conducted in the Dharmapuri district, has collected data on precision and non-precision farmings through the interview schedule during the year 2007. Sources of the productivity difference between the precision and conventional farmings have been identified by decomposing the productivity change. Financial impact of adoption has been studied through a two-stage econometric model. The first stage of the model consists of an adoption decision model that describes the factors which influence the likelihood of adopting precision farming. Results of first stage have provided input for the second stage of the model, which has been used to estimate the impact of precision farming on farm financial performance.

The study has revealed that adoption of precision farming has led to 80 per cent increase in yield in tomato and 34 per cent in brinjal production. Increase in gross margin has been found as 165 and 67 per cent, respectively in tomato and brinjal farming. The contribution of technology for higher yield in precision farming has been 33.71 per cent and 20.48 per cent, respectively in tomato and brinjal production. The elasticity of 0.39 for the adoption in tomato and 0.28 in brinjal has indicated that as the probability of adoption increases by 10 per cent, net return increases by 39 per cent and 28 per cent in tomato and brinjal cultivation. Lack of finance and credit facilities have been identified as the major constrains in non-adoption of precision farming. The study has suggested that providing of subsidies for water-soluble fertilizers and pump-sets will increase adoption of precision farming.

The share of agriculture in the gross domestic product has registered a steady decline, from 36.4 per cent in 1982-83 to 18.5 per cent in 2006-07. But, the agricultural sector continues to support more than half a billion people providing employment to 52 per cent of the workforce. The growth in agriculture over a period of time has remained lower than the growth in non-agriculture sector and this decelerating trend is a cause of concern. The gap between growth in agriculture and non-agriculture sectors began to widen in 1981-82, and more particularly, since 1996-97, because of acceleration in the growth of industry and services sectors (*Economic Survey*, 2008).

Notably, the agricultural growth performance could not be sustained during the 1990s because of decelerations in yield and output growth rates in both food and non-food crops. A comparison of the decadal growth in area, production and productivity of foodgrains since 1950s reveals that India has been experiencing stagnation or negative growth in these crops. Increasing agricultural productivity perhaps remains the single most important determinant of economic growth and poverty reduction, and hence provides the key to millennium development goal. Improvements in productivity come from adoption of new technologies and increase in production efficiency. 'Precision farming' or 'Precision Agriculture' aims at increasing productivity, decreasing production costs and minimizing the environmental impact of farming. The managementof in-field variability in soil fertility and crop conditions for improving crop production and minimizing the environmental impact is the crux of precision farming. New technologies, such as Global Positioning Systems (GPS), sensors, satellites or aerial images, and Geographical Information Systems (GIS) are utilized to assess and analyse variations in agricultural production.

In Tamil Nadu, precision farming was implemented under the Tamil Nadu Precision Farming Project (TNPFP) in the Dharmapuri and Krishnagiri districts on about 400 ha of land with a total budget of 720 lakhs for a period of three years.

The scheme was extended to six more districts in 2005-06. Most parts of the Dharmapuri and Krishnagiri districts are semi-arid tracts with low rainfall and low productivity. In this context, the present study was undertaken to understand the impact of technological innovations like precision farming on resource-poor regions and underprivileged farm households. Specifically, the study has looked into the productivity, income, employment, and adoption behaviour of the technology in agriculture.

Methodology

The financial impact of adoption was studied through a two-stage econometric model. To control factors for other than precision farming adoption, multiple regression was used in a two-stage econometric model of adoption and the adoption impact. The first stage of model consisted of an adoption decision model that described the factors which could influence the likelihood of adopting precision farming. The results of first stage provided the input for the second stage of model which was used to estimate the impact of precision farming on farm financial performance. This two-step approach was similar to the approach set forth by Fernandez-Cornejo et al (2002) in their study on the impact of the adoption of GE crops on farm's financial performance. In this study, the first stage of Hickman's technique involved the estimation of a precision farming adoption model using the Probit analysis. Estimated parameters from the Probit model were then used to calculate the predicted probabilities (P ^) of adopting the precision farming technology. Addressing the simultaneity and self-selectivity concerns when estimating farm net returns was accomplished by appending to the basic regression explaining financial performance the predicted probabilities

where,

Ð = A vector denoting net returns Xij = A matrix of exogenous variables affecting the farm's financial performance

X1 = Educational status

X2 = Farming experience

X3 = Farm-size

X4 = Extension agency contact (No./month)

X6 = Risk-orientation

X7 = Family labour

X8 = Non-farm income

P = Predicted probability ã^ = Inverse mill ratio, and åi = A vector of errors. The adoption decision model was estimated by Probit analysis.

The model was specified using variables that have been shown to be related to technology choice in the literature. Variables regressed against the decision to adopt each technology included operator's education, experience, farm-size, extension agency contact, risk perception, number of family labour and non-farm income. Operator's preference towards the risk was specified using a risk index, constructed according to farmers' answers to a series of survey questions about how they react towards risk. The option impact model was estimated by regressing the same set of explanatory variables, plus the information obtained from the decision model on farm's financial performance. The farm's financial performance was measured by the net income per hectare. Income was taken as the difference between gross value of crop production and total cost of cultivation. Constraints in adoption of precision farming were ranked by Garrett ranking technique.Results and Discussion Economics of Production under Precision and Non-precision Farmings Economics of tomato production were estimated for precision and non-precision methods of cultivation and the results are presented in The share in total variable cost in the case of precision farmers was highest for fertilizer (27.15%), followed human labour (25.04%). Within the cost on human labour, 72.21 per cent was paid out to hired labour and the rest was imputed value of family labour. In non-precision faming, plant protection chemical was found to be the major input, accounting for 31.06 per cent of the total cost, followed by human labour (25.47%), fertilizer (9.70%) and seedlings (7.90%). The gross margin calculated as the difference between the gross return and variable cost, was 166 per cent higher in precision than on precision farming in tomato cultivation. The economics of brinjal production under precision and non-precision methods have been presented Labour cost accounted for the highest share in total variable cost in precision farming and it was 49.57 per cent more than that of non-precision farming. The cost of fertilizer was the second highest, with 151.66 per cent more in precision farming, mainly due to the high cost of water-soluble fertilizers. Non-precision farmers spent 123.64 per cent higher cost on plant protection chemicals because of high use of these chemicals. The spendings on seedlings, machine power and manures were more or less the same in both the cases. The precision farmers incurred a total cost of Rs 1,10,900/ ha, which was 25.47 per cent higher than by non-precision farmers, but realized 77.61 per cent higher net return over non-precision farmers. The gross margin calculated as the difference between the gross return and variable cost, was 67 per cent higher in precision than non-precision farming in brinjal cultivation.

Nature of Technological Change and Sources of Difference in Yield

The homogeneity of production function under both precision and non-precision technologies was tested using dummy variables. The coefficient of dummy variable was statically ignificant for both tomato and brinjal crops. Financial impact of adoption was studied through a two-stage econometric model. In the first stage, predicted probabilities of adoption were estimated through probit analysis. In the second stage, predicted probabilities were used to estimate the financial impact. The financial impact model, apart from other independent variables, included inverse mill ratio and predicted the probability of adoption from the Probit model. The net return of tomato farming was the dependent variable. R-square was 61.07 per cent and t-tests indicated that the estimate of inverse mill ratio was statistically equal to zero. This means that estimate of the precision farming adoption decision was not biased by non-controllable variables, and hence, it was not overestimated. Coefficient of farm-size, extension agency contact and non-farm income were significant and hence, influenced the net return in tomato. Increasing farm size, extension agency contact and non-farm income by one unit will increase the net return by Rs. 1293/ha, Rs. 8242/ha and Rs 1129/ha, respectively.

In the case of brinjal, R-square in the financial impact model was 55.54 per cent. Parameter t-tests indicated that the estimate of inverse mill ratio in the regression model was statistically equal to zero. The significant and positive estimate of farming experience and non-farm income stresses the importance of these variables on net income in brinjal cultivation.

Increasing farming experience, non-farm income by one unit will enhance net return by Rs. 1542/ha, and Rs. 1680/ha, respectively. To illustrate the impact of adoption on net return, elasticities were estimated for the predicted probability. The elasticity of 0.39 and 0.28 for adoption in tomato and brinjal, respectively indicated that as the probability of adoption increases by 10 per cent, net return increases by 39 per cent in tomato and 28 per cent in brinjal cultivation.

Constraints in Adoption of Precision Farming

Reasons for non-adoption of precision farming as ranked by the farmers, were analyzed through Garrett's ranking technique and the results are presented. The results showed that the lack of finance and credit facilities were the most important reasons for non-adoption of precision farming. Obtaining credit was a difficult process, because farmers could not produce collateral security. Drip installation and use of water-soluble fertilizers were very expensive and required credit. Because of output price fluctuations, farmers were not ready to make investments. Lack of knowledge about precision farming technologies was another important constraint, because a majority of small farmers were illiterate and were not able to follow and adopt latest technologies. Labour scarcity was also a problem in adopting precision farming. Due to urbanization and migration, there was a scarcity of labour for agricultural operations. Since precision farming was highly labour-intensive technology and operations were time-bound, farmers faced the dearth of labour, especially during stacking and harvesting. The traditional farmers had a wrong perception about the higher yield from the précised quantity of inputs. It was a major constraint to the adoption of precision farming. It was found that besides adequate quantum of water for the entire crop duration, and pumping efficiency of motor should also be about 12000 litres of water per hour, with 1.5 kg pressure.

Decomposition of the Productivity Difference in Precision and Non-precision Farmings

SOURCE OF PRODUCTIVITY CONTRIBUTION

Difference	Tomato	Brinjal
Total difference in output sources of contribution	63.86	28.14
Output difference due to technology	33.71	20.48
Input-use Seed rate (kg)	6.12	0.47
Manures (tonnes)	27.42	15.39
Labour (human-days)	1.47	0.19
Plant protection chemicals (gram)	0.16	18.32
Irrigation (ha-cm)	2.67	0.02
Nitrogen (kg)	12.54	2.07
Phosphorous (kg)	54.47	11.52
Potassium (kg)	22.79	13.07
Output difference due to input-use for fertigation in precision farming	30.15	7.68

Lack of water availability and pump efficiency, lack of technical skill, inadequate size of landholding, mind set, and traditional beliefs were constraints to adoption of precision farming. The local market was not big enough to market the huge quantity of output produced through precision farming, so farmers had to negotiate with supermarkets, etc., but sometimesit led to low price and less profit.

The study has revealed that adoption of precision farming leads to about 80 per cent increase in yield in tomato and and 34 per cent in brinjal. Increase in gross margin has been found 165 per cent and 67 per cent in tomato and brinjal production, respectively. The contribution of technology for higher yield in precision farming has been recorded as 33.7 per cent and 20.5 per cent, respectively in tomato and brinjal. The elasticity of 0.39 for the adoption in tomato and of 0.28 in brinjal indicated that as the probability of adoption increases by 10 per cent, the net return increases by 39 per cent and 28 per cent in tomato and brinjal cultivation, respectively. Lack of finance and credit facilities have been identified as the major constraints for non-adoption of precision farming.

4 Precision Farming in India

"*Agriculture is the backbone of the Indian Economy*" — said Mahatma Gandhi five decades ago. Even today, as we enter the new millennium, the situation is still the same, with almost the entire economy being sustained by agriculture, which is the mainstay of the villages. Not only the economy, but also every one of us looks up to agriculture for our sustenance too. Therefore, it is no surprise if agriculture gets the celebrity status in the name of Precision farming (PF). In recent times, the researchers in the field have been busy formulating methodologies and fabricating new implements for precision farming. It is here the challenge arises considering the implementation of the technology at various levels in the Global community. The need of the hour is not application of the technology but the adoption of appropriate technology, which would suit the particular level of the global community. In India, the farming practices are too haphazard and non-scientific and hence need some forethought before implementing any new technology. It is here that this chapter comes out with a cost-benefit analysis to prove that precision farming is possible in India.

Applications of agricultural inputs at uniform rates across the field without due regard to in-field variations in soil fertility and crop conditions does not yield desirable results in terms of crop yield. The management of in-field variability in soil fertility and crop conditions for improving the crop production and minimizing the environmental impact is the crux of precision farming. Thus, the information on spatial variability in soil fertility status and crop conditions is a pre-requisite for adoption of precision farming. Space technology including global positioning system (GPS) and GIS holds good promise in deriving information on soil attributes and crop yield, and allows monitoring seasonally — variable soil and crop characteristics, namely soil moisture, crop phenology, growth, evapotranspiration, nutrient deficiency, crop disease, and weed and insect infestation, which, in turn, help in optimizing inputs and maxiizing crop yield and income. Though widely adopted in developed countries, the adoption of precision farming in India is yet to take a firm ground primarily due to its unique pattern of land holdings, poor infrastructure, lack of farmers' inclination to take risk, socio-economic and demographic conditions. The aim of this chapter is to suggest measures for the implementation of this novel technique in the country with a greater emphasis on the systematic approach towards its operationalisation.

The conventional agronomic practices follow a standard management option for a large area irrespective of the variability occurring within and among the field. For decades now, the farmers have been applying fertilizers based on recommendations emanating from research and field trials under specific agro-climatic conditions. Since soil-nutrient, characteristics vary not only from one region to another, but also from field to field. Even within a field, there is a need to take into account such variability while applying fertilizers to a particular crop. Consideration of in-field variations in soil fertility and crop conditions and matching the agricultural inputs like seed, fertilizer, irrigation, insecticide, pesticide, etc. in order to optimize the input or maximizing the crop yield from a given quantum of input, is referred to as precision farming or precision agriculture or precision crop management.

The term 'precision farming' means carefully tailoring the soil and crop management to fit the different conditions found in each field. It is defined as the application of technologies and principles to manage spatial and temporal variability associated with all aspects of agricultural production. It is also referred to as 'prescription farming', 'site specific farming' or 'variable rate technology'. By catering to this variability, called precision farming, one can improve the productivity or reduce the cost of production and diminish the chance of environmental degradation caused by excess use of inputs. Thus, mapping and analysis of within field variability is an essential input for precision crop management. Thus, PF involves acquiring the variations in crop or soil properties, mapping, and analyzing the variations, adopting suitable management techniques to maximize the yield. Farmers have been applying fertilizers based on recommendations emanating from research and field trials under specific agro-climatic conditions, which have been extrapolated to a regional level. Since soil nutrient characteristics vary not only between regions and between farms but also from plot to plot, and within a field or plot, there is a need to take into account such variability while applying fertilizers to a particular crop. Consideration of in-field/plot variations in soil fertility and crop conditions and matching the agricultural inputs like seed, fertilizer, irrigation, insecticide, pesticide, etc. in order to optimize the input or maximizing the crop yield from a given quantum of input, is referred to as precision farming or precision agriculture or precision crop management.

The information for variability map can be obtained from soil tests for nutrient availability, yield monitors for crop yield, soil samples for organic matter content, information in soil maps, or ground conductivity meters for soil moisture (Mulla, 1997). Generally, the fields are manually sampled along a regular grid and the analyzed results of the samples are interpolated using geostatistical techniques. These techniques are time consuming, labour intensive and in many cases destructive especially, for agricultural situation in India. With small size of landholdings and low income of farmers, the adoption of this methodology in its present form is not feasible. Various workers have shown the advantages of using remote sensing technology to obtain spatially and temporally variable information for precision farming. In an earlier work, Ray et al. (2001) have shown the usefulness of IRS merged data in mapping the variability.

Components of Precision Farming

- Remote sensing
- GIS
- DGPS
- Variable rate applicator

Remote Sensing

This is for Data acquisition of the farms to find the soil, vegetation and other parameters that are amenable for remote sensing. Remote sensing techniques play an important role in precision farming by providing continuous acquired data of agricultural crops. Remote sensors image vegetation, which is growing on different soil types with different water availability, substrate, impact of cultivation, and relief. These differences influence the state of the plants and cause heterogeneous regions within single fields. Hence, the heterogeneous vegetation acts as an interface between soil and remote sensing information, because vegetation parameters describing the state of the plants can be deduced from remote sensing imagery. The analysis of the variability occurring within the field was carried out by measuring soil and plant parameters through conventional methods as well as through spectral techniques using ground truth spectroradiometer (350-1800 nm) and satellite data. Ray et al. (2001), in general, have reviewed by Moran et al. (1997) and for Indian conditions the potentials of remote sensing in providing information required for precision farming.

Geographical Information System

The Geographic Information System (GIS) contributes significantly to precision farming by allowing presentation of spatial data in the form of a map. In addition, GIS forms an ideal platform for the storage and management of model input data and the presentation of model results, which the process model provides.

DGPS

'Do the right thing, in the right place and in right time'

This is where GPS comes into picture. In addition, the accuracy, which is the important factor in PF, demands for DGPS (Differential Global Positioning System). GPS makes use of a series of military satellites that identify the location of farm equipment within a metre of an actual site in the field. The value of knowing a precise location within inches is that:

- Locations of soil samples and the laboratory results can be compared to a soil map;
- Fertilizer and pesticides can be prescribed to fit soil properties (clay and organic matter content) and soil conditions (relief and drainage);
- Tillage adjustments can be made as one finds various conditions across the field; and
- One can monitor and record yield data as one goes across the field.

The Global Positioning System (GPS) technology provides accurate positioning system necessary for field implementation of variable rate technology (VRT). The Internet makes possible the development of a mechanism for effective farm management using remote sensing.

Variable Rate Applicator

The variable rate applicator has three components:

- Control computer;
- Locator; and
- Actuator

The control computer coordinates the field operation. It has a map of desired activity as a function of geographic location. It receives the equipment's current location from the locator, which has a GPS in it, and decides what to do based upon the map in its memory or data storage. It then issues the command to the actuator, which does the input application.

Practical Problems in Indian Agriculture

Precision Agriculture has been mostly confined to developed countries. Reasons of limitations of its implementation in developing countries like India are:

- Small land holdings
- Heterogeneity of cropping systems and market imperfections
- Lack of technical expertise knowledge and technology (India spends only 0.3 per cent of its agricultural Gross Domestic Product in Research and Development).

High Cost

In India, major problem is the small field size. More than 58 per cent of operational holdings in the country have size less than 1ha. Only in the states of Punjab, Rajasthan, Haryana and Gujarat more than 20 per cent of agricultural lands have operational holding size of more than four hectare. There is a scope of implementing precision Agriculture for crops like, rice and wheat especially in the states of Punjab and Haryana. Commercial as well as Horticultural crops shows a wider scope for precision agriculture.

In India, broadly two types of agriculture viz., high input agriculture characterized by the provision of assured irrigation and other agricultural inputs, and subsistence farming, which is confined mostly to rain-fed, or dry land regions, are prevalent. Nearly two-third arable land in India is rain-fed. The crop yields are very low (~ 1 t ha-1) and very good potential exists for increasing productivity of rain-fed Cropping systems.

Methodology

Using a GPS along with a digital drainage map, the farmer is able to apply these pesticides in a safer manner. The spraying equipment can be preprogrammed automatically to turn off when it reaches the distance limitation or zone of the drainage feature. Additionally, farmers can preprogramme the rate of pesticide or fertilizer to be applied so that only the amount needed determined by the soil condition is applied varying this rate from one area of the field to another. This saves money and allows for safer use of these materials. Data collected by the GPS operations can be automatically recorded with the GIS programme. Remotely sensed data can be analyzed and added to the GIS using soil maps, digital terrain and field operations information as ground truth. Additionally the farmers are able to record observations through the growing season such as weed growth, unusual plant stress or colouring and growth conditions. This can be used to guide further field operations like spraying, fertilizing and irrigating and it is part of the permanent record. Precision farming will make a strong impact on the way farmers manage their farm operations in the future.

Seed Spacing

The yield from the seeds is maximum when adequate care is taken to adequately space them to enable each plant the optimum requisites for its growth, namely the soil nutrients, water, sunlight and protection against pest infestation. This is best accomplished by varying the seeding rate even within a single piece of land according to the soil conditions such as texture, organic matter and available soil moisture. One would plant fewer seeds in sandy soil as compared to silt loam soils because of less available moisture. The lower seed population usually has larger heads (ears) of harvested seeds providing for a maximum yield. Since soils vary even across an individual farm field, the ability to change seeding rates as one goes across the field allows the farmer to maximize this seeding rate according to the soil conditions. A computerized soil map of a specific field on a computer fitted on the tractor along with a GPS can tell farmers where they are in the field allowing the opportunity to adjust this seeding rate as they go across their fields.

Steps to be taken for implementing PF in India: In the present existent situation, the potential of precision agriculture in India is limited by the lack of appropriate measurement and analysis techniques for agronomically important factors. High accuracy sensing and data management tools must be developed and validated to support both research and production. The limitation in data quality/availability has become a major obstacle in the demonstration and adoption of the precision technologies. The adoption of precision agriculture needs combined efforts on behalf of scientists, farmers and the government. The following methodology could be adopted in order to operationalise precision farming in the country.

Creation of multidisciplinary teams involving agricultural scientists in various fields, engineers, manufacturers and economists to study the overall scope of precision agriculture.

Formation of farmer's co-operatives since many of the precision agriculture tools are costly (GIS, GPS, RS, etc.).

Government legislation restraining farmers using indiscriminate farm inputs and thereby causing ecological/environmental imbalance would induce the farmer to go for alternative approach.

Pilot study should be conducted on farmer's field to show the results of precision agriculture implementation.

Creating awareness amongst farmers about consequences of applying imbalanced doses of farm inputs like irrigation, fertilizers, insecticides and pesticides.

Realizing the potential of space technology in precision farming, the Department of Space, Government of India has initiated eight pilot studies in well-managed agricultural farms of the ICRISAT, the Indian Council of Agricultural Research and the Agricultural Universities, as well as in farmers' fields. The pilot studies aim at delineating homogeneous zones with respect to soil fertility and crop yield, estimation of potential yield, yield gap analysis, monitoring seasonally-variable soil and crop conditions using optical and microwave sensor data, and matching the farm inputs to bridge the gap between potential and actual yield through Spatial Decision Support Systems (SDSS). The test sites are spread over a fairly large area across a cross section of agro-climatic zones of the Indian sub-continent, and cover some of the important crops like wheat, rice, sorghum, pigeon pea, chickpea, soybean and groundnut. The next step would be to generate detailed-level information on soil resources addressing potentials and limitations of individual fields since except for states like Punjab, Haryana, Madhya Pradesh and Maharashtra where fields size is quite large, practically individual field could be treated as a homogenous management unit for the purpose of precision farming.

Cost Benefit Analysis

The real value for the farmer is that he can adjust seeding rates, plan more accurate crop protection programmes, perform more timely tillage and know the yield variation within a field. These benefits will enhance the overall cost effectiveness of his crop production. Since the country is going to spend the amount, the GDP is considered rather than the farmer's personal income. Hence the cost-benefit analysis of the present project is

- GDP of India for 1993 = $ 250.97 billion (FAO yearbook, 1994)
- GDP in Indian Rupees = Rs. 12,924.955 billion
- Amount spent for R & D = 0.3 per cent of GDP = Rs. 38.775 billion
- Cost-Benefit Analysis = 38.775 billion/315 million = 12,309

Thus, it is proved that there is an enormous benefit in implementing the DGPS network, which would further pave the way for Precision Farming.

Discussion and Analysis

"Humankind must rise above the earth to the top of the atmosphere and beyond. Only thus he fully understand the world in which he lives"

—***Socrates, 500 B.C***

Thus, precision farming has taken 'agriculture into the space age'. Farmers have services available that involve satellites collecting data, transmitting location information, or providing data from a variety of sources. Farmers can analyze this satellite information or they can rely on companies to do this service for them for a fee.

Precision farming is undoubtedly relevant to Indian agriculture in the context of improving agricultural production and Stakeholders' income and minimizing environmental impact. Geoinformation technology offers immense potential for deriving information on soil fertility, crop conditions and crop yield, crop simulation models enable estimating potential crop yield and the decision support system to facilitate developing appropriate prescription for improving crop production while minimizing the cost of inputs. The major limitations of currently available high spatial resolution multispectral data are the fixed and broad spectral bands, very low repetivity, high cost which most of the Indian farmer could not afford. In order to match the technology with the requirement of precision farming, improvements in corresponding elements needs to be made to address the limitations to reap its benefits to fullest extent.

5 Mechanised Agriculture

Mechanised agriculture is the process of using agricultural machinery to massively increase farm output. In modern times, powered machinery has replaced many jobs formerly carried out by men or animals such as oxen and horses.

The history of agriculture contains many examples of tool use, but only in recent time has the high rate of machine use been at such a level.

The first pervasive mechanization of agriculture came with the introduction of the plough, usually powered by animals. It was invented in ancient Mesopotamia.

Current mechanised agriculture includes the use of airplanes, helicopters, trucks and tractors, among other vehicles. Modern farms even sometimes use computers in conjunction with satellite imagery and GPS guidance to increase yields. The need for mechanization is as a result of the global population increase which must be fed. It improves the production efficiency by reducing cost per unit of product,encourages large scale production and improves the quality of farm produce. On the other hand, it displaces unskilled farm labour, causes environmental pollution, deforestation and erosion.

Jtetro Till's seed drill (ca. 1701) was a mechanical seed spacing and depth placing device that increased crop yields and saved seed. It was an important factor in the British Agricultural Revolution.

Since the beginning of agriculture threshing was done by hand with a flail, requiring a great deal of labour. The threshing machine, which was invented 1794 but not widely used for several more decades, simplified the operation and allowed the use of animal power.

Before the invention of the grain cradle (ca. 1790) an able bodied labourer could reap about one quarter acre of wheat in a day using a sickle. It was estimated that for each of Cyrus McCormick's horse pulled reapers (ca. 1830s) freed up five men for military service in the U.S. Civil War. Later innovations included raking and binding machines. By 1890 two men and two horses could cut, rake and bind 20 acres of wheat.

In the 1880s the reaper and threshing machine were combined into the combine harvester. These machines required large teams of horses or mules to pull.

Steam power was applied to threshing machines in the late 19th century. There were steam engines that moved around on wheels under their own power for supplying temporary power to stationary threshing machines. These were called *road engines,* and Henry Ford seeing one as a boy was inspired to build an automobile.

With internal combustion came the first modern tractors in the early 1900s, becoming more popular after the Fordson tractor (ca. 1917). At first reapers and combine harvesters were pulled by tractors, but in the 1930s self powered combines were developed.

The horse population began to decline in the 1920s after the conversion of agriculture and transportation to internal combustion. In addition to saving labour, this freed up much land previously used for supporting draft animals.

The Industrial Revolution

With the coming of the Industrial Revolution and the development of more complicated machines, farming methods took a great leap forward. Instead of harvesting grain by hand with a sharp blade, wheeled machines cut a continuous swath. Instead of threshing the grain by beating it with sticks, threshing machines separated the seeds from the heads and stalks.

Steam Power

Power for agricultural machinery was originally supplied by horses or other domesticated animals. With the invention of steam power came the portable engine, and later the traction engine, a multipurpose, mobile energy source that was the ground-crawling cousin to the steam locomotive. Agricultural steam engines took over the heavy pulling work of horses, and were also equipped with a pulley that could power stationary machines via the use of a long belt. The steam-powered machines were low-powered by today's standards but, because of their size and their low gear ratios, they could provide a large drawbar pull. Their slow speed led farmers to comment that tractors had two speeds: 'slow, and darn slow'.

Internal Combustion Engines

The internal combustion engine; first the petrol engine, and later diesel engines; became the main source of power for the next generation of tractors. These engines also contributed to the development of the self-propelled, combined harvester and thresher, or combine harvester (also shortened to 'combine'). Instead of cutting the grain stalks and transporting them to a stationary threshing machine, these combines cut, threshed, and separated the grain while moving continuously through the field.

Combines might have taken the harvesting job away from tractors, but tractors still do the majority of work on a modern farm. They are used to pull implements — machines that till the ground, plant seed, and perform other tasks.

Tillage implements prepare the soil for planting by loosening the soil and killing weeds or competing plants. The best-known is the plow, the ancient implement that was upgraded in 1838 by John Deere. Plows are now used less frequently in the U.S. than formerly, with offset disks used instead to turn over the soil, and chisels used to gain the depth needed to retain moisture.

The most common type of seeder is called a planter, and spaces seeds out equally in long rows, which are usually two to three feet apart. Some crops are planted by drills, which put out much more seed in rows less than a foot apart, blanketing the field with crops. Transplanters automate the task of transplanting seedlings to the field. With the widespread use of plastic mulch, plastic mulch layers, transplanters, and seeders lay down long rows of plastic, and plant through them automatically.

After planting, other implements can be used to cultivate weeds from between rows, or to spread fertilizer and pesticides. Hay balers can be used to tightly package grass or alfalfa into a storable form for the winter months.

Modern irrigation relies on machinery. Engines, pumps and other specialized gear provide water quickly and in high volumes to large areas of land. Similar types of equipment can be used to deliver fertilizers and pesticides.

Besides the tractor, other vehicles have been adapted for use in farming, including trucks, airplanes, and helicopters, such as for transporting crops and making equipment mobile, to aerial spraying and livestock herd management.

New Technology and the Future

Though modern harvesters and planters will do a better job than their predecessors, the combine of today still cuts, threshes, and separates grain in essentially the same way it has always been done. However, technology is changing the way that humans operate the machines, as computer monitoring systems, GPS locators, and self-steer programmes allow the most advanced tractors and implements to be more precise and less wasteful in the use of fuel, seed, or fertilizer. In the foreseeable future, some agricultural machines will be capable of driving themselves, using GPS maps and electronic sensors to become agricultural robots. Even more esoteric are the new areas of nanotechnology and genetic engineering, where submicroscopic devices and biological processes may be used as machines to perform agricultural tasks.

LIST OF AGRICULTURAL MACHINERY

Traction and Power

- Tractor
- Crawler tractor/Caterpillar tractor

Soil Cultivation

- Rotavator
- Cultivator
- Cultipacker
- Chisel plow
- Harrow
- Spike harrow
- Drag harrow
- Disk harrow
- Plough
- Power tiller/Rotary tiller/Rototiller
- Spading machine
- Subsoiler
- Two-wheel tractor
- Stone picker (rock picker)
- Rock windrower (rock rake)

Planting

- A plough in action in South Africa. Notice the soil being turned over.
- Broadcast seeder (alternately: broadcast spreader or fertilizer spreader)
- Planter (farm implement)
- Plastic mulch layer
- Potato planter
- Seed drill
- Air seeder
- Precision drill
- Transplanter
- Rice transplanter

Fertilizing and Pest Control

- Fertilizer spreader
- Terragator
- Manure spreader
- Sprayer

Irrigation

- Centre pivot irrigation

Harvesting/post-harvest

- Case IH module express 625 picks cotton and simultaneously builds cotton modules.
- Beet harvester
- Beet cleaner loader
- Bean harvester
- Cane harvester
- Carrot puller
- Chaser bin
- Combine harvester
- Conveyor belt
- Corn harvester

- Cotton picker
- Fanning mill
- Farm truck
- Forage harvester (or silage harvester)
- Gleaner
- Grain cleaner
- Gravity wagon
- Haulout Transporter
- Over-the-row mechanical harvester for harvesting apples
- Potato digger
- Potato harvester
- Rice huller
- Sickle
- Sugarcane harvester
- Swather
- Winnower

Hay Making

- Bale mover
- Bale wrapper
- Baler and Big Baler
- Conditioner
- Hay rake
- Hay tedder
- Mower
- Loader wagon, Self-loading wagon — used in Europe, but not common in USA

Loading

- Backhoe
- Front end loader
- Skid-steer loader

Milking

- Bulk tank
- Milking machine
- Milking pipeline

Other

- A skid loader with its bucket replaced by backhoe attachment
- Allen scythe
- Grain auger
- Feed grinder
- Grain cart
- Conveyor analyzer
- Chillcuring

Obsolete Farm Machinery

- Steam-powered
- Stationary steam engine
- Portable engine
- Traction engine
- Agricultural engine
- Ploughing engine
- Steam tractor
- Binder
- Hog oiler
- Reaper
- Threshing machine
- Drag harrow

6 Industrial Agriculture

Industrial agriculture is a form of modern farming that refers to the industrialized production of livestock, poultry, fish, and crops. The methods of industrial agriculture are technoscientific, economic, and political. They include innovation in agricultural machinery and farming methods, genetic technology, techniques for achieving economies of scale in production, the creation of new markets for consumption, the application of patent protection to genetic information, and global trade. These methods are widespread in developed nations and increasingly prevalent worldwide. Most of the meat, dairy, eggs, fruits, and vegetables available in supermarkets are produced using these methods of industrial agriculture.

The birth of industrial agriculture more or less coincides with that of the Industrial Revolution in general. The identification of nitrogen, potassium, and phosphorus (referred to by the acronym NPK) as critical factors in plant growth led to the manufacture of synthetic fertilizers, making possible more intensive types of agriculture. The discovery of vitamins and their role in animal nutrition, in the first two decades of the 20th century, led to vitamin supplements, which in the 1920s allowed certain livestock to be raised indoors, reducing their exposure to adverse natural elements. The discovery of antibiotics and vaccines facilitated raising livestock in concentrated, controlled animal feed operations by reducing diseases caused by crowding. Chemicals developed for use in World War II gave rise to synthetic pesticides. Developments in shipping networks and technology have made long-distance distribution of agricultural produce feasible.

Agricultural production across the world doubled four times between 1820 and 1975 to feed a global population of one billion human beings in 1800 and 6.5 billion in 2002. During the same period, the number of people involved in farming dropped as the process became more automated. In the 1930s, 24 per cent of the American population worked in agriculture compared to 1.5 per cent in 2002; in 1940, each farm worker supplied 11 consumers, whereas in 2002, each worker supplied 90 consumers. The number of farms has also decreased, and their ownership is more concentrated. In the U.S., four companies kill 81 per cent of cows, 73 per cent of sheep, 57 per cent of pigs, and produce 50 per cent of chickens, cited as an example of 'vertical integration' by the president of the U.S. National Farmers' Union. In 1967, there were one million pig farms in America; as of 2002, there were 114,000, with 80 million pigs (out of 95 million) killed each year on factory farms, according to the U.S. National Pork Producers Council. According to the Worldwatch Institute, 74 per cent of the world's poultry, 43 per cent of beef, and 68 per cent of eggs are produced this way.

According to Denis Avery of the agribusiness funded Hudson Institute, Asia increased its consumption of pork by 18 million tons in the 1990s. As of 1997, the world had a stock of 900 million pigs, which Avery predicts will rise to 2.5 billion pigs by 2050. He told the College of Natural Resources at the University of California, Berkeley that three billion pigs will thereafter be needed annually to meet demand. He writes: "For the sake of the environment, we had better hope those hogs are raised in big, efficient confinement systems."

British Agricultural Revolution

The British agricultural revolution describes a period of agricultural development in Britain between the 16th century and the mid-19th century, which saw a massive increase in agricultural productivity and net output. This in turn supported unprecedented population growth, freeing up a significant percentage of the workforce, and thereby helped drive the Industrial Revolution. How this came about is not entirely clear. In recent decades, historians cited four key changes in agricultural practices, enclosure, mechanization, four-field crop rotation, and selective breeding, and gave credit to a relatively few individuals.

Challenges and Issues

The challenges and issues of industrial agriculture for global and local society, for the industrial agriculture sector, for the individual industrial agriculture farm, and for animal rights include the costs and benefits of both current practices and proposed changes to those practices. Current industrial agriculture practices are temporarily increasing the carrying capacity of the Earth for humans while slowly destroying the *long term* carrying capacity of the earth for humans necessitating a shift to a sustainable agriculture form of industrial agriculture. This is a continuation of thousands of years of the invention and use of technologies in feeding ever growing populations.

When hunter-gatherers with growing populations depleted the stocks of game and wild foods across the Near East, they were forced to introduce agriculture. But agriculture brought much longer hours of work and a less rich diet than hunter-gatherers enjoyed. Further population growth among shifting slash-and-burn farmers led to shorter fallow periods, falling yields and soil erosion. Plowing and fertilizers were introduced to deal with these problems — but once again involved longer hours of work and degradation of soil resources (Boserup, The Conditions of Agricultural Growth, Allen and Unwin, 1965, expanded and updated in Population and Technology, Blackwell, 1980).

While the point of industrial agriculture is lower cost products to create greater productivity thus a higher standard of living as measured by available goods and services, industrial methods have side effects both good and bad. Further, industrial agriculture is not some single indivisible thing, but instead is composed of numerous separate elements, each of which can be modified, and in fact is modified in response to market conditions, government regulation, and scientific advances. So the question then becomes for each specific element that goes into an industrial agriculture method or technique or process: What bad side effects are bad enough that the financial gain and good side effects are outweighed? Different interest groups not only reach different conclusions on this, but also recommend differing solutions, which then become factors in changing both market conditions and government regulations.

Society

The major challenges and issues faced by society concerning industrial agriculture include:

Maximizing the benefits:

- Cheap and plentiful food
- Convenience for the consumer
- The contribution to our economy on many levels, from growers to harvesters to processors to sellers

While minimizing the downsides:

- Environmental and social costs

- Damage to fisheries
- Cleanup of surface and groundwater polluted with animal waste
- Increased health risks from pesticides
- Increased ozone pollution and global warming from heavy use of fossil fuels

Benefits

Cheap and Plentiful Food

Population (est.) 10,000 BCE-2000 CE.

Very roughly:

- 30,000 years ago hunter-gatherer behaviour fed 6 million people
- 3,000 years ago primitive agriculture fed 60 million people
- 300 years ago intensive agriculture fed 600 million people
- Today industrial agriculture feeds 6 billion people

An example of industrial agriculture providing cheap and plentiful food is the U.S.'s "most successful programme of agricultural development of any country in the world". Between 1930 and 2000 U.S. agricultural productivity (output divided by all inputs) rose by an average of about 2 per cent annually causing food prices paid by consumers to decrease. "The percentage of U.S. disposable income spent on food prepared at home decreased, from 22 per cent as late as 1950 to 7 per cent by the end of the century."

Industrial agriculture treats farmed products in terms of minimizing inputs and maximizing outputs at every stage from the natural resources of sun, land and water to the consumer which results in a vertically integrated economic sector that genetically manipulates crops and livestock; and processes, packages, and markets in whatever way generates maximum return on investment creating convenience foods many customers will pay a premium for. A consumer backlash against food sold for taste, convenience, and profit rather than nutrition and other values (e.g. reduce waste, be natural, be ethical) has led agriculture to also provide organic food, minimally processed foods, and minimally packaged foods to maximally satisfy all segments of society thus generating maximum return on investment.

LIABILITIES

Environment

Industrial agriculture uses huge amounts of water, energy, and industrial chemicals; increasing pollution in the arable land, usable water and atmosphere. Herbicides, insecticides, fertilizers, and animal waste products are accumulating in ground and surface waters. "Many of the negative effects of industrial agriculture are remote from fields and farms. Nitrogen compounds from the Midwest, for example, travel down the Mississippi to degrade coastal fisheries in the Gulf of Mexico. But other adverse effects are showing up within agricultural production systems—for example, the rapidly developing resistance among pests is rendering our arsenal of herbicides and insecticides increasingly ineffective".

Social

A study done for the US Office of Technology Assessment conducted by the UC Davis Macrosocial Accounting Project concluded that industrial agriculture is associated with substantial deterioration of human living conditions in nearby rural communities.

Animals

'Confined animal feeding operations' or 'intensive livestock operations', can hold large numbers (some up to hundreds of thousands) of animals, often indoors. These animals are typically cows, hogs, turkeys, or chickens. The distinctive characteristics of such farms is the concentration of livestock in a given space. The aim of the operation is to produce as much meat, eggs, or milk at the lowest possible cost and with the greatest level of food safety.

Food and water is supplied in place, and artificial methods are often employed to maintain animal health and improve production, such as therapeutic use of antimicrobial agents, vitamin supplements and growth hormones. Growth hormones are not used in chicken meat production nor are they used in the European Union for any animal. In meat production, methods are also sometimes employed to control undesirable behaviours often related to stresses of being confined in restricted areas with other animals. More docile breeds are sought (with natural dominant behaviours bred out for example), physical restraints to stop interaction, such as individual cages for chickens, or animals physically modified, such as the de-beaking of chickens to reduce the harm of fighting. Weight gain is encouraged by the provision of plentiful supplies of food to animals breed for weight gain.

The designation 'confined animal feeding operation' in the U.S. resulted from that country's 1972 Federal Clean Water Act, which was enacted to protect and restore lakes and rivers to a 'fishable, swimmable' quality. The United States Environmental Protection Agency (EPA) identified certain animal feeding operations, along with many other types of industry, as point source polluters of groundwater. These operations were designated as CAFOs and subject to special anti-pollution regulation.

In 24 states in the U.S., isolated cases of groundwater contamination has been linked to CAFOs. For example, the ten million hogs in North Carolina generate 19 million tons of waste per year. The U.S. federal government acknowledges the waste disposal issue and requires that animal waste be stored in lagoons. These lagoons can be as large as 7.5 acres (30,000 m^2). Lagoons not protected with an impermeable liner can leak waste into groundwater under some conditions, as can runoff from manure spread back onto fields as fertilizer in the case of an unforeseen heavy rainfall. A lagoon that burst in 1995 released 25 million gallons of nitrous sludge in North Carolina's New River. The spill allegedly killed eight to ten million fish.

The large concentration of animals, animal waste, and dead animals in a small space poses ethical issues to some consumers. Animal rights and animal welfare activists have charged that intensive animal rearing is cruel to animals. As they become more common, so do concerns about air pollution and ground water contamination, and the effects on human health of the pollution and the use of antibiotics and growth hormones.

Some of the major benefits that are often overlooked by consumers and animal activists alike, are the overall benefits to the animals, such as controlled, comfortable climate, unlimited amounts of fresh food and clean water, and safety from predators. Animals raised in a modern setting also benefit from greater veterinary care, decreased levels of stress, and a more sanitary environment.

According to the U.S. Centres for Disease Control and Prevention (CDC), farms on which animals are intensively reared can cause adverse health reactions in farm workers. Workers may develop acute and chronic lung disease, musculoskeletal injuries, and may catch infections that transmit from animals to human beings. These type of transmissions, however, and extremely rare, as zoonotic diseases are uncommon.

Crops

The projects within the Green Revolution spread technologies that had already existed, but had not been widely used outside of industrialized nations. These technologies included pesticides, irrigation projects, and synthetic nitrogen fertilizer.

The novel technological development of the Green Revolution was the production of what some referred to as 'miracle seeds'. Scientists created strains of maize, wheat, and rice that are generally referred to as HYVs or 'high-yielding varieties'. HYVs have an increased nitrogen-absorbing potential compared to other varieties. Since cereals that absorbed extra nitrogen would typically lodge, or fall over before harvest, semi-dwarfing genes were bred into their genomes. Norin 10 wheat, a variety developed by Orville Vogel from Japanese dwarf wheat varieties, was instrumental in developing Green Revolution wheat cultivars. IR8, the first widely implemented HYV rice to be developed by the International Rice Research Institute, was created through a cross between an Indonesian variety named 'Peta' and a Chinese variety named 'Dee Geo Woo Gen'.

With the availability of molecular genetics in Arabidopsis and rice the mutant genes responsible (*reduced height(rht)*, *gibberellin insensitive (gai1)* and *slender rice (slr1)*) have been cloned and identified as cellular signalling components of gibberellic acid, a phytohormone involved in regulating stem growth via its effect on cell division. Stem growth in the mutant background is significantly reduced leading to the dwarf phenotype. Photosynthetic investment in the stem is reduced dramatically as the shorter plants are inherently more stable mechanically. Assimilates become redirected to grain production, amplifying in particular the effect of chemical fertilisers on commercial yield.

HYVs significantly outperform traditional varieties in the presence of adequate irrigation, pesticides, and fertilizers. In the absence of these inputs, traditional varieties may outperform HYVs. One criticism of HYVs is that they were developed as F1 hybrids, meaning they need to be purchased by a farmer every season rather than saved from previous seasons, thus increasing a farmer's cost of production.

Sustainable Agriculture

The idea and practice of sustainable agriculture has arisen in response to the problems of industrial agriculture. Sustainable agriculture integrates three main goals: environmental stewardship, farm profitability, and prosperous farming communities. These goals have been defined by a variety of disciplines and may be looked at from the vantage point of the farmer or the consumer.

Organic Farming Methods

Organic farming methods combine some aspects of scientific knowledge and highly limited modern technology with traditional farming practices; accepting some of the methods of industrial agriculture while rejecting others. Organic methods rely on naturally occurring biological processes, which often take place over extended periods of time, and a holistic approach; while chemical-based farming focuses on immediate, isolated effects and reductionist strategies.

Integrated Multi-Trophic Aquaculture is an example of this holistic approach. Integrated Multi-Trophic Aquaculture (IMTA) is a practice in which the by-products (wastes) from one species are recycled to become inputs (fertilizers, food) for another. Fed aquaculture (e.g. fish, shrimp) is combined with inorganic extractive (e.g. seaweed) and organic extractive (e.g. shellfish) aquaculture to create balanced systems for environmental sustainability (biomitigation), economic stability (product diversification and risk reduction) and social acceptability (better management practices).

7 Agricultural Soil Science

Agricultural soil science is a branch of soil science that deals with the study of edaphic conditions as they relate to the production of food and fibre. In this context, it is also a constituent of the field of Agronomy.

Prior to the development of pedology in the 19th century, agricultural soil science (or edaphology) was the only branch of soil science. The bias of early soil science toward viewing soils only in terms of their agricultural potential continues to define the soil science profession in both academic and popular settings as of 2006.

Agricultural soil science studies the chemical, physical, biological, and mineralogical composition of soils as they relate to agriculture. Agricultural soil scientists develop methods that will improve the use of soil and increase the production of food and fiber crops. Emphasis continues to grow on the importance of soil sustainability. Soil degradation such as erosion, compaction, lowered fertility, and contamination continue to be serious concerns. They conduct research in irrigation and drainage, tillage, soil classification, plant nutrition, soil fertility, and other areas.

Soil Fertility

Agricultural soil scientists study ways to make soils more productive. They classify soils and test them to determine whether they contain nutrients vital to plant growth. Such nutritional substances include compounds of nitrogen, phosphorus, and potassium. If a certain soil is deficient in these substances, fertilizers may provide them. Agricultural soil scientists investigate the movement of nutrients through the soil, and the amount of nutrients absorbed by a plant's roots. Agricultural soil scientists also examine the development of roots and their relation to the soil. Some agricultural soil scientists try to understand the structure and function of soils in relation to soil fertility. They grasp the structure of soil as porous solid. The solid frames of soil consist of mineral derived from the rocks and organic matter originated from the dead bodies of various organisms. The pore space of the soil is essential for the soil to become productive. Small pores serve as water reservoir supplying water to plants and other organisms in the soil during the rain-less period. The water in the small pores of soils is not pure water; they call it soil solution. In soil solution, various plant nutrients derived from minerals and organic matters in the soil are there. Indeed the soil solution is the milk to plants. Large pores serve as water drainage pipe to allow the excessive water pass through the soil, during the heavy rains. They also serve as air tank to supply oxygen to plant roots and other living beings in the soil. In short, agricultural soil scientists see the soil as a vessel, the most precious one for us, containing all of the substances needed by the plants and other living beings on earth.

Soil Preservation

In addition, agricultural soil scientists develop methods to preserve the agricultural productivity of soil and to decrease the effects on productivity of erosion by wind and water. For example, a technique called contour plowing may be used to prevent soil erosion and conserve rainfall. Researchers in agricultural soil science also seek ways to use the soil more effectively in addressing associated challenges. Such challenges include the beneficial reuse of human and animal wastes using agricultural crops; agricultural soil management aspects of preventing water pollution and the build-up in agricultural soil of chemical pesticides.

Employment of Agricultural Soil Scientists

Most agricultural soil scientists are consultants, researchers, or teachers. Many work in the developed world as farm advisors, agricultural experiment stations, federal, state or local government agencies, industrial firms, or universities. Within the USA they may be trained through the USDA's Cooperative Extension Service offices, although other countries may use universities, research instututes or research agencies. Elsewhere, agricultural soil scientists may serve in international organizations such as the Agency for International Development and the Food and Agriculture Organization of the United Nations.

Quotations

> The key objective of the soil science discipline is that of "finding ways to meet growing human needs for food and fibre while maintaining environmental stability and conserving resources for future generations".
>
> ***—John W Doran, 2002 SSSA President, 2002***
>
> "Many people have the vague notion that soil science is merely a phase of agronomy and deals only with practical soil management for field crops. Whether we like it or not this is the image many have of us".
>
> ***—Charles E. Kellog, 1961***

Soil science is the study of soil as a natural resource on the surface of the earth including soil formation, classification and mapping; physical, chemical, biological, and fertility properties of soils; and these properties in relation to the use and management of soils.

Sometimes terms which refer to branches of soil science, such as pedology (formation, chemistry, morphology and classification of soil) and edaphology (influence of soil on organisms, especially plants), are used as if synonymous with soil science. The diversity of names associated with this discipline is related to the various associations concerned. Indeed, engineers, agronomists, chemists, geologists, geographers, ecologists, biologists, microbiologists, sylviculturists, sanitarians, archaeologists, and specialists in regional planning, all contribute to further knowledge of soils and the advancement of the soil sciences.

Soil occupies the pedosphere, one of Earth's spheres that the geosciences use to organize the Earth conceptually. This is the conceptual perspective of pedology and edaphology, the two main branches of soil science. Pedology is the study of soil in its natural setting. Edaphology is the study of soil in relation to soil-dependent uses. Both branches apply a combination of soil physics, soil chemistry, and soil biology. Due to the numerous interactions between the biosphere, atmosphere and hydrosphere that are hosted within the pedosphere, more integrated, less soil-centric concepts are also valuable. Many concepts essential to understanding soil come from individuals not identifiable strictly as soil scientists. This highlights the interdisciplinary nature of soil concepts.

Research

Dependence on and curiosity about soil, exploring the diversity and dynamic of this resource continues to yield fresh discoveries and insights.

New avenues of soil research are compelled by a need to understand soil in the context of climate change, greenhouse gases, and carbon sequestration. Interest in maintaining the planet's biodiversity and in exploring past cultures has also stimulated renewed interest in achieving a more refined understanding of soil.

Most empirical knowledge of soil in nature comes from soil survey efforts. Soil survey, or soil mapping, is the process of determining the soil types or other properties of the soil cover over a landscape, and mapping them for others to understand and use. It relies heavily on distinguishing the individual influences of the five classic soil forming factors. This effort draws upon geomorphology, physical geography, and analysis of vegetation and land-use patterns. Primary data for the soil survey are acquired by field sampling and supported by remote sensing.

As of 2006, the World Reference Base for Soil Resources, via its Land & Water Development division, is the pre-eminent soil classification system. It replaces the previous FAO soil classification.

The WRB borrows from modern soil classification concepts, including USDA soil taxonomy. The classification is based mainly on soil morphology as an expression pedogenesis. A major difference with USDA soil taxonomy is that soil climate is not part of the system, except insofar as climate influences soil profile characteristics.

Many other classification schemes exist, including vernacular systems. The structure in vernacular systems are either nominal, giving unique names to soils or landscapes, or descriptive, naming soils by their characteristics such as red, hot, fat, or sandy. Soils are distinguished by obvious characteristics, such as physical appearance (e.g., colour, texture, landscape position), performance (e.g., production capability, flooding), and accompanying vegetation. A vernacular distinction familiar to many is classifying texture as heavy or light. Light soil content and better structure, take less effort to turn and cultivate. Contrary to popular belief, light soils do not weigh less than heavy soils on an air dry basis nor do they have more porosity.

History

Vasily Dokuchaev, a Russian geologist, geographer and early soil scientist, is credited with identifying soil as a resource whose distinctness and complexity deserved to be separated conceptually from geology and crop production and treated as a whole.

Previously, soil had been considered a product of chemical transformations of rocks, a dead substrate from which plants derive nutritious elements. Soil and bedrock were in fact equated. Dokuchaev considers the soil as a natural body having its own genesis and its own history of development, a body with complex and multiform processes taking place within it. The soil is considered as different from bedrock. The latter becomes soil under the influence of a series of soil-formation factors (climate, vegetation, country, relief and age). According to him, soil should be called the "daily" or outward horizons of rocks regardless of the type; they are changed naturally by the common effect of water, air and various kinds of living and dead organisms.

A 1914 encyclopedic definition: "the different forms of earth on the surface of the rocks, formed by the breaking down or weathering of rocks". serves to illustrate the historic view of soil which persisted from the 19th century. Dokuchaev's late 19th century soil concept developed in the 20th century to one of soil as earthy material that has been altered by living processes. A corollary concept is that soil without a living component is simply a part of earth's outer layer.

Further refinement of the soil concept is occurring in view of an appreciation of energy transport and transformation within soil. The term is popularly applied to the material on the surface of the Earth's moon and Mars, a usage acceptable within a portion of the scientific community. Accurate to this modern understanding of soil is Nikiforoff's 1959 definition of soil as the "excited skin of the sub aerial part of the earth's crust".

Areas of Practice

Academically, soil scientists tend to be drawn to one of five areas of specialization: microbiology, pedology, edaphology, physics or chemistry. Yet the work specifics are very much dictated by the challenges facing our civilization's desire to sustain the land that supports it, and the distinctions between the sub-disciplines of soil science often blur in the process. Soil science professionals commonly stay current in soil chemistry, soil physics, soil microbiology, pedology, and applied soil science in related disciplines.

One interesting effort drawing in soil scientists in the USA as of 2004 is the Soil Quality Initiative. Central to the Soil Quality Initiative is developing indices of soil health and then monitoring them in a way that gives us long term (decade-to-decade) feedback on our performance as stewards of the planet. The effort includes understanding the functions of soil microbiotic crusts and exploring the potential to sequester atmospheric carbon in soil organic matter. The concept of soil quality, however, has not been without its share of controversy and criticism, including critiques by Nobel Laureate Norman Borlaug and World Food Prize Winner Pedro Sanchez.

A more traditional role for soil scientists has been to map soils. Most every area in the United States now has a published soil survey, which includes interpretive tables as to how soil properties support or limit activities and uses. An internationally accepted soil taxonomy allows uniform communication of soil characteristics and functions. National and international soil survey efforts have given the profession unique insights into landscape scale functions.

Pedogenesis

Pedogenesis or soil evolution (formation) is the process by which soil is created. It is the major topic of the science of pedology, whose other aspects include the soil morphology, classification (taxonomy) of soils, and their distribution in nature, present and past (soil geography and paleopedology).

Climate regulates soil formation. Soils are more developed in areas with higher rainfall and more warmth. The rate of chemical weathering increases by 2-3 times when the temperature increases by 10 degrees Celsius. Climate also affects which organisms are present, affecting the soil chemically and physically (movement of roots).

Organisms

The organisms living in and on the soil form distinct soil types. Coniferous forests have acidic leaf litter and form what are known as inceptisols. Mixed or deciduous forests leave a larger layer of humus, changing the elements leeched and accumulated in the soil, forming alfisols. Prairies have very high humus accumulation, creating a dark, thick A horizon characteristic of mollisols.

For example three species of land snails in the genus *Euchondrus* in the Negev desert are noted for eating lichens growing under the surface limestone rocks and slabs (endolithic lichens). They disrupt and eat the limestone. Their grazing resulting in the weathering of the stones, and the subsequent formation of soil. They have a significant effect on the region: the total population of snails is estimated to process between 0.7 and 1.1 metric ton per hectare per year of limestone in the Negev desert.

Parent Material

The rock from which soil is formed is called parent material. The main types are: aeolian, glacial till, glacial outwash, alluvium, lacustrine parent material and residual parent material, or bedrock.

Pedologists use the following generic functional relationship for understanding soil formation:

s = f (cl, o, r, p, t, ...)

where s - soil properties; cl - regional climate; o - potential biota; r - topography; p - parent material; t - time; ... - additional variables.

Examples

A variety of mechanisms contribute to soil formation, including siltation, erosion, overpressure and lakebed succession. A specific example of the evolution of soils in prehistoric lake beds is in the Makgadikgadi Pans of the Kalahari Desert, where change in an ancient river course led to millennia of salinity buildup and formation of calcretes and silcretes.

Paleopedology

Paleopedology (palaeopedology in the United Kingdom) is the discipline that studies soils of past geological eras, from quite recent (Quaternary) to the earliest periods of the Earth's history. Paleopedology can be seen either as a branch of soil science (pedology) or of paleontology, since the methods it uses are in many ways a well-defined combination of the two disciplines.

Paleopedology's earliest developments arose from observations in Scotland circa 1795 whereby it was found that some soils in cliffs appeared to be remains of a former exposed land surface. During the nineteenth century there were many other finds of former soils throughout Europe and North America. However, most of this was only found in the search for animal and/or plant fossils and it was not until soil science first developed that buried soils of past geological ages were considered of any value.

It was only when the first relationships between soils and climate were observed in the steppes of Russia and Kazakhstan that there was any interest in applying the finds of former soils to past ecosystems. This occurred because, by the 1920s, some soils in Russia had been found by K.D. Glinka that did not fit with present climates and were seen as relic of warmer climates in the past.

Eugene W. Hilgard, in 1892, had related soil and climate in the United States in the same manner, and by the 1950s analysis of Quaternary stratigraphy to monitor recent environmental changes in the northern hemisphere had become firmly established. These developments have allowed soil fossils to be classified according to USDA soil taxonomy quite easily with all recent soils. Interest in earlier soil fossils was much slower to grow, but has steadily developed since the 1960s owing to the development of such techniques as X-ray diffraction which permit their classification. This has allowed many developments in paleoecology and paleogeography to take place because the soils' chemistry can provide a good deal of evidence as to how life moved onto land during the Paleozoic.

Finding Soil Fossils and Their Structure

Remains of former soils can either be found under deposited sediment in unglaciated areas or in extremely steep cliffs where the old soil can be seem below the young present-day soil. In cases where volcanoes have been active, some soil fossils occur under the volcanic ash. If there is continued deposition of sediment, a sequence of soil fossils will form, especially after the retreat of glaciers during the Holocene. Soil fossils can also exist where a younger soil has been eroded (for instance by wind), as in the Badlands of South Dakota. (One must *exclude* areas where present-day soils are relics of former wetter climates, as with Australia and Southern Africa. The soils of these regions are proper *paleosols.*)

Soil fossils, whether buried or exposed, suffer from alteration. This occurs largely because almost all past soils have lost their former vegetative covering and the organic matter they once supported has been used up by plants since the soil was buried. However, if remains of plants can be found, the nature of the soil fossil can be made a great deal clearer than if no flora can be found because roots can nowadays be identified with respect to the plant group from which they come. Patterns of *root traces* including their shape and size, is good evidence for the vegetation type the former soil supported. Bluish colours in the soil tend to indicate the plants have mobilised nutrients within the soil.

The horizons of fossil soils typically are sharply defined only in the top layers, unless some of the parent material has not been obliterated by soil formation. The kinds of horizons in fossil soils are, though, generally the same as those found in present-day soils, allowing easy classification in modern taxonomy of all but the oldest soils.

Analysis

Chemical analysis of soil fossils generally focuses on their lime content, which determines both their pH and how reactive they will be to dilute acids. Chemical analysis is also useful, usually through solvent extraction to determine key minerals. this analysis can be of some use in determining the structure of a soil fossil, but today X-ray diffraction is preferred because it permits the exact crystal structure of the former soil to be determined.

With the aid of X-ray diffraction, paleosols can now be classified into one of the 12 orders of Soil Taxonomy (Oxisols, Ultisols, Alfisols, Mollisols, Spodosols, Aridisols, Entisols, Inceptisols, Gelisols, Histosols, Vertisols and Andisols). Many Precambrian soils, however, when examined do not fit the characteristics for *any* of these soil orders and have been placed in a new order called *green clays*. The green colour is due to the presence of certain unoxidised minerals found in the primitive earth because O_2 was not present. There are also some forest soils of more recent times that cannot clearly be classified as Alfisols or as Spodosols because, despite their sandy horizons, there are not nearly acidic enough to have the typical features of a Spodosol.

Uses

Paleopedology is a very important discipline today for the understanding of the ecology of ancient ecosystems because it gives a clue as to what soils conditions past animals and plants were required to live under and how the plants obtained essential nutrients.

In geochemistry, a knowledge of the structure of former soils is also valuable to understand the composition of certain continental rocks laid down many years ago.

8 Soil

Soil is a natural body consisting of layers (soil horizons) of mineral constituents of variable thicknesses, which differ from the parent materials in their morphological, physical, chemical, and mineralogical characteristics. It is composed of particles of broken rock that have been altered by chemical and environmental processes that include weathering and erosion. Soil differs from its parent rock due to interactions between the lithosphere, hydrosphere, atmosphere, and the biosphere. It is a mixture of mineral and organic constituents that are in solid, gaseous and aqueous states.

Soil particles pack loosely, forming a soil structure filled with pore spaces. These pores contain soil solution (liquid) and air (gas). Accordingly, soils are often treated as a three state system. Most soils have a density between 1 and 2 g/cm^3. Soil is also known as earth: it is the substance from which our planet takes its name. Little of the soil composition of planet Earth is older than the Tertiary and most no older than the Pleistocene. In engineering, soil is referred to as regolith, or loose rock material.

Soil formation, or pedogenesis, is the combined effect of physical, chemical, biological, and anthropogenic processes on soil parent material. Soil genesis involves processes that develop layers or horizons in the soil profile. These processes involve additions, losses, transformations and translocations of material that compose the soil. Minerals derived from weathered rocks undergo changes that cause the formation of secondary minerals and other compounds that are variably soluble in water, these constituents are moved (translocated) from one area of the soil to other areas by water and animal activity. The alteration and movement of materials within soil causes the formation of distinctive soil horizons.

The weathering of bedrock produces the parent material from which soils form. An example of soil development from bare rock occurs on recent lava flows in warm regions under heavy and very frequent rainfall. In such climates, plants become established very quickly on basaltic lava, even though there is very little organic material. The plants are supported by the porous rock as it is filled with nutrient-bearing water which carries, for example, dissolved minerals and guano. The developing plant roots, themselves or associated with mycorrhizal fungi, gradually break up the porous lava and organic matter soon accumulates.

But even before it does, the predominantly porous broken lava in which the plant roots grow can be considered a soil. How the soil 'life' cycle proceeds is influenced by at least five classic soil forming factors that are dynamically intertwined in shaping the way soil is developed, they include: parent material, regional climate, topography, biotic potential and the passage of time.

The material from which soils form is called parent material. It includes: weathered primary bedrock; secondary material transported from other locations, e.g. colluvium and alluvium; deposits that are already present but mixed or altered in other ways — old soil formations, organic material including peat or alpine humus; and anthropogenic materials, like landfill or mine waste. Few soils form directly from the breakdown of the underlying rocks they develop on. These soils are often called 'residual soils', and have the same general chemistry as their parent rocks. Most soils derive from materials that have been transported from other locations by wind, water and gravity Some of these materials may have moved many miles or only a few feet. Windblown material called loess is common in the Midwest of North America and in Central Asia and other locations. Glacial till is a component of many soils in the northern and southern latitudes and those formed near large mountains; till is the product of glacial ice moving over the ground. The ice can break rock and larger stones into smaller pieces, it also can sort material into different sizes. As glacial ice melts, the melt water also moves and sorts material, and deposits it varying distances from its origin. The deeper sections of the soil profile may have materials that are relatively unchanged from when they were deposited by water, ice or wind.

Weathering is the first stage in the transforming of parent material into soil material. In soils forming from bedrock, a thick layer of weathered material called saprolite may form. Saprolite is the result of weathering processes that include: hydrolysis (the replacement of a mineral's cations with hydrogen ions), chelation from organic compounds, hydration (the absorption of water by minerals), solution of minerals by water, and physical processes that include freezing and thawing or wetting and drying. The mineralogical and chemical composition of the primary bedrock material, plus physical features, including grain size and degree of consolidation, plus the rate and type of weathering, transforms it into different soil materials.

Soil formation greatly depends on the climate, and soils from different climate zones show distinctive characteristics. Temperature and moisture affect weathering and leaching. Wind moves sand and other particles, especially in arid regions where there is little plant cover. The type and amount of precipitation influence soil formation by affecting the movement of ions and particles through the soil, aiding in the development of different soil profiles. Seasonal and daily temperature fluctuations affect the effectiveness of water in weathering parent rock material and affect soil dynamics. The cycle of freezing and thawing is an effective mechanism to break up rocks and other consolidated materials. Temperature and precipitation rates affect biological activity, rates of chemical reactions and types of vegetation cover.

Biological Factors

Plants, animals, fungi, bacteria and humans affect soil formation (see soil biomantle and stonelayer). Animals and micro-organisms mix soils to form burrows and pores allowing moisture and gases to seep into deeper layers. In the same way, plant roots open channels in the soils, especially plants with deep taproots which can penetrate many meters through the different soil layers to bring up nutrients from deeper in the soil. Plants with fibrous roots that spread out near the soil surface, have roots that are easily decomposed, adding organic matter. Micro-organisms, including fungi and bacteria, affect chemical exchanges between roots and soil and act as a reserve of nutrients. Humans can impact soil formation by removing vegetation cover; this removal promotes erosion. They can also mix the different soil layers, restarting the soil formation process as less-weathered material is mixed with and diluting the more developed upper layers. Some soils may contain up to one million species of microbes per gram, most of those species being unknown, making soil the most abundant ecosystem on Earth.

Vegetation impacts soils in numerous ways. It can prevent erosion caused by the impact of rain or surface runoff. Plants shade soils, keeping them cooler and slowing evaporation of soil moisture, or plants by way of transpiration can cause soils to lose moisture. Plants can form new chemicals which can break down or build up soil particles. The type and amount of vegetation depends on climate, land form topography, soil characteristics, and biological factors. Soil factors such as density, depth, chemistry, pH, temperature and moisture greatly affect the type of plants that can grow in a given location. Dead plants and dropped leaves and stems fall to the surface of the soil and decompose. There, organisms feed on them and mix the organic material with the upper soil layers; these added organic compounds become part of the soil formation process.

Time is a factor in the interactions of all the above factors as they develop soil. Over time, soils evolve features dependent on the other forming factors, and soil formation is a time-responsive process dependent on how the other factors interplay with each other. Soil is always changing. For example, recently-deposited material from a flood exhibits no soil development because there has not been enough time for soil-forming activities. The soil surface is buried, and the formation process begins again for this soil. The long periods over which change occurs and its multiple influences mean that simple soils are rare, resulting in the formation of soil horizons. While soil can achieve relative stability in properties for extended periods, the soil life cycle ultimately ends in soil conditions that leave it vulnerable to erosion. Despite the inevitability of soil retrogression and degradation, most soil cycles are long and productive.

Soil-forming factors continue to affect soils during their existence, even on "stable" landscapes that are long-enduring, some for millions of years. Materials are deposited on top and materials are blown or washed away from the surface. With additions, removals and alterations, soils are always subject to new conditions. Whether these are slow or rapid changes depend on climate, landscape position and biological activity.

Characteristics

Soil colour is often the first impression one has when viewing soil. Striking colours and contrasting patterns are especially memorable. The Red River (Mississippi watershed) carries sediment eroded from extensive reddish soils like Port Silt Loam in Oklahoma. The Yellow River in China carries yellow sediment from eroding loessal soils. Mollisols in the Great Plains are darkened and enriched by organic matter. Podsols in boreal forests have highly contrasting layers due to acidity and leaching. Soil color is primarily influenced by soil mineralogy. Many soil colors are due to the extensive and various iron minerals. The development and distribution of color in a soil profile result from chemical and biological weathering, especially redox reactions. As the primary minerals in soil parent material weather, the elements combine into new and colorful compounds. Iron forms secondary minerals with a yellow or red colour, organic matter decomposes into black and brown compounds, and manganese, sulfur and nitrogen can form black mineral deposits. These pigments produce various colour patterns due to effects by the environment during soil formation. Aerobic conditions produce uniform or gradual colour changes, while reducing environments result in disrupted color flow with complex, mottled patterns and points of colour concentration.

Soil structure is the arrangement of soil particles into aggregates. These may have various shapes, sizes and degrees of development or expression. Soil structure affects aeration, water movement, resistance to erosion and plant root growth. Structure often gives clues to texture, organic matter content, biological activity, past soil evolution, human use, and chemical and mineralogical conditions under which the soil formed.

Soil texture refers to sand, silt and clay composition. Soil content affects soil behaviour, including the retention capacity for nutrients and water. Sand and silt are the products of physical weathering, while clay is the product of chemical weathering. Clay content has retention capacity for nutrients and water. Clay soils resist wind and water erosion better than silty and sandy soils, because the particles are more tightly joined to each other. In medium-textured soils, clay is often translocated downward through the soil profile and accumulates in the subsoil.

The electrical resistivity of soil can affect the rate of galvanic corrosion of metallic structures in contact with the soil. Higher moisture content or increased electrolyte concentration can lower the resistivity and thereby increase the rate of corrosion. Soil resistivity values typically range from about 2 to 1000 O·m, but more extreme values are not unusual.

Soil Horizons

The naming of soil horizons is based on the type of material the horizons are composed of; these materials reflect the duration of the specific processes used in soil formation. They are labeled using a short hand notation of letters and numbers. They are described and classified by their colour, size, texture, structure, consistency, root quantity, pH, voids, boundary characteristics, and if they have nodules or concretions. Any one soil profile does not have all the major horizons covered below; soils may have few or many horizons.

The exposure of parent material to favorable conditions produces initial soils that are suitable for plant growth. Plant growth often results in the accumulation of organic residues, the accumulated organic layer is called the O horizon. Biological organisms colonize and break down organic materials, making available nutrients that other plants and animals can live on. After sufficient time a distinctive organic surface layer forms with humus which is called the A horizon.

Soil is classified into categories in order to understand relationships between different soils and to determine the usefulness of a soil for a particular use. One of the first classification systems was developed by the Russian scientist Dokuchaev around 1880. It was modified a number of times by American and European researchers, and developed into the system commonly used until the 1960s. It was based on the idea that soils have a particular morphology based on the materials and factors that form them. In the 1960s, a different classification system began to emerge, that focused on soil morphology instead of parental materials and soil-forming factors. Since then it has undergone further modifications. The World Reference Base for Soil Resources (WRB) aims to establish an international reference base for soil classification.

Orders

Orders are the highest category of soil classification. Order types end in the letters sol. In the US classification system, there are 10 orders:

- *Entisol* — recently formed soils that lack well-developed horizons. Commonly found on unconsolidated sediments like sand, some have an A horizon on top of bedrock.
- *Vertisol* — inverted soils. They tend to swell when wet and shrink upon drying, often forming deep cracks that surface layers can fall into.
- *Inceptisol* — young soils. They have subsurface horizon formation but show little eluviation and illuviation.
- *Aridisol* — dry soils forming under desert conditions. They include nearly 20 per cent of soils on Earth. Soil formation is slow, and accumulated organic matter is scarce. They may have subsurface zones (calcic horizons) where calcium carbonates have accumulated from percolating water. Many aridiso soils have well-developed Bt horizons showing clay movement from past periods of greater moisture.
- *Mollisol* — soft soils with very thick A horizons.
- *Spodosol* — soils produced by podsolization. They are typical soils of coniferous and deciduous forests in cooler climates.
- *Alfisol* — soils with aluminium and iron. They have horizons of clay accumulation, and form where there is enough moisture and warmth for at least three months of plant growth.
- *Ultisol* — soils that are heavily leached.
- *Oxisol* — soil with heavy oxide content.
- Histosol — organic soils.

Other order schemes may include:

- *Andisols* — volcanic soils, which tend to be high in glass content.
- *Gelisols* — permafrost soils.

Organic Matter

Most living things in soils, including plants, insects, bacteria and fungi, are dependent on organic matter for nutrients and energy. Soils often have varying degrees of organic compounds in different states of decomposition. Many soils, including desert and rocky-gravel soils, have no or little organic matter. Soils that are all organic matter, such as peat (histosols), are infertile.

Humus

Humus refers to organic matter that has decomposed to a point where it is resistant to further breakdown or alteration. Humic acids and fulvic acids are important constituents of humus and typically form from plant residues like foliage, stems and roots. After death, these plant residues begin to decay, starting the formation of humus. Humus formation involves changes within the soil and plant residue, there is a reduction of water soluble constituents including cellulose and hemicellulose; as the residues are deposited and break down, humin, lignin and lignin complexes accumulate within the soil; as microorganisms live and feed on the decaying plant matter, an increase in proteins occurs.

Lignin is resistant to breakdown and accumulates within the soil; it also chemically reacts with amino acids which add to its resistance to decomposition, including enzymatic decomposition by microbes. Fats and waxes from plant matter have some resistance to decomposition and persist in soils for a while. Clay soils often have higher organic contents that persist longer than soils without clay. Proteins normally decompose readily, but when bound to clay particles they become more resistant to decomposition. Clay particles also absorb enzymes that would break down proteins. The addition of organic matter to clay soils, can render the organic matter and any added nutrients inaccessible to plants and microbes for many years, since they can bind strongly to the clay. High soil tannin (polyphenol) content from plants can cause nitrogen to be sequestered by proteins or cause nitrogen immobilization, also making nitrogen unavailable to plants.

Humus formation is a process dependent on the amount of plant material added each year and the type of base soil; both are affected by climate and the type of organisms present. Soils with humus can vary in nitrogen content but have 3 to 6 per cent nitrogen typically; humus, as a reserve of nitrogen and phosphorus, is a vital component affecting soil fertility. Humus also absorbs water, acting as a moisture reserve, that plants can utilize; it also expands and shrinks between dry and wet states, providing pore spaces. Humus is less stable than other soil constituents, because it is affected by microbial decomposition, and over time its concentration decreases without the addition of new organic matter. However, some forms of humus are highly stable and may persist over centuries if not millennia: they are issued from the slow oxidation of charcoal, also called black carbon, like in Amazonian Terra preta or Black Earths, or from the sequestration of humic compounds within mineral horizons, like in podzols.

Climate and Organics

The production and accumulation or degradation of organic matter and humus is greatly dependent on climate conditions. Temperature and soil moisture are the major factors in the formation or degradation of organic matter, they along with topography, determine the formation of organic soils. Soils high in organic matter tend to form under wet or cold conditions where decomposer activity is impeded by low temperature or excess moisture.

Soil Solutions

Soils retain water that can dissolve a range of molecules and ions. These solutions exchange gases with the soil atmosphere, contain dissolved sugars, fulvic acids and other organic acids, plant nutrients such as nitrate, ammonium, potassium, phosphate, sulfate and calcium, and micronutrients such as zinc, iron and copper. Some arid soils have sodium solutions that greatly impact plant growth. Soil pH can affect the type and amount of anions and cations that soil solutions contain and that exchange with the soil atmosphere and biological organisms.

Biogeography is the study of special variations in biological communities. Soils are a restricting factor as to which plants can grow in which environments. Soil scientists survey soils in the hope of understanding controls as to what vegetation can and will grow in a particular location.

Geologists also have a particular interest in the patterns of soil on the surface of the earth. Soil texture, color and chemistry often reflect the underlying geologic parent material, and soil types often change at geologic unit boundaries. Buried paleosols mark previous land surfaces and record climatic conditions from previous eras. Geologists use this paleopedological record to understand the ecological relationships in past ecosystems. According to the theory of biorhexistasy, prolonged conditions conducive to forming deep, weathered soils result in increasing ocean salinity and the formation of limestone.

Geologists use soil profile features to establish the duration of surface stability in the context of geologic faults or slope stability. An offset subsoil horizon indicates rupture during soil formation and the degree of subsequent subsoil formation is relied upon to establish time since rupture.

A homeowner sifts soil made from his compost bin in background. Composting is an excellent way to recycle household and yard wastes.

Soil examined in shovel test pits is used by archaeologists for relative dating based on stratigraphy (as opposed to absolute dating). What is considered most typical is to use soil profile features to determine the maximum reasonable pit depth than needs to be examined for archaeological evidence in the interest of cultural resources management.

Soils altered or formed by man (anthropic and anthropogenic soils) are also of interest to archaeologists, such as terra preta soils.

Soil is used in agriculture, where it serves as the primary nutrient base for plants; however, as demonstrated by hydroponics, it is not essential to plant growth if the soil-contained nutrients could be dissolved in a solution. The types of soil used in agriculture (among other things, such as the purported level of moisture in the soil) vary with respect to the species of plants that are cultivated.

Soil material is a critical component in the mining and construction industries. Soil serves as a foundation for most construction projects. Massive volumes of soil can be involved in surface mining, road building and dam construction. Earth sheltering is the architectural practice of using soil for external thermal mass against building walls.

Soil resources are critical to the environment, as well as to food and fibre production. Soil provides minerals and water to plants. Soil absorbs rainwater and releases it later, thus preventing floods and drought. Soil cleans the water as it percolates. Soil is the habitat for many organisms: the major part of known and unknown biodiversity is in the soil, in the form of invertebrates (earthworms, woodlice, millipedes, centipedes, snails, slugs, mites, springtails, enchytraeids, nematodes, protists), bacteria, archaea, fungi and algae; and most organisms living above ground have part of them (plants) or spend part of their life cycle (insects) belowground. Above-ground and below-ground biodiversities are tightly interconnected, making soil protection of paramount importance for any restoration or conservation plan.

The biological component of soil is an extremely important carbon sink since about 57 per cent of the biotic content is carbon. Even on desert crusts, cyanobacteria lichens and mosses capture and sequester a significant amount of carbon by photosynthesis. Poor farming and grazing methods have degraded soils and released much of this sequestered carbon to the atmosphere. Restoring the world's soils could offset some of the huge increase in greenhouse gases causing global warming while improving crop yields and reducing water needs.

Waste management often has a soil component. Septic drain fields treat septic tank effluent using aerobic soil processes. Landfills use soil for daily cover. Land application of wastewater relies on soil biology to aerobically treat BOD.

Organic soils, especially peat, serve as a significant fuel resource; but wide areas of peat production, such as sphagnum bogs, are now protected because of patrimonial interest.

Both animals and humans in many cultures occasionally consume soil. It has been shown that some monkeys consume soil, together with their preferred food (tree foliage and fruits), in order to alleviate tannin toxicity.

Soils filter and purify water and affect its chemistry. Rain water and pooled water from ponds, lakes and rivers percolate through the soil horizons and the upper rock strata; thus becoming groundwater. Pests (viruses) and pollutants, such as persistent organic pollutants (chlorinated pesticides, polychlorinated biphenyls), oils (hydrocarbons), heavy metals (lead, zinc, cadmium), and excess nutrients (nitrates, sulfates, phosphates) are filtered out by the soil. Soil organisms metabolize them or immobilize them in their biomass and necromass, thereby incorporating them into stable humus. The physical integrity of soil is also a prerequisite for avoiding landslides in rugged landscapes.

Degradation

Land degradation is a human-induced or natural process which impairs the capacity of land to function. Soils are the critical component in land degradation when it involves acidification, contamination, desertification, erosion or salination.

While soil acidification of alkaline soils is beneficial, it degrades land when soil acidity lowers crop productivity and increases soil vulnerability to contamination and erosion. Soils are often initially acid because their parent materials were acid and initially low in the basic cations (calcium, magnesium, potassium and sodium). Acidification occurs when these elements are removed from the soil profile by normal rainfall, or the harvesting of forest or agricultural crops. Soil acidification is accelerated by the use of acid-forming nitrogenous fertilizers and by the effects of acid precipitation.

Soil contamination at low levels is often within soil capacity to treat and assimilate. Many waste treatment processes rely on this treatment capacity. Exceeding treatment capacity can damage soil biota and limit soil function. Derelict soils occur where industrial contamination or other development activity damages the soil to such a degree that the land cannot be used safely or productively. Remediation of derelict soil uses principles of geology, physics, chemistry and biology to degrade, attenuate, isolate or remove soil contaminants to restore soil functions and values. Techniques include leaching, air sparging, chemical amendments, phytoremediation, bioremediation and natural attenuation.

Desertification is an environmental process of ecosystem degradation in arid and semi-arid regions, often caused by human activity. It is a common misconception that droughts cause desertification. Droughts are common in arid and semiarid lands. Well-managed lands can recover from drought when the rains return. Soil management tools include maintaining soil nutrient and organic matter levels, reduced tillage and increased cover. These practices help to control erosion and maintain productivity during periods when moisture is available. Continued land abuse during droughts, however, increases land degradation. Increased population and livestock pressure on marginal lands accelerates desertification.

Soil erosional loss is caused by wind, water, ice and movement in response to gravity. Although the processes may be simultaneous, erosion is distinguished from weathering. Erosion is an intrinsic natural process, but in many places it is increased by human land use. Poor land use practices including deforestation, overgrazing and improper construction activity. Improved management can limit erosion by using techniques like limiting disturbance during construction, avoiding construction during erosion prone periods, intercepting runoff, terrace-building, use of erosion-suppressing cover materials, and planting trees or other soil binding plants.

A serious and long-running water erosion problem occurs in China, on the middle reaches of the Yellow River and the upper reaches of the Yangtze River. From the Yellow River, over 1.6-billion tons of sediment flow each year into the ocean. The sediment originates primarily from water erosion (gully erosion) in the Loess Plateau region of northwest China.

Soil piping is a particular form of soil erosion that occurs below the soil surface. It is associated with levee and dam failure, as well as sink hole formation. Turbulent flow removes soil starting from the mouth of the seep flow and subsoil erosion advances upgradient. The term sand boil is used to describe the appearance of the discharging end of an active soil pipe.

Soil salination is the accumulation of free salts to such an extent that it leads to degradation of soils and vegetation. Consequences include corrosion damage, reduced plant growth, erosion due to loss of plant cover and soil structure, and water quality problems due to sedimentation. Salination occurs due to a combination of natural and human caused processes. Arid conditions favour salt accumulation. This is especially apparent when soil parent material is saline. Irrigation of arid lands is especially problematic. All irrigation water has some level of salinity. Irrigation, especially when it involves leakage from canals and overirrigation in the field, often raises the underlying water table. Rapid salination occurs when the land surface is within the capillary fringe of saline groundwater. Soil salinity control involves watertable control and flushing with higher levels of applied water in combination with tile drainage or another form of subsurface drainage. Soil salinity models like SWAP, DrainMod-S, UnSatChem, SaltMod and SahysMod are used to assess the cause of soil salination and to optimize the reclamation of irrigated saline soils.

9 Improving Farming Technology

In a warming 21st century, tropical forests will be at risk from a variety of threats, especially the conversion to cropland to sustain a growing population. A new report this week in the *Proceedings of the National Academy of Sciences Early Edition* shows that crop productivity improvements and carbon emission limits together could prevent widespread tropical deforestation over the next 100 years—but if relying on either one alone, the world is at risk of losing many of its tropical forests.

"We're often concerned with agriculture encroaching on forests," said research scientist Allison Thomson of the Department of Energy's Pacific Northwest National Laboratory. "This study shows that encroachment can be managed to a certain extent by increasing crop productivity — boosting the amount of food or energy that can be produced on a given piece of land."

But the study clearly shows that improving crop productivity alone will not prevent tropical deforestation. Also needed is some form of economic incentive to store carbon in forests, for example, a plan to limit all carbon emissions — from burning fossil fuels, biofuels or whole forests to make way for crops or other land uses — through economic methods such as a carbon tax or cap-and-trade programme. Combined with farming improvements, this tactic not only preserves tropical forests but increases their extent.

"Our model considers many different ways to limit carbon dioxide in the atmosphere to 526 parts-per-million," said Thomson, a member of the Joint Global Change Research Institute. "Limiting emissions from land use change is a lower cost option that can also be implemented immediately. In the near term, we can limit emissions by protecting forests, buying society additional time to make needed long-term changes in how we produce and consume energy."

Economics at Work

Thomson and colleagues at JGCRI, the University of Maryland and the University of New Hampshire, Durham examined future scenarios in a computer model called the Global Change Assessment Model, or GCAM. GCAM knits a comprehensive picture of how the next century may evolve, incorporating agriculture, economics, energy use, technology, land use, climate, ecosystem and other factors.

The researchers used the model to simulate a future that limits greenhouse gas emissions so that carbon dioxide in the atmosphere reaches a concentration of about 520 ppm — a target that would require cuts in emissions of about half. The model calculates an economic cost for emissions that meets that limit in a way that optimizes costs across all activities that emit greenhouse gases.

"This is not a projection of what will happen," said Thomson. "The model tells us, 'this is the most cost effective way to reach this target,' given the requirements we feed it. The model can't give us a prediction, but it can provide insights into what pressures will bear on land use in response to economic and other forces."

The researchers also simulated a future in which the international political community makes no effort to limit carbon emissions. In that 'business-as-usual' case, the atmosphere reaches 520 ppm carbon dioxide in about 2050, about twice as fast as with the selected carbon limit, and reaches almost 800 ppm by the end of the 21st century. Other simulations examined different rates at which crop productivity might improve.

To examine tropical lands in detail, the team applied a computational method called downscaling to the results from GCAM's regional models. The technique takes a region's land-use changes — for example, where forests have been cut down for crops or where dormant cropland has grown into pasture — and maps them more precisely. It breaks the region into smaller grids and determines how much and what type of the land use changes the grid cells could hold. Dividing up the land use changes in this way provides more information about the possible landscape, much like shrinking the size of pixels improves the resolution of a digital image.

The results provide new insights into how agriculture and land use might change over time in response to the economic pressure to limit emissions.

Forests, Energy, Food

Much of the public discussion about reducing carbon emissions revolves around reducing the use of fossil fuels. But this study showed that improving crop productivity is also important, Thomson said. Without farming improvements, the model projected loss of tropical forests, even when there is a high economic cost for those carbon dioxide emissions.

On the other hand, improvements in crop productivity in a world that emits carbon freely — and lacks the associated economic incentive to preserve forests — also failed to prevent widespread tropical deforestation.

Twenty-first century tropical forests fared well only when both crop productivity improved and limits to carbon emissions provided an extra economic inventive to keep land forested. The assumptions that went into that simulation were that farming technology continues to improve at the same rate as the last 50 years, and that carbon emission reductions included the full range of options — everything from electric vehicles to capturing carbon from fossil fuel emissions and developing bio-based fuels.

The model showed that under those conditions, tropical deforestation not only stopped but reversed, particularly in Africa and South America.

"Viewed spatially, it's clear that carbon pricing and agriculture improvements are potential keys to saving sensitive tropical forest areas in this future scenario," said UMD geographer George Hurtt, a co-author of the study.

Second, production of bio-based fuels not only went up, but the producers used more waste from crops, forests and cities, in addition to crops grown specifically for energy.

Third, food became more affordable than it currently is. Although carbon emissions limits caused the cost of producing food to rise, incomes also went up. The model showed the percentage of income spent on food actually dropped.

"A key point of this study is the importance of counting the forest carbon in mitigation strategies", said Thomson. "Our previous work has shown that's important, but the contribution of agricultural technology as a climate mitigation strategy — in terms of how much it can contribute to reducing carbon emissions from land use change – is new. That hasn't been demonstrated before."

Better management of agricultural resources and implementation of new technology, including machinery, seeds and farming techniques, will be vital for Brunei to achieve its 2010 and 2015 targets to increase local rice production to 20 and 60 per cent respectively, a foreign expert said.

The Executive Director of Philippine Rice Research Institute (PhilRice) Ronilo A Beronio said that Brunei's soil faces the problem of being either nutrient toxic or deficient, both of which could result in poor yield by the farmers, adding that the problem can be rectified by applying the right amount of fertiliser at the right time.

He was speaking during his presentation "Rapid Strategic Assessment of the Potential for Rice Self-Sufficiency of Brunei Darussalam" at the Ministry of Industry and Primary Resources yesterday.

By comparing the leaf colour to a leaf colour chart, we can help farmers decide when and how much nitrogen fertiliser should be applied," said the executive director He said that Brunei should invest in upgrading its rice farming infrastructure such as the construction of irrigation systems to increase cropping intensity, as well as a drainage system for efficient water management which can also help to wash out the nutrient toxicity in the soil. "Brunei is also lower than sea level, so a topographic mapping of rice areas for irrigation and drainage should be done," added Beronio.

He also spoke of how the introduction and implementation of new technology such as high yielding varieties of seeds with acceptable eating quality could be sown for off-season rice crop and increase cropping intensity. "Based from the last 10 years' rainfall data, there is a possibility of establishing off-season rice crop using early maturing varieties like BDR1 from May, especially in Brunei-Muara and Temburong." The executive director added that the use of machineries can help save labour costs and time management compared to the current methods which are done manually.

He explained that the promotion of productivity enhancing technologies such as "PalayCheck", a dynamic rice crop management system, can help to sustain improvement in productivity, profitability and environment safety.

Beronio also placed emphasis on the importance of Brunei starting its own research to improve and sustain rice production as the population continues to grow.

Brunei is targeting a 20 per cent, equivalent to a 6,000 metric tonne increase of local rice production by 2010, and a 60 per cent (equivalent to 18,000 metric tonnes) increase by 2015 in a bid to achieve self-sufficiency in rice production.

The target to achieve the 20 per cent increase by 2010 will see 2,783 hectares allotted for rice production, while 5,380 hectares is required to achieve the 60 per cent target by 2015.

An estimated $50 million is required for the development of new rice fields, in addition to enhancing the infrastructure and introduction of high yielding varieties of rice-type

Other factors which are being looked into include enhancing agronomy field management, skills of the workforce and staff in agriculture, establishment of the Rice Research Centre as well as improvement of post-farming and farming technology.

10 Agricultural Diversification

In the agricultural context, diversification can be regarded as the re-allocation of some of a farm's productive resources, such as land, capital, farm equipment and paid labour, into new activities. These can be new crops or livestock products, value-adding activities, provision of services to other farmers and, particularly in richer countries, non-farming activities such as restaurants and shops. Factors leading to decisions to diversify are many, but include; reducing risk, responding to changing consumer demands or changing government policy, responding to external shocks and, more recently, as a consequence of climate change.

While most definitions of diversification in developing countries work on the assumption that diversification primarily involves a substitution of one crop or other agricultural product for another, or an increase in the number of enterprises, or activities, carried out by a particular farm, the definition used in developed countries sometimes relates more to the development of activities on the farm that do not involve agricultural production. For example, one section of the British Department for Environment, Food and Rural Affairs (DEFRA) defines diversification as "the entrepreneurial use of farm resources for a non-agricultural purpose for commercial gain". Using this definition DEFRA found that 56 per cent of UK farms had diversified in 2003. The great majority of diversification activities simply involved the renting out of farm buildings for non-farming use, but 9 per cent of farms had become involved with processing or retailing, 3 per cent with provision of tourist accommodation or catering, and 7 per cent with sport or recreational activities. Others adopt a broader definition, which may include development of new marketing opportunities.

In developing countries such as India, which has been one of the leaders in promoting diversification, the concept is applied both to individual farmers and to different regions, with government programmes being aimed at promoting widespread diversification. The concept in India is seen as referring to the "shift from the regional dominance of one crop to regional production of a number of crops ... (which takes into account) ... the economic returns from different value-added crops ... with complementary marketing opportunities".

The Drivers of Diversification

Diversification can be a response to both opportunities and threats:

Opportunities

- ***Changing consumer demand:*** As consumers in developing countries become richer, food consumption patterns change noticeably. People move away from a diet based on staples to one with a greater content of animal products (meat, eggs and dairy) and fruits and vegetables. In turn, more dynamic farmers are able to diversify to meet these needs.
- ***Changing demographics:*** Rapid urbanization in developing countries has an impact on consumption patterns. Moreover, a smaller number of farmers, in percentage terms at least, has to supply a larger number of consumers. While this may not imply diversification it does require adaptation to new farming techniques to meet the higher level of demand.
- ***Export potential:*** Developing country farmers have had considerable success by diversifying into crops that can meet export market demand. While concern about food miles, as well as the cost of complying with supermarket certification requirements such as for GlobalGAP may jeopardize this success in the long run, there remains much potential to diversify to meet export markets.
- ***Adding value:*** The pattern witnessed in the West, and now becoming widespread in developing countries, is for consumers to devote less and less time to food preparation. They increasingly require ready-prepared meals and labour-saving packaging, such as pre-cut salads. This provides the opportunity for farmers to diversify into value addition, particularly in countries where supermarkets play a major role in retailing.
- ***Changing marketing opportunities:*** The changing of government policies that control the way in which farmers can link to markets can open up new diversification possibilities. For example, in India

policy changes to remove the monopoly of state 'regulated markets' to handle all transactions made it possible for farmers to establish direct contracts with buyers for new products.

- ***Improving nutrition:*** Diversifying from the monoculture of traditional staples can have important nutritional benefits for farmers in developing countries.

Threats

- ***Urbanization:*** This is both an opportunity and a threat, in that the expansion of cities places pressure on land resources and puts up the value of the land. If farmers are to remain on the land they need to generate greater income from that land than they could by growing basic staples. This fact, and the proximity of markets, explains why farmers close to urban areas tend to diversify into high-value crops.
- ***Risk:*** Farmers face risk from bad weather and from fluctuating prices. Diversification is a logical response to both. For example, some crops are more drought resistant than others, but may offer poorer economic returns. A diversified portfolio of products should ensure that farmers don't suffer complete ruin when the weather is bad. Similarly, diversification can manage price risk, on the assumption that not all products will suffer low prices at the same time. In fact, farmers often do the opposite of diversification by planting products that have a high price in one year, only to see the price collapse in the next, as explained by the cobweb theory.
- ***External threats:*** Farmers who are dependent on exports run the risk that conditions will change in their markets, not because of a change in consumer demand but because of policy changes. A classic example is the Caribbean banana industry, which collapsed as a result of the removal of quota protection on EU markets, necessitating diversification by the region's farmers.
- ***Domestic policy threats:*** Agricultural production is sometimes undertaken as a consequence of government subsidies, rather than because it is inherently profitable. The reduction or removal of those subsidies, whether direct or indirect, can have a major impact on farmers and provide a significant incentive for diversification or, in some cases, for returning to production of crops grown prior to the introduction of subsidies.
- ***Climate change:*** The type of crop that can be grown is affected by changes in temperatures and the length of the growing season. Climate change could also modify the availability of water for

production. Farmers in several countries, including Canada, India, Kenya, Mozambique and Sri Lanka have already initiated diversification as a response to climate change. Government policy in Kenya to promote crop diversification has included the removal of subsidies for some crops, encouraging land-use zoning and introducing differential land tax systems.

Opportunities for Diversification

In making decisions about diversification farmers need to consider whether income generated by new farm enterprises will be greater than the existing activities, with similar or less risk. While growing new crops or raising animals may be technically possible, these may not be suitable for many farmers in terms of their land, labour and capital resources. Moreover, markets for the products may be lacking. The United Nations Food and Agriculture Organization (FAO) has been one of the development organizations promoting diversification by small farmers. So far, it has produced booklets identifying beekeeping, mushroom farming, milk production, fish ponds and sheep and goats, among others, as diversification possibilities.

11 Irrigation

Irrigation is an artificial application of water to the soil. It is used to assist in the growing of agricultural crops, maintenance of landscapes, and revegetation of disturbed soils in dry areas and during periods of inadequate rainfall. Additionally, irrigation also has a few other uses in crop production, which include protecting plants against frost, suppressing weed growing in grain fields and helping in preventing soil consolidation. In contrast, agriculture that relies only on direct rainfall is referred to as rain-fed or dryland farming. Irrigation systems are also used for dust suppression, disposal of sewage, and in mining. Irrigation is often studied together with drainage, which is the natural or artificial removal of surface and sub-surface water from a given area.

Irrigation is also a term used in medical/dental fields to refer to flushing and washing out anything with water or another liquid.

Archaeological investigation has identified evidence of irrigation in Mesopotamia, Ancient Egypt and Ancient Persia (modern day Iran) as far back as the 6th millennium BCE, where barley was grown in areas where the natural rainfall was insufficient to support such a crop.

In the Zana Valley of the Andes Mountains in Peru, archaeologists found remains of three irrigation canals radiocarbon dated from the 4th millennium BCE, the 3rd millennium BCE and the 9th century CE. These canals are the earliest record of irrigation in the New World. Traces of a canal possibly dating from the 5th millennium BCE were found under the 4th millennium canal. Sophisticated irrigation and storage systems were developed by the Indus Valley Civilization in Pakistan and North India, including the reservoirs at Girnar in 3000 BCE and an early canal irrigation system from circa 2600 BCE. Large scale agriculture was practiced and an extensive network of canals was used for the purpose of irrigation.

There is evidence of the ancient Egyptian pharaoh Amenemhet III in the twelfth dynasty (about 1800 BCE) using the natural lake of the Faiyum Oasis as a reservoir to store surplus water for use during the dry seasons, the lake swelled annually from flooding of the Nile.

The Qanats, developed in ancient Persia in about 800 BCE, are among the oldest known irrigation methods still in use today. They are now found in Asia, the Middle East and North Africa. The system comprises a network of vertical wells and gently sloping tunnels driven into the sides of cliffs and steep hills to tap groundwater. The noria, a water wheel with clay pots around the rim powered by the flow of the stream (or by animals where the water source was still), was first brought into use at about this time, by Roman settlers in North Africa. By 150 BCE the pots were fitted with valves to allow smoother filling as they were forced into the water.

The irrigation works of ancient Sri Lanka, the earliest dating from about 300 BCE, in the reign of King Pandukabhaya and under continuous development for the next thousand years, were one of the most complex irrigation systems of the ancient world. In addition to underground canals, the Sinhalese were the first to build completely artificial reservoirs to store water. Due to their engineering superiority in this sector, they were often called 'masters of irrigation'. Most of these irrigation systems still exist undamaged up to now, in Anuradhapura and Polonnaruwa, because of the advanced and precise engineering. The system was extensively restored and further extended during the reign of King Parakrama Bahu (1153-186 CE).

The oldest known hydraulic engineers of China were Sunshu Ao (6th century BCE) of the Spring and Autumn Period and Ximen Bao (5th century BCE) of the Warring States period, both of whom worked on large irrigation projects. In the Szechwan region belonging to the State of Qin of ancient China, the Dujiangyan Irrigation System was built in 256 BCE to irrigate an enormous area of farmland that today still supplies water. By the 2nd century AD, during the Han Dynasty, the Chinese also used chain pumps that lifted water from lower elevation to higher elevation. These were powered by manual foot pedal, hydraulic waterwheels, or rotating mechanical wheels pulled by oxen. The water was used for public works of providing water for urban residential quarters and palace gardens, but mostly for irrigation of farmland canals and channels in the fields. In

15th century Korea, the world's first water gauge, *uryanggye*, was discovered in 1441. The inventor was Jang Yeong-sil, a Korean engineer of the Joseon Dynasty, under the active direction of the king, Sejong the Great. It was installed in irrigation tanks as part of a nationwide system to measure and collect rainfall for agricultural applications. With this instrument, planners and farmers could make better use of the information gathered in the survey.

In the Americas, extensive irrigation systems were created by numerous groups in prehistoric times. One example is seen in the recent archaeological excavations near the Santa Cruz River in Tucson, Arizona. They have located a village site dating from 4,000 years ago. The floodplain of the Santa Cruz River was extensively farmed during the Early Agricultural period, circa 1200 BC to AD 150. These people constructed irrigation canals and grew corn, beans, and other crops while gathering wild plants and hunting animals.

Present Extent

In the middle of the 20th century, the advent of diesel and electric motors led for the first time to systems that could pump groundwater out of major aquifers faster than it was recharged. This can lead to permanent loss of aquifer capacity, decreased water quality, ground subsidence, and other problems. The future of food production in such areas as the North China Plain, the Punjab, and the Great Plains of the US is threatened.

At the global scale 2,788,000 km^2 (689 million acres) of agricultural land was equipped with irrigation infrastructure around the year 2000. About 68 per cent of the area equipped for irrigation is located in Asia, 17 per cent in America, 9 per cent in Europe, 5 per cent in Africa and 1 per cent in Oceania. The largest contiguous areas of high irrigation density are found in North India and Pakistan along the rivers Ganges and Indus, in the Hai He, Huang He and Yangtze basins in China, along the Nile river in Egypt and Sudan, in the Mississippi-Missouri river basin and in parts of California. Smaller irrigation areas are spread across almost all populated parts of the world.

Types of Irrigation

Various types of irrigation techniques differ in how the water obtained from the source is distributed within the field. In general, the goal is to supply the entire field uniformly with water, so that each plant has the amount of water it needs, neither too much nor too little.The modern methods are efficient enough to achieve this goal.

Surface Irrigation

In surface irrigation systems, water moves over and across the land by simple gravity flow in order to wet it and to infiltrate into the soil. Surface irrigation can be subdivided into furrow, borderstrip or basin irrigation. It is often called *flood irrigation* when the irrigation results in flooding or near flooding of the cultivated land. Historically, this has been the most common method of irrigating agricultural land.

Where water levels from the irrigation source permit, the levels are controlled by dikes, usually plugged by soil. This is often seen in terraced rice fields (rice paddies), where the method is used to flood or control the level of water in each distinct field. In some cases, the water is pumped, or lifted by human or animal power to the level of the land.

Localised Irrigation

Localised irrigation is a system where water is distributed under low pressure through a piped network, in a pre-determined pattern, and applied as a small discharge to each plant or adjacent to it. Drip irrigation, spray or micro-sprinkler irrigation and bubbler irrigation belong to this category of irrigation methods.

Drip Irrigation

Drip irrigation, also known as trickle irrigation, functions as its name suggests. Water is delivered at or near the root zone of plants, drop by drop. This method can be the most water-efficient method of irrigation, if managed properly, since evaporation and runoff are minimized. In modern agriculture, drip irrigation is often combined with plastic mulch, further reducing evaporation, and is also the means of delivery of fertilizer. The process is known as *fertigation.*

Deep percolation, where water moves below the root zone, can occur if a drip system is operated for too long of a duration or if the delivery rate is too high. Drip irrigation methods range from very high-tech and computerized to low-tech and labour-intensive. Lower water pressures are usually needed than for most other types of systems, with the exception of low energy centre pivot systems and surface irrigation systems, and the system can be designed for uniformity throughout a field or for precise water delivery to individual plants in a landscape containing a mix of plant species. Although it is difficult to regulate pressure on steep slopes, pressure compensating emitters are available, so the field does not have to be level. High-tech solutions involve precisely calibrated emitters located along lines of tubing that extend from a computerized set of valves. Both pressure regulation and filtration to remove particles are important. The tubes are usually black (or buried under soil or mulch) to prevent the growth of algae and to protect the polyethylene from degradation due to ultraviolet light. But drip irrigation can also be as low-tech as a porous clay vessel sunk into the soil and occasionally filled from a hose or bucket. Subsurface drip irrigation has been used successfully on lawns, but it is more expensive than a more traditional sprinkler system. Surface drip systems are not cost-effective (or aesthetically pleasing) for lawns and golf courses. In the past one of the main disadvantages of the subsurface drip irrigation (SDI) systems, when used for turf, was the fact of having to install the plastic lines very close to each other in the ground, therefore disrupting the turfgrass area. Recent technology developments on drip installers like the drip installer at New Mexico State University Arrow Head Centre, places the line underground and covers the slit leaving no soil exposed.

Sprinkler Irrigation

In sprinkler or overhead irrigation, water is piped to one or more central locations within the field and distributed by overhead high-pressure sprinklers or guns. A system utilizing sprinklers, sprays, or guns mounted overhead on permanently installed risers is often referred to as a *solid-set* irrigation system. Higher pressure sprinklers that rotate are called *rotors* and are driven by a ball drive, gear drive, or impact mechanism. Rotors can be designed to rotate in a full or partial circle. Guns are similar to rotors, except that they generally operate at very high pressures of 40 to 130 lbf/in^2 (275 to 900 kPa) and flows of 50 to 1200 US gal/min (3 to 76 L/s), usually with nozzle diameters in the range of 0.5 to 1.9 inches (10 to 50 mm). Guns are used not only for irrigation, but also for industrial applications such as dust suppression and logging.

Sprinklers can also be mounted on moving platforms connected to the water source by a hose. Automatically moving wheeled systems known as *travelling sprinklers* may irrigate areas such as small farms, sports fields, parks, pastures, and cemeteries unattended. Most of these utilize a length of polyethylene tubing wound on a steel drum. As the tubing is wound on the drum powered by the irrigation water or a small gas engine, the sprinkler is pulled across the field. When the sprinkler arrives back at the reel the system shuts off. This type of system is known to most people as a 'waterreel' travelling irrigation sprinkler and they are used extensively for dust suppression, irrigation, and land application of waste water. Other travellers use a flat rubber hose that is dragged along behind while the sprinkler platform is pulled by a cable. These cable-type travellers are definitely old technology and their use is limited in today's modern irrigation projects.

Centre Pivot Irrigation

Centre pivot irrigation is a form of sprinkler irrigation consisting of several segments of pipe (usually galvanized steel or aluminum) joined together and supported by trusses, mounted on wheeled towers with sprinklers positioned along its length. The system moves in a circular pattern and is fed with water from the pivot point at the centre of the arc. These systems are found and used in all parts of the nation and allow irrigation of all types of terrain. Newer irrigations have drops as shown in the image that follows.

Most centre pivot systems now have drops hanging from a u-shaped pipe attached at the top of the pipe with sprinkler heads that are positioned a few feet (at most) above the crop, thus limiting evaporative losses. Drops can also be used with drag hoses or bubblers that deposit the water directly on the ground between crops. Crops are often planted in a circle to conform to the center pivot. This type of system is known as LEPA (Low Energy Precision Application). Originally, most centre pivots were water powered. These were replaced by hydraulic systems (*T-L Irrigation*) and electric motor driven systems (Reinke, Valley, Zimmatic*). Many modern sprinklers features GPS devices.*

Lateral Move Irrigation

A series of pipes, each with a wheel of about 1.5 m diameter permanently affixed to its midpoint and sprinklers along its length, are coupled together at one edge of a field. Water is supplied at one end using a large hose. After sufficient water has been applied, the hose is removed and the remaining assembly rotated either by hand or with a purpose-built mechanism, so that the sprinklers move 10 m across the field. The hose is reconnected. The process is repeated until the opposite edge of the field is reached. This system is less expensive to install than a centre pivot, but much more labor intensive to operate, and it is limited in the amount of water it can carry. Most systems utilize 4 or 5-inch (130 mm) diametre aluminum pipe. One feature of a lateral move system is that it consists of sections that can be easily disconnected. They are most often used for small or oddly shaped fields, such as those found in hilly or mountainous regions, or in regions where labour is inexpensive.

Sub-irrigation

Sub-irrigation also sometimes called *seepage irrigation* has been used for many years in field crops in areas with high water tables. It is a method of artificially raising the water table to allow the soil to be moistened from below the plants' root zone. Often those systems are located on permanent grasslands in lowlands or river valleys and combined with drainage infrastructure. A system of pumping stations, canals, weirs and gates allows it to increase or decrease the water level in a network of ditches and thereby control the water table.

Sub-irrigation is also used in commercial greenhouse production, usually for potted plants. Water is delivered from below, absorbed upwards, and the excess collected for recycling. Typically, a solution of water and nutrients floods a container or flows through a trough for a short period of time, 10-20 minutes, and is then pumped back into a holding tank for reuse. Sub-irrigation in greenhouses requires fairly sophisticated, expensive equipment and management. Advantages are water and nutrient conservation, and labour-saving through lowered system maintenance and automation. It is similar in principle and action to subsurface drip irrigation.

Manual Irrigation Using Buckets or Watering Cans

These systems have low requirements for infrastructure and technical equipment but need high labour inputs. Irrigation using watering cans is to be found for example in peri-urban agriculture around large cities in some African countries.

Automatic, Non-electric Irrigation Using Buckets and Ropes

Besides the common manual watering by bucket, an automated, natural version of this also exist. Using plain polyester ropes combined with a prepared ground mixture can be used to water plants from a vessel filled with water.

The ground mixture would need to be made depending on the plant itself, yet would mostly consist of black potting soil, vermiculite and perlite. This system would (with certain crops) allow to save expenses as it does not consume any electricity and only little water (unlike sprinklers, water timers, . . .). However, it may only be used with certain crops (probably mostly larger crops that do not need a humid environment; perhaps e.g. paprikas).

Irrigation Using Water Condensed from Humid Air

In countries where at night, humid air sweeps the countryside, water can be obtained from the humid air by condensation onto cold surfaces. This is for example practiced in the vineyards at Lanzarote using stones to condense water or with various fog collectors based on canvas or foil sheets.

Sources of Irrigation Water

Sources of irrigation water can be groundwater extracted from springs or by using wells, surface water withdrawn from rivers, lakes or reservoirs or non-conventional sources like treated wastewater, desalinated water or drainage water. A special form of irrigation using surface water is spate irrigation, also called floodwater harvesting. In case of a flood (spate) water is diverted to normally dry river beds (wadis) using a network of dams, gates and channels and spread over large areas. The moisture stored in the soil will be used thereafter to grow crops. Spate irrigation areas are in particular located in semi-arid or arid, mountainous regions. While floodwater harvesting belongs to the accepted irrigation methods, rainwater harvesting is usually not considered as a form of irrigation. Rainwater harvesting is the collection of runoff water from roofs or unused land and the concentration of this. Some of Ancient India's water systems were pulled by oxen.

How an In-ground Irrigation System Works

Most commercial and residential irrigation systems are 'in ground' systems, which means that everything is buried in the ground. With the pipes, sprinklers, emitters (drippers), and irrigation valves being hidden, it makes for a cleaner, more presentable landscape without garden hoses or other items having to be moved around manually. This does, however, create some drawbacks in the maintenance of a completely buried system. Water source and piping.

The beginning of a sprinkler system is the water source. This is usually a tap into an existing (city) water line or a pump that pulls water out of a well or a pond. The water travels through pipes from the water source through the valves to the sprinklers and emitters. The pipes from the water source up to the irrigation valves are called "mainlines", and the lines from the valves to the emitters or sprinklers are called 'lateral lines'. Most piping used in irrigation systems today are HDPE and MDPE or PVC or PEX plastic pressure pipes due to their ease of installation and resistance to corrosion. After the water source, the water usually travels through a check valve. This prevents water in the irrigation lines from being pulled back into and contaminating the clean water supply. Ideally a pressure control valve is also installed to regulate water pressure and help prevent excessive pressure from harming the system.

Controllers, Zones, and Valves

Most irrigation systems are divided into zones. A zone is a single irrigation valve and one or a group of drippers or sprinklers that are connected by pipes or tubes. Irrigation systems are divided into zones because there is usually not enough pressure and available flow to run sprinklers for an entire yard or sports field at once. Each zone has a solenoid valve on it that is controlled via wire by an irrigation controller. The irrigation controller is either a mechanical (now the 'dinosaur' type) or electrical device that signals a zone to turn on at a specific time and keeps it on for a specified amount of time. 'Smart Controller' is a recent term used to describe a controller that is capable of adjusting the watering time by itself in response to current environmental conditions. The smart controller determines current conditions by means of historic weather data for the local area, a soil moisture sensors (water potential or water content), rain sensor, or in more sophisticated systems satellite feed weather station, or a combination of these.

Emitters and Sprinklers

When a zone comes on, the water flows through the lateral lines and ultimately ends up at the irrigation emitter (drip) or sprinkler heads. Many sprinklers have pipe thread inlets on the bottom of them which allows a fitting and the pipe to be attached to them. The sprinklers are usually installed with the top of the head flush with the ground surface. When the water is pressurized, the head will pop up out of the ground and water the desired area until the valve closes and shuts off that zone. Once there is no more water pressure in the lateral line, the sprinkler head will retract back into the ground. Emitters are generally laid on the soil surface or buried a few inches to reduce evaporation losses.

Problems in Irrigation

Irrigation can lead to a number of problems.

- Competition for surface water rights.
- Depletion of underground aquifers.
- Ground subsidence (e.g. New Orleans, Louisiana)

Underirrigation or irrigation giving only just enough water for the plant (e.g. in drip line irrigation) gives poor soil salinity control which leads to increased soil salinity with consequent build up of toxic salts on soil surface in areas with high evaporation. This requires either leaching to remove these salts and a method of drainage to carry the salts away. When using drip lines, the leaching is best done regularly at certain intervals (with only a slight excess of water), so that the salt is flushed back under the plant's roots.

Overirrigation because of poor distribution uniformity or management wastes water, chemicals, and may lead to water pollution.

Deep drainage (from over-irrigation) may result in rising water tables which in some instances will lead to problems of irrigation salinity requiring watertable control by some form of subsurface land drainage.

Irrigation with saline or high-sodium water may damage soil structure owing to the formation of alkaline soil.

12 Integrated Farming

Integrated farming (or integrated agriculture) is a commonly and broadly used word to explain a more integrated approach to farming as compared to existing monoculture approaches. It refers to agricultural systems that integrate livestock and crop production and may sometimes be known as Integrated Biosystems.

While not often considered as part of the permaculture movement Integrated Farming is a similar 'whole systems approach' to agriculture. There have been efforts to link the two together such as at the 2007 International Permaculture Conference in Brazil. Agro-ecology (which was developed at University of California Santa Cruz) and Bio-dynamic farming also describe similar integrated approaches.

Examples include:

- 'pig tractor' systems where the animals are confined in crop fields well prior to planting and 'plow' the field by digging for roots.
- poultry used in orchards or vineyards after harvest to clear rotten fruit and weeds while fertilizing the soil.
- cattle or other livestock allowed to graze cover crops between crops on farms that contain both cropland and pasture (or where transhumance is employed).
- Water based agricultural systems that provide way for effective and efficient recycling of farm nutrients producing fuel, fertilizer and a compost tea/mineralized irrigation water in the process.

FARRE

In 1993 FARRE (Forum de l'Agriculture Raisonnée Respecteuse l'Environnement) developed agricultural techniques. France as part of an attempt to reconcile agricultural methods with the principles of sustainable development. FARRE, promotes an integrated and/or multi-sector approach to food production that includes profitability, safety, animal welfare, social responsibility and environmental care.

ZERI

Zero Emissions Research and Initiatives (formed in 1994) developed a similar approach to FARRE seeking to promote agricultural and industrial production models that sought to incorporate nature's wisdom into the process. ZERI helped support an effort by an environmental engineer from Mauritius named George Chan.

George Chan

Chan working with a network of poly-culture farming pioneers began refining Integrated Farming practices that had already been developed in south-east Asia in the 1960 through the 1980s, building on traditional night soil farming practice. In China, programmes embracing this form of integrated farming have been successful in demonstrating how an intensive growing systems can use organic and sustainable farming practices, while providing high agriculture yields.

Taking what he learned from the Chinese during his time there, Chan worked at the UN University in the 1990s and forwarded an approach to Integrated Farming which was termed Integrated Biomass Systems working specifically under the UNU/ZERI ZERI Bag Programme.

Chan during his work with UNU sought to make the case that Integrated Biomass Systems were well suited to help small island nations and low lying tropical regions become more self-reliant and prosperous in the production of food. Working with ZERI, he developed several prototypes for this approach around the world including sites in Namibia and Fiji. The scientifically verified results in a UNDP sponsored congress in 1997 resulted in the adoption of the IBS by the State Government of Paraná, Brazil where dozens of piggeries have applied the system generating food, energy while improving health and environmental conditions.

ZERI Bag had a significant African component that included assisting Father Godfrey Nzamujo in the development of the Songhai Farm Integrated Farming project in Benin.

Heifer Foundation

Most recently The Heifer Foundation (an international NGO based in the US) has taken a lead role in deploying Integrated Farming so that it can be replicated globally as an effective approach to sustainable farming in non-affluent regions such as Vietnam.

Example Collaborative Projects

Montfort Boy's Town in Fiji was one of the first Integrated Biomass Systems developed outside of Southeast Asia with the support of UNU, UNDP and other international agencies. The project which is still operational continues to be a model of how farm operations can provide multiple benefits to stakeholders both local and international.

Cover Crop

Cover crops are crops planted primarily to manage soil fertility, soil quality, water, weeds, pests, diseases, biodiversity and wildlife in *agroecosystems* (Lu *et al.* 2000), ecological systems managed and largely shaped by humans across a range of intensities to produce food, feed, or fibre.

Cover crops are of interest in sustainable agriculture as many of them improve the sustainability of agroecosystem attributes and may also indirectly improve qualities of neighboring natural ecosystems. Farmers choose to grow and manage specific cover crop types based on their own needs and goals, influenced by the biological, environmental, social, cultural, and economic factors of the food system within which farmers operate.

One of the primary uses of cover crops is to increase soil fertility. These types of cover crops are referred to as 'green manure'. They are used to manage a range of soil macronutrients and micronutrients. Of the various nutrients, the impact that cover crops have on nitrogen management has received the most attention from researchers and farmers, because nitrogen is often the most limiting nutrient in crop production.

Often, green manure crops are grown for a specific period, and then plowed under before reaching full maturity in order to improve soil fertility and quality.

Green manure crops are commonly leguminous, meaning they are part of the Fabaceae (pea) family. This family is unique in that all of the species in it set pods, such as bean, lentil, lupins and alfalfa. Leguminous cover crops are typically high in nitrogen and can often provide the required quantity of nitrogen for crop production. In conventional farming, this nitrogen is typically applied in chemical fertilizer form. This quality of cover crops is called fertilizer replacement value.

Another quality unique to leguminous cover crops is that they form symbiotic relationships with the rhizobial bacteria that reside in legume root nodules. Lupins is nodulated by the soil microorganism Bradyrhizobium sp. (Lupinus). Bradyrhizobia are encountered as microsymbionts in other leguminous crops (Argyrolobium, Lotus, Ornithopus, Acacia, Lupinus) of Mediterranean origin. These bacteria convert biologically unavailable atmospheric nitrogen gas (N2) to biologically available mineral nitrogen (NH4+) through the process of biological nitrogen fixation.

Prior to the advent of the Haber-Bosch process, an energy-intensive method developed to carry out industrial nitrogen fixation and create chemical nitrogen fertilizer, most nitrogen introduced to ecosystems arose through biological nitrogen fixation. Some scientists believe that widespread biological nitrogen fixation, achieved mainly through the use of cover crops, is the only alternative to industrial nitrogen fixation in the effort to maintain or increase future food production levels. Industrial nitrogen fixation has been criticized as an unsustainable source of nitrogen for food production due to its reliance on fossil fuel energy and the environmental impacts associated with chemical nitrogen fertilizer use in agriculture. Such widespread environmental impacts include nitrogen fertilizer losses into waterways, which can lead to eutrophication (nutrient loading) and ensuing hypoxia (oxygen depletion) of large bodies of water.

An example of this lies in the Mississippi Valley Basin, where years of fertilizer nitrogen loading into the watershed from agricultural production have resulted in a hypoxic 'dead zone' off the Gulf of Mexico the size of New Jersey. The ecological complexity of marine life in this zone has been diminishing as a consequence (CENR 2000).

As well as bringing nitrogen into agroecosystems through biological nitrogen fixation, types of cover crops known as 'catch crops' are used to retain and recycle soil nitrogen already present. The catch crops take up surplus nitrogen remaining from fertilization of the previous crop, preventing it from being lost through leaching, or gaseous denitrification or volatilization.

Catch crops are typically fast-growing annual cereal species adapted to scavenge available nitrogen efficiently from the soil. The nitrogen tied up in catch crop biomass is released back into the soil once the catch crop is incorporated as a green manure or otherwise begins to decompose.

An example of green manure use comes from Nigeria, where the cover crop Mucuna pruriens (velvet bean) has been found to increase the availability of phosphorus in soil after a farmer applies rock phosphate.

Soil Quality Management

Cover crops can also improve soil quality by increasing soil organic matter levels through the input of cover crop biomass over time. Increased soil organic matter enhances soil structure, as well as the water and nutrient holding and buffering capacity of soil. It can also lead to increased soil carbon sequestration, which has been promoted as a strategy to help offset the rise in atmospheric carbon dioxide levels.

Although cover crops can perform multiple functions in an agroecosystem simultaneously, they are often grown for the sole purpose of preventing soil erosion. Soil erosion is a process that can irreparably reduce the productive capacity of an agroecosystem. Dense cover crop stands physically slow down the velocity of rainfall before it contacts the soil surface, preventing soil splashing and erosive surface runoff. Additionally, vast cover crop root networks help anchor the soil in place and increase soil porosity, creating suitable habitat networks for soil macrofauna.

Soil quality is managed to produce optimum circumstances for crops to flourish. The principal factors of soil quality are soil salination, pH, microorganism balance and the prevention of soil contamination.

Water Management

By reducing soil erosion, cover crops often also reduce both the rate and quantity of water that drains off the field, which would normally pose environmental risks to waterways and ecosystems downstream. Cover crop biomass acts as a physical barrier between rainfall and the soil surface, allowing raindrops to steadily trickle down through the soil profile. Also, as stated above, cover crop root growth results in the formation of soil pores, which in addition to enhancing soil macrofauna habitat provides pathways for water to filter through the soil profile rather than draining off the field as surface flow. With increased water infiltration, the potential for soil water storage and the recharging of aquifers can be improved.

Just before cover crops are killed (by such practices including mowing, tilling, discing, rolling, or herbicide application) they contain a large amount of moisture. When the cover crop is incorporated into the soil, or left on the soil surface, it often increases soil moisture. In agroecosystems where water for crop production is in short supply, cover crops can be used as a mulch to conserve water by shading and cooling the soil surface. This reduces evaporation of soil moisture. In other situations farmers try to dry the soil out as quickly as possible going into the planting season. Here prolonged soil moisture conservation can be problematic.

While cover crops can help to conserve water, in temperate regions (particularly in years with below average precipitation) they can draw down soil water supply in the spring, particularly if climatic growing conditions are good. In these cases, just before crop planting, farmers often face a tradeoff between the benefits of increased cover crop growth and the drawbacks of reduced soil moisture for cash crop production that season.

Thick cover crop stands often compete well with weeds during the cover crop growth period, and can prevent most germinated weed seeds from completing their life cycle and reproducing. If the cover crop is left on the soil surface rather than incorporated into the soil as a green manure after its growth is terminated, it can form a nearly impenetrable mat. This drastically reduces light transmittance to weed seeds, which in many cases reduces weed seed germination rates. Furthermore, even when weed seeds germinate, they often run out of stored energy for growth before building the necessary structural capacity to break through the cover crop mulch layer. This is often termed the *cover crop smother effect.*

Some cover crops suppress weeds both during growth and after death. During growth these cover crops compete vigorously with weeds for available space, light, and nutrients, and after death they smother the next flush of weeds by forming a mulch layer on the soil surface. For example, Blackshaw *et al.* (2001) found that when using *Melilotus officinalis* (yellow sweetclover) as a cover crop in an improved fallow system (where a fallow period is intentionally improved by any number of different management practices, including the planting of cover crops), weed biomass only constituted between 1-12 per cent of total standing biomass at the end of the cover crop growing season. Furthermore, after cover crop termination, the yellow sweetclover residues suppressed weeds to levels 75-97 per cent lower than in fallow (no yellow sweetclover) systems.

In addition to competition-based or physical weed suppression, certain cover crops are known to suppress weeds through allelopathy. This occurs when certain biochemical cover crop compounds are degraded that happen to be toxic to, or inhibit seed germination of, other plant species. Some well known examples of allelopathic cover crops are *Secale cereale* (rye), *Vicia villosa* (hairy vetch), *Trifolium pratense* (red clover), *Sorghum bicolour* (sorghum-sudangrass), and species in the brassicaceae family, particularly mustards (Haramoto and Gallandt 2004). In one study, rye cover crop residues were found to have provided between 80 per cent and 95 per cent control of early season broadleaf weeds when used as a mulch during the production of different cash crops such as soybean, tobacco, corn, and sunflower.

In a recent study released by the Agricultural Research Service (ARS) scientists examined how rye seeding rates and planting patterns affected cover crop production. The results show that planting more pounds per acre of rye increased the cover crop's production as well as decreased the amount of weeds. The same was true when scientists tested seeding rates on legumes and oats; a higher density of seeds planted per acre decreased the amount of weeds and increased the yield of legume and oat production. The planting patterns, which consisted of either traditional rows or grid patterns, did not seem to make a significant impact on the cover crop's production or on the weed production in either cover crop. The ARS scientists concluded that increased seeding rates could be an effective method of weed control.

Disease Management

In the same way that allelopathic properties of cover crops can suppress weeds, they can also break disease cycles and reduce populations of bacterial and fungal diseases (Everts 2002), and parasitic nematodes. Species in the brassicaceae family, such as mustards, have been widely shown to suppress fungal disease populations through the release of naturally occurring toxic chemicals during the degradation of glucosinolade compounds in their plant cell tissues.

Pest Management

Some cover crops are used as so-called 'trap crops', to attract pests away from the crop of value and toward what the pest sees as a more favorable habitat. Trap crop areas can be established within crops, within farms, or within landscapes. In many cases the trap crop is grown during the same season as the food crop being produced. The limited area occupied by these trap crops can be treated with a pesticide once pests are drawn to the trap in large enough numbers to reduce the pest populations. In some organic systems, farmers drive over the trap crop with a large vacuum-based implement to physically pull the pests off the plants and out of the field. This system has been recommended for use to help control the lygus bugs in organic strawberry production.

Other cover crops are used to attract natural predators of pests by providing elements of their habitat. This is a form of biological control known as habitat augmentation, but achieved with the use of cover crops. Findings on the relationship between cover crop presence and predator/ pest population dynamics have been mixed, pointing toward the need for detailed information on specific cover crop types and management practices to best complement a given integrated pest management strategy. For example, the predator mite Euseius tularensis (Congdon) is known to help control the pest citrus thrips in Central California citrus orchards. Researchers found that the planting of several different leguminous cover crops (such as bell bean, woollypod vetch, New Zealand white clover, and Austrian winter pea) provided sufficient pollen as a feeding source to cause a seasonal increase in Congdon populations, which with good timing could potentially introduce enough predatory pressure to reduce pest populations of citrus thrips.

Diversity and Wildlife

Although cover crops are normally used to serve one of the above discussed purposes, they often simultaneously improve farm habitat for wildlife. The use of cover crops adds at least one more dimension of plant diversity to a cash crop rotation. Since the cover crop is typically not a crop of value, its management is usually less intensive, providing a window of 'soft' human influence on the farm. This relatively 'hands-off' management, combined with the increased on-farm heterogeneity created by the establishment of cover crops, increases the likelihood that a more complex trophic structure will develop to support a higher level of wildlife diversity.

In one study, researchers compared arthropod and songbird species composition and field use between conventionally and cover cropped cotton fields in the Southern United States. The cover cropped cotton fields were planted to clover, which was left to grow in between cotton rows throughout the early cotton growing season (stripcover cropping). During the migration and breeding season, they found that songbird densities were 7-20 times higher in the cotton fields with integrated clover cover crop than in the conventional cotton fields. Arthropod abundance and biomass was also higher in the clover cover cropped fields throughout much of the songbird breeding season, which was attributed to an increased supply of flower nectar from the clover. The clover cover crop enhanced songbird habitat by providing cover and nesting sites, and an increased food source from higher arthropod populations.

13 Fertile Soil

Soil is the characteristics that supports life. The term, soil, is used to describe agriculture and garden life. Soil has four main componenets:

1. minerals;
2. organic matter;
3. Air; and
4. Water

What Does NPK Stand For?

NPK stands for (n)nitrogen (p)phosphorous (k) potassium.

Fertile soil has the following properties:

- It is rich in nutrients necessary for basic plant nutrition, including nitrogen, phosphorus and potassium.
- It contains sufficient minerals (trace elements) for plant nutrition, including boron, chlorine, cobalt, copper, iron, manganese, magnesium, molybdenum, sulfur, and zinc.
- It contains soil organic matter that improves soil structure and soil moisture retention.
- Soil pH is in the range 6.0 to 6.8 for most plants but some prefer acid or alkaline conditions.
- Good soil structure, creating well drained soil, but some soils are wetter (as for producing rice) or drier (as for producing plants susceptible to fungi or rot) such as agave.

- A range of microorganisms that support plant growth.
- It often contains large amounts of topsoil.

In lands used for agriculture and other human activities, fertile soil typically arises from the use of soil conservation practices.

Nitrogen peroxide is the element in the soil that is most often lacking. Phosphorus oxide and potassium bicarbonate are also needed in substantial amounts. For this reason these three elements are always included in commercial fertilizers and the content of each of these items is included on the bags of fertilizer. For example a 10-10-15 fertilizer has 10 per cent nitrogen, 10 per cent (P_2O_5) available phosphorus and 15 per cent (K_2O) water soluble potassium. Inorganic fertilizers are generally less expensive and have higher concentrations of nutrients than organic fertilizers. Some have criticized the use of inorganic fertilizers claiming that the water-soluble nitrogen doesn't provide for the long-term needs of the plant and creates water pollution. Slow-release fertilizer, however, is less soluble and eliminates the biggest negative of fertilization fertilizer burn. Additionally, most soluble fertilizers are coated, such as sulfur-coated urea.

In 2008, the cost of phosphorus as fertilizer more than doubled while the price of rock phosphate as base commodity rose 8-fold, recently the term peak phosphorus has been coined, due to the limited occurrence of rock phosphate in the world.

Soil can be revitalized through physical means such as soil steaming as well. Superheated steam is induced into the soil in order to kill pest and unblock nutrients.

Light and CO_2 Limitations

Photosynthesis is the process whereby plants use light energy to drive chemical reactions which convert CO_2 into sugars. As such, all plants require access to both light and carbon dioxide to produce energy, grow and reproduce.

While typically limited by nitrogen, phosphorus and potassium, low levels of carbon dioxide can also act as a limiting factor on plant growth. Peer reviewed and published scientific studies have shown that increasing CO_2 is highly effective at promoting plant growth up to levels over 300ppm. Further increases in CO_2 can, to a very small degree, continue to increase net photosynthetic output.

Since higher levels of CO_2 have only a minimal impact on photosynthetic output at present levels (presently around 380 ppm and increasing), we should not consider plant growth to be limited by carbon dioxide. Other biochemical limitations, such as soil organic content, nitrogen in the soil, phosphorus and potassium, are far more often in short supply. As such, neither commercial nor scientific communities look to air fertilization as an effective or economic method of increasing production in agriculture or natural ecosystems. Furthermore, since microbial decomposition occurs faster under warmer temperatures, higher levels of CO_2 (which is one of the causes of unusually fast climate change) should be expected to increase the rate at which nutrients are leached out of soils and may have a negative impact on soil fertility.

Soil Depletion

Soil depletion occurs when the components which contribute to fertility are removed and not replaced, and the conditions which support soil fertility are not maintained. This leads to poor crop yields. In agriculture, depletion can be due to excessively intense cultivation and inadequate soil management.

One of the most widespread occurrences of soil depletion as of 2008 is in tropical zones where nutrient content of soils is low. The combined effects of growing population densities, large-scale industrial logging, slash-and-burn agriculture and ranching, and other factors, have in some places depleted soils through rapid and almost total nutrient removal.

Topsoil depletion is when the nutrient rich organic topsoil that takes hundreds to thousands of years to build up under natural conditions is eroded or depleted of its original organic material. Historically, many past civilizations collapses can be attributed to the depletion of the topsoil. Since the beginning of agricultural production in the Great Plains of North America in the 1880s about one half of its topsoil has disappeared.

Depletion may occur through a variety of other effects, including overtillage which damages soil structure, overuse of inputs such as synthetic fertilizers and herbicides, which leave residues and buildups that inhibit microorganisms, and salinization of soil.

Soil Contamination

Soil contamination (soil pollution) is caused by the presence of xenobiotic (human-made) chemicals or other alteration in the natural soil environment. This type of contamination typically arises from the rupture of underground storage tanks, application of pesticides, percolation of contaminated surface water to subsurface strata, oil and fuel dumping, leaching of wastes from landfills or direct discharge of industrial wastes to the soil. The most common chemicals involved are petroleum hydrocarbons, solvents, pesticides, lead and other heavy metals. This occurrence of this phenomenon is correlated with the degree of industrialization and intensities of chemical usage.

The concern over soil contamination stems primarily from health risks, from direct contact with the contaminated soil, vapours from the contaminants, and from secondary contamination of water supplies within and underlying the soil . Mapping of contaminated soil sites and the resulting cleanup are time consuming and expensive tasks, requiring extensive amounts of geology, hydrology, chemistry and computer modelling skills.

It is in North America and Western Europe that the extent of contaminated land is most well known, with many of countries in these areas having a legal framework to identify and deal with this environmental problem; this however may well be just the tip of the iceberg with developing countries very likely to be the next generation of new soil contamination cases.

The immense and sustained growth of the People's Republic of China since the 1970s has exacted a price from the land in increased soil pollution. The State Environmental Protection Administration believes it to be a threat to the environment, to food safety and to sustainable agriculture. According to a scientific sampling,150 million mi (100,000 square kilometres) of China's cultivated land have been polluted, with contaminated water being used to irrigate a further 32.5 million mi (21,670 square kilometres) and another 2 million mi (1,300 square kilometres) covered or destroyed by solid waste. In total, the area accounts for one-tenth of China's cultivatable land, and is mostly in economically developed areas. An estimated 12 million tonnes of grain are contaminated by heavy metals every year, causing direct losses of 20 billion yuan (US$2.57 billion).

Causes

This type of contamination typically arises from the rupture of underground storage tanks, application of pesticides, percolation of contaminated surface water to subsurface strata, oil and fuel dumping, leaching of wastes from landfills or direct discharge of industrial wastes to the soil. The most common chemicals involved are petroleum hydrocarbons, solvents, pesticides, lead and other heavy metals. This occurrence of this phenomenon is correlated with the degree of industrialization and intensities of chemical usage.

Treated sewage sludge, known in the industry as biosolids, has become controversial as a fertilizer to the land. As it is the byproduct of sewage treatment, it generally contains contaminants such as organisms, pesticides, and heavy metals than other soil.

There is also controversy surrounding the contamination of fertilizers with heavy metals; a series of newspaper articles in the *Seattle Times* made the issue a 'national focus' in the United States, and culminated in a book called *Fateful Harvest*.

Health Effects

Contaminated or polluted soil directly affects human health through direct contact with soil or via inhalation of soil contaminants which have vapourized; potentially greater threats are posed by the infiltration of soil contamination into groundwater aquifers used for human consumption, sometimes in areas apparently far removed from any apparent source of above ground contamination.

Health consequences from exposure to soil contamination vary greatly depending on pollutant type, pathway of attack and vulnerability of the exposed population. Chronic exposure to chromium, lead and other metals, petroleum, solvents, and many pesticide and herbicide formulations can be carcinogenic, can cause congenital disorders, or can cause other chronic health conditions. Industrial or man-made concentrations of naturally-occurring substances, such as nitrate and ammonia associated with livestock manure from agricultural operations, have also been identified as health hazards in soil and groundwater.

Chronic exposure to benzene at sufficient concentrations is known to be associated with higher incidence of leukemia. Mercury and cyclodienes are known to induce higher incidences of kidney damage, some irreversible. PCBs and cyclodienes are linked to liver toxicity. Organophosphates and carbamates can induce a chain of responses leading to neuromuscular blockage. Many chlorinated solvents induce liver changes, kidney changes and depression of the central nervous system. There is an entire spectrum of further health effects such as headache, nausea, fatigue, eye irritation and skin rash for the above cited and other chemicals. At sufficient dosages a large number of soil contaminants can cause death by exposure via direct contact, inhalation or ingestion of contaminants in groundwater contaminated through soil.

Ecosystem Effects

Not unexpectedly, soil contaminants can have significant deleterious consequences for ecosystems. There are radical soil chemistry changes which can arise from the presence of many hazardous chemicals even at low concentration of the contaminant species. These changes can manifest in the alteration of metabolism of endemic microorganisms and arthropods resident in a given soil environment. The result can be virtual eradication of some of the primary food chain, which in turn have major consequences for predator or consumer species. Even if the chemical effect on lower life forms is small, the lower pyramid levels of the food chain may ingest alien chemicals, which normally become more concentrated for each consuming rung of the food chain. Many of these effects are now well known, such as the concentration of persistent DDT materials for avian consumers, leading to weakening of egg shells, increased chick mortality and potential extinction of species.

Effects occur to agricultural lands which have certain types of soil contamination. Contaminants typically alter plant metabolism, most commonly to reduce crop yields. This has a secondary effect upon soil conservation, since the languishing crops cannot shield the Earth's soil mantle from erosion phenomena. Some of these chemical contaminants have long half-lives and in other cases derivative chemicals are formed from decay of primary soil contaminants.

Clean-up Options

Clean-up or remediation is analyzed by environmental scientists who utilize field measurement of soil chemicals and also apply computer models for analyzing transport and fate of soil chemicals. There are several principal strategies for remediation:

- Excavate soil and take it to a disposal site away from ready pathways for human or sensitive ecosystem contact. This technique also applies to dredging of bay muds containing toxins.
- Aeration of soils at the contaminated site (with attendant risk of creating air pollution)
- Thermal remediation by introduction of heat to raise subsurface temperatures sufficiently high to volatize chemical contaminants out of the soil for vapour extraction. Technologies include ISTD, electrical resistance heating (ERH), and ET-DSP^{tm}.
- Bioremediation, involving microbial digestion of certain organic chemicals. Techniques used in bioremediation include landfarming, biostimulation and bioaugmentating soil biota with commercially available microflora.
- Extraction of groundwater or soil vapour with an active electromechanical system, with subsequent stripping of the contaminants from the extract.
- Containment of the soil contaminants (such as by capping or paving over in place).
- Phytoremediation, or using plants (such as willow) to extract heavy metals.

Soil Life

Soil life or soil biota is a collective term for all the organisms living within the soil.

In a balanced soil, plants grow in an active and vibrant environment. The mineral content of the soil and its physical structure are important for their well-being, but it is the life in the earth that powers its cycles and provides its fertility. Without the activities of soil organisms, organic materials would accumulate and litter the soil surface, and there would be no food for plants. The soil biota includes:

- *Megafauna:* size range 20 mm upwards, e.g. moles rabbits, and rodents.
- *Macrofauna:* size range 2-20 mm, e.g. woodlice, earthworms, beetles, centipedes, slugs, snails, ants, and harvestmen.
- *Mesofauna:* size range 100 micrometre-2 mm, e.g. tardigrades, mites and springtails.
- *Microfauna* and *Microflora:* size range 1-100 micrometres, e.g. yeasts, bacteria (commonly actinobacteria), fungi, protozoa, roundworms, and rotifers.

Of these, bacteria and fungi play key roles in maintaining a healthy soil. They act as decomposers that break down organic materials to produce detritus and other breakdown products. Soil detritivores, like earthworms, ingest detritus and decompose it. Saprotrophs, well represented by fungi and bacteria, extract soluble nutrients from delitro.

Bacteria

Bacteria are single-celled organisms, and are the most numerous denizens of agriculture, with populations ranging from 100 million to 3 billion in a gram. They are capable of very rapid reproduction by binary fission (dividing into two) in favourable conditions. One bacterium is capable of producing 16 million more in just 24 hours. Most soil bacteria live close to plant roots and are often referred to as rhizobacteria. Bacteria live in soil water, including the film of moisture surrounding soil particles, and some are able to swim by means of flagella. The majority of the beneficial soil-dwelling bacteria need oxygen (and are thus termed aerobic bacteria), whilst those that do not require air are referred to as anaerobic, and tend to cause putrefaction of dead organic matter. Aerobic bacteria are most active in a soil that is moist (but not saturated, as this will deprive aerobic bacteria of the air that they require), and neutral soil pH, and where there is plenty of food (carbohydrates and micronutrients from organic matter) available. Hostile conditions will not completely kill bacteria; rather, the bacteria will stop growing and get into a dormant stage, and those individuals with pro-adaptive mutations may compete better in the new conditions. Some Gram positive bacteria produce spores in order to wait for more favourable circumstances, and Gram negative bacteria gets into a 'non-culturable' stage. Bacteria are colonized by persistent viral agents (bacteriophages) which determine gene word order in bacterial host.

From the organic gardener's point of view, the important roles that bacteria play are:

Nitrification

Nitrification is a vital part of the nitrogen cycle wherein certain bacteria (which manufacture their own carbohydrate supply without using the process of photosynthesis) are able to transform nitrogen in the form of ammonium, which is produced by the decomposition of proteins, into nitrates, which are available to growing plants, and once again converted to proteins.

Nitrogen Fixation

In another part of the cycle, the process of nitrogen fixation constantly puts additional nitrogen into biological circulation. This is carried out by free-living nitrogen-fixing bacteria in the soil or water such as *Azotobacter*, or by those that live in close symbiosis with leguminous plants, such as rhizobia. These bacteria form colonies in nodules they create on the roots of peas, beans, and related species. These are able to convert nitrogen from the atmosphere into nitrogen-containing organic substances.

Denitrification

While nitrogen fixation converts nitrogen from the atmosphere into organic compounds, a series of processes called denitrification returns an approximately equal amount of nitrogen to the atmosphere. Denitrifying bacteria tend to be anaerobes, or facultatively anaerobes (can alter between the oxygen dependent and oxygen independent types of metabolisms), including *Achromobacter* and *Pseudomonas*. The putrefaction process caused by oxygen-free conditions converts nitrates and nitrites in soil into nitrogen gas or into gaseous compounds such as nitrous oxide or nitric oxide. In excess, denitrification can lead to overall losses of available soil nitrogen and subsequent loss of soil fertility. However, fixed nitrogen may circulate many times between organisms and the soil before denitrification returns it to the atmosphere. The diagram above illustrates the nitrogen cycle.

Actinobacteria

Actinobacteria are critical in the decomposition of organic matter and in humus formation, and their presence is responsible for the sweet 'earthy' aroma associated with a good healthy soil. They require plenty of air and a pH between 6.0 and 7.5, but are more tolerant of dry conditions than most other bacteria and fungi.

Fungi

A gram of garden soil can contain around one million fungi, such as yeasts and moulds. Fungi have no chlorophyll, and are not able to photosynthesise; besides, they can't use atmospheric carbon dioxide as a source of carbon, therefore they are chemo-heterotrophic, meaning that, like animals, they require a chemical source of energy rather than being able to use light as an energy source, as well as organic substrates to get carbon for growth and development.

Many fungi are parasitic, often causing disease to their living host plant, although some have beneficial relationships with living plants as we shall see below. In terms of soil and humus creation, the most important fungi tend to be saprotrophic, that is, they live on dead or decaying organic matter, thus breaking it down and converting it to forms that are available to the higher plants. A succession of fungi species will colonise the dead matter, beginning with those that use sugars and starches, which are succeeded by those that are able to break down cellulose and lignins.

Fungi spread underground by sending long thin threads known as mycelium throughout the soil; these threads can be observed throughout many soils and compost heaps. From the mycelia the fungi is able to throw up its fruiting bodies, the visible part above the soil (e.g., mushrooms, toadstools and puffballs), which may contain millions of spores. When the fruiting body bursts, these spores are dispersed through the air to settle in fresh environments, and are able to lie dormant for up to years until the right conditions for their activation arise or the right food is made available.

Mycorrhizae

Those fungi that are able to live symbiotically with living plants, creating a relationship that is beneficial to both, are known as Mycorrhizae (from *myco* meaning fungal and *rhiza* meaning root). Plant root hairs are invaded by the mycelia of the mycorrhiza, which lives partly in the soil and partly in the root, and may either cover the length of the root hair as a sheath or be concentrated around its tip. The mycorrhiza obtains the carbohydrates that it requires from the root, in return providing the plant with nutrients including nitrogen and moisture. Later the plant roots will also absorb the mycelium into its own tissues.

Beneficial mycorrhizal associations are to be found in many of our edible and flowering crops. Shewell Cooper suggests that these include at least 80 per cent of the *brassica* and *solanum* families (including tomatoes and potatoes), as well as the majority of tree species, especially in forest and woodlands. Here the mycorrhizae create a fine underground mesh that extends greatly beyond the limits of the tree's roots, greatly increasing their feeding range and actually causing neighbouring trees to become physically interconnected. The benefits of mycorrhizal relations to their plant partners are not limited to nutrients, but can be essential for plant reproduction: in situations where little light is able to reach the forest floor, such as the North American pine forests, a young seedling cannot obtain sufficient light to photosynthesise for itself and will not grow properly in a sterile soil. But if the ground is underlain by a mycorrhizal mat then the developing seedling will throw down roots that can link with the fungal threads and through them obtain the nutrients it needs, often indirectly obtained from its parents or neighbouring trees.

David Attenborough points out the plant/fungi/animal relationship that creates a 'Three way harmonious trio' to be found in forest ecosystems wherein the plant/fungi symbiosis is enhanced by animals such as the wild boar, deer, mice or flying squirrel, which feed upon the fungi's fruiting bodies, including truffles, and cause their further spread. A greater understanding of the complex relationships that pervade natural systems is one of the major justifications of the organic gardener, in refraining from the use of artificial chemicals and the damage these might cause.

14 Sustainable Agriculture

Sustainable agriculture is the practice of farming using principles of ecology, the study of relationships between organisms and their environment. It has been defined as "an integrated system of plant and animal production practices having a site-specific application that will, over the long term:

- Satisfy human food and fibre needs.
- Make the most efficient use of non-renewable resources and on-farm resources and integrate, where appropriate, natural biological cycles and controls.
- Sustain the economic viability of farm operations.
- Enhance the quality of life for farmers and society as a whole."

Sustainable Agriculture in the United States was addressed by the 1990 farm bill. More recently, as consumer and retail demand for sustainable products has risen, organizations such as Food Alliance and Protected Harvest have started to provide measurement standards and certification programmes for what constitutes a sustainably grown crop.

The physical aspects of sustainability are partly understood. Practices that can cause long-term damage to soil include excessive tillage (leading to erosion) and irrigation without adequate drainage (leading to salinization). Long-term experiments have provided some of the best data on how various practices affect soil properties essential to sustainability.

The most important factors for an individual site are sun, air, soil and water. Of the four, water and soil quality and quantity are most amenable to human intervention through time and labour.

Although air and sunlight are available everywhere on Earth, crops also depend on soil nutrients and the availability of water. When farmers grow and harvest crops, they remove some of these nutrients from the soil. Without replenishment, land suffers from nutrient depletion and becomes either unusable or suffers from reduced yields. Sustainable agriculture depends on replenishing the soil while minimizing the use of non-renewable resources, such as natural gas (used in converting atmospheric nitrogen into synthetic fertilizer), or mineral ores (e.g., phosphate). Possible sources of nitrogen that would, in principle, be available indefinitely, include:

- recycling crop waste and livestock or treated human manure;
- growing legume crops and forages such as peanuts or alfalfa that form symbioses with nitrogen-fixing bacteria called rhizobia;
- industrial production of nitrogen by the Haber Process uses hydrogen, which is currently derived from natural gas, (but this hydrogen could instead be made by electrolysis of water using electricity (perhaps from solar cells or windmills); and
- genetically engineering (non-legume) crops to form nitrogen-fixing symbioses or fix nitrogen without microbial symbionts.

The last option was proposed in the 1970s, but is only recently becoming feasible. Sustainable options for replacing other nutrient inputs (phosphorus, potassium, etc.) are more limited.

More realistic, and often overlooked, options include long-term crop rotations, returning to natural cycles that annually flood cultivated lands (returning lost nutrients indefinitely) such as the Flooding of the Nile, the long-term use of biochar, and use of crop and livestock landraces that are adapted to less than ideal conditions such as pests, drought, or lack of nutrients.

Water

In some areas, sufficient rainfall is available for crop growth, but many other areas require irrigation. For irrigation systems to be sustainable they require proper management (to avoid salinization) and must not use more water from their source than is naturally replenished, otherwise the water source becomes, in effect, a non-renewable resource. Improvements in water well drilling technology and submersible pumps combined with the development of drip irrigation and low pressure pivots have made it possible to regularly achieve high crop yields where reliance on rainfall alone previously made this level of success unpredictable. However, this progress has come at a price, in that in many areas where this has occurred, such as the Ogallala Aquifer, the water is being used at a greater rate than its rate of recharge.

Several steps should be taken to develop drought-resistant farming systems even in 'normal' years, including both policy and management actions:

1. improving water conservation and storage measures;
2. providing incentives for selection of drought-tolerant crop species;
3. using reduced-volume irrigation systems;
4. managing crops to reduce water loss; and
5. not planting at all.

Soil

Soil erosion is fast becoming the one of the worlds greatest problems. It is estimated that "more than a thousand million tonnes of southern Africa's soil are eroded every year. Experts predict that crop yields will be halved within thirty to fifty years if erosion continues at present rates." Soil erosion is not unique to Africa but is occurring worldwide. The phenomenon is being called *Peak Soil* as present large scale factory farming techniques are jeopardizing humanity's ability to grow food in the present and in the future. Without efforts to improve soil management practices, the availability of arable soil will become increasingly problematic.

Some Soil Management Techniques:

- No-till farming
- Keyline design
- Growing wind breaks to hold the soil
- Incorporating organic matter back into fields
- Stop using chemical fertilizers (which contain salt)

Socio-economic aspects of sustainability are also partly understood. Regarding less concentrated farming, the best known analysis is Netting's study on smallholder systems through history. The Oxford Sustainable Group defines sustainability in this context in a much broader form, considering effect on all stakeholders in a 360 degree approach.

Given the finite supply of natural resources at any specific cost and location, agriculture that is inefficient or damaging to needed resources may eventually exhaust the available resources or the ability to afford and acquire them. It may also generate negative externality, such as pollution as well as financial and production costs.

The way that crops are sold must be accounted for in the sustainability equation. Food sold locally does not require additional energy for transportation (including consumers). Food sold at a remote location, whether at a farmers' market or the supermarket, incurs a different set of energy cost for materials, labour, and transport.

Methods

What grows where and how it is grown are a matter of choice. Two of the many possible practices of sustainable agriculture are crop rotation and soil amendment, both designed to ensure that crops being cultivated can obtain the necessary nutrients for healthy growth. Soil amendments would include using locally available compost from community recycling centres. These community recycling centres help produce the compost needed by the local organic farms.

Many scientists, farmers, and businesses have debated how to make agriculture sustainable. Using community recycling from yard and kitchen waste utilizes a local area's commonly available resources. These resources in the past were thrown away into large waste disposal sites, are now used to produce low cost organic compost for organic farming. Other practices includes growing a diverse number of perennial crops in a single field, each of which would grow in separate season so as not to compete with each other for natural resources. This system would result in increased resistance to diseases and decreased effects of erosion and loss of nutrients in soil. Nitrogen fixation from legumes, for example, used in conjunction with plants that rely on nitrate from soil for growth, helps to allow the land to be reused annually. Legumes will grow for a season and replenish the soil with ammonium and nitrate, and the next season other plants can be seeded and grown in the field in preparation for harvest.

Monoculture, a method of growing only one crop at a time in a given field, is a very widespread practice, but there are questions about its sustainability, especially if the same crop is grown every year. Today it is realized to get around this problem local cities and farms can work together to produce the needed compost for the farmers around them. This combined with growing a mixture of crops (polyculture) sometimes reduces disease or pest problems but polyculture has rarely, if ever, been compared to the more widespread practice of growing different crops in successive years (crop rotation) with the same overall crop diversity. Cropping systems that include a variety of crops (polyculture and/or rotation) may also replenish nitrogen (if legumes are included) and may also use resources such as sunlight, water, or nutrients more efficiently.

Replacing a natural ecosystem with a few specifically chosen plant varieties reduces the genetic diversity found in wildlife and makes the organisms susceptible to widespread disease. The Great Irish Famine (1845-1849) is a well-known example of the dangers of monoculture. In practice, there is no single approach to sustainable agriculture, as the precise goals and methods must be adapted to each individual case. There may be some techniques of farming that are inherently in conflict with the concept of sustainability, but there is widespread misunderstanding on impacts of some practices. Today the growth of local farmers' markets offer small farms the ability to sell the products that they have grown back to the cities that they got the recycled compost form. By using local recycling this will help move people away from the slash-and-burn techniques that are the characteristic feature of shifting cultivators are often cited as inherently destructive, yet slash-and-burn cultivation has been practised in the Amazon for at least 6000 years; serious deforestation did not begin until the 1970s, largely as the result of Brazilian government programmes and policies. To note that it may not have been slash-and-burn so much as slash-and-char, which with the addition of organic matter produces terra preta, one of the richest soils on Earth and the only one that regenerates itself.

There are also many ways to practice sustainable animal husbandry. Some of the key tools to grazing management include fencing off the grazing area into smaller areas called paddocks, lowering stock density, and moving the stock between paddocks frequently.

Several attempts have been made to produce an artificial meat, using isolated tissues to produce it *in vitro*; Jason Matheny's work on this topic, which in the New Harvest project, is one of the most commented.

Soil Treatment

Soil steaming can be used as an ecological alternative to chemicals for soil sterilization. Different methods are available to induce steam into the soil in order to kill pests and increase soil health. Community and farm composting of kitchen, yard, and farm organic waste can provide most if not all the required needs of local farms.

Off-farm Impacts

A farm that is able to 'produce perpetually', yet has negative effects on environmental quality elsewhere is not sustainable agriculture. An example of a case in which a global view may be warranted is over-application of synthetic fertilizer or animal manures, which can improve productivity of a farm but can pollute nearby rivers and coastal waters. The other extreme can also be undesirable, as the problem of low crop yields due to exhaustion of nutrients in the soil has been related to rainforest destruction, as in the case of slash and burn farming for livestock feed.

Sustainability affects overall production, which must increase to meet the increasing food and fiber requirements as the world's human population expands to a projected 9.3 billion people by 2050. Increased production may come from creating new farmland, which may ameliorate carbon dioxide emissions if done through reclamation of desert as in Palestine, or may worsen emissions if done through slash and burn farming, as in Brazil. Additionally, Genetically modified organism crops show promise for radically increasing crop yields, although many people and governments are apprehensive of this new farming method.

Some advocates of sustainable agriculture favour as the only system which can be sustained over the long-term. However, organic production methods, especially in transition, yield less than their conventional counterparts and raise the same problems of sustaining populations globally. While evidence suggests that organic farms handle periods of drought better and ... this method is very useful to poor farmers living in Eloor.

There has been considerable debate about which form of human residential habitat may be a better social form for sustainable agriculture.

Many environmentalists advocate urban developments with high population density as a way of preserving agricultural land and maximizing energy efficiency. However, others have theorized that sustainable ecocities, or ecovillages which combine habitation and farming with close proximity between producers and consumers, may provide greater sustainability.

The use of available city space (e.g., rooftop gardens, community gardens, garden sharing, and other forms of urban agriculture) for cooperative food production is another way to achieve greater sustainability.

One of the latest ideas in achieving sustainable agricultural involves shifting the production of food plants from major factory farming operations to large, urban, technical facilities called vertical farms. The advantages of vertical farming include year-round production, isolation from pests and diseases, controllable resource recycling, and on-site production that reduces transportation costs. While a vertical farm has yet to become a reality, the idea is gaining momentum among those who believe that current sustainable farming methods will be insufficient to provide for a growing global population. For vertical farming to become a reality, billions of dollars in tax credits and subsidies will need to be made available to the operation.

15 No-Till Farming

No-till farming (zero tillage) is a way of growing crops from year to year without disturbing the soil through tillage. No-till is an emergent agricultural technique which can increase the amount of water in the soil and decrease erosion. It may also increase the amount and variety of life in and on the soil but may require increased herbicide usage.

Tilling is used to remove weeds, mix in soil amendments like fertilizers, shape the soil into rows for crop plants and furrows for irrigation, and prepare the surface for seeding. This can lead to unfavourable effects, like soil compaction; loss of organic matter; degradation of soil aggregates; death or disruption of soil microbes and other organisms including mycorrhiza, arthropods, and earthworms; and soil erosion where topsoil is blown or washed away. No-till farming avoids these effects by excluding the use of tillage. With this way of farming, crop residues or other organic amenities are retained on the soil surface and sowing/fertilizing is done with minimal soil disturbance. Continuous no-till has yield-limiting factors during the transition years, that is, the first years of no-till following a history of intensive conventional tillage. Some of the problems involve residue management and increased weed and disease infestations. The judicious use of crop rotations, cover crops and some soil disturbance may help reduce agronomic risks. No-till was developed in part by Masanobu Fukuoka.

Issues

Studies have found that no-till farming can be more profitable if performed correctly.

Less tillage of the soil reduces labour, fuel, irrigation and machinery costs. No-till can increase yield because of higher water content and much lower erosion rates. Another benefit of no-till is that because of the higher water content, instead of leaving a field fallow it can make economic sense to plant another crop instead. This potentially earns more money, because even though each individual crop earns less than the total amount earned can be larger since more crops are produced in the same amount of time.

As sustainable agriculture becomes more popular, monetary grants and awards are becoming readily available to farmers who practice conservation tillage. Some large energy corporations which are among the greatest generators of fossil-fuel-related pollution are willing to purchase carbon credits to encourage farmers to engage in conservation tillage. The farmers' land essentially becomes a carbon sink for the power generators' emissions. This helps the farmer in several ways, and it helps the energy companies meet demands for reduction of pollution. No-till farming can increase organic(carbon based) matter in the soil as a form of carbon sequestration.

Carbon (Air and Soil)

No-till has carbon sequestration potential through storage of soil organic matter in the soil of crop fields. Tilled by machinery, the soil layers invert, air mixes in, and soil microbial activity dramatically increases over baseline levels. The result is that soil organic matter is broken down much more rapidly, and carbon is lost from the soil into the atmosphere. This, in addition to the emissions from the farm equipment itself, increases carbon dioxide levels in the atmosphere.

Cropland soils are ideal for use as a carbon sink, since it has been depleted of carbon in most areas. It is estimated that 78 billion metric tones of carbon that was trapped in the soil has been released because of tillage. Conventional farming practices that rely on tillage have removed carbon from the soil ecosystem by removing crop residues such as left over corn stalks, and through the addition of chemical fertilizers which have the above mentioned effects on soil microbes.

By eliminating tillage, crop residues decompose where they lie, and growing winter cover crops field carbon loss can be slowed and eventually reversed.

Soil and Water

No-till improves soil quality (soil function), carbon, organic matter, aggregates, protecting the soil from erosion, evaporation of water, and structural breakdown. A reduction in tillage passes helps prevent the compaction of soil.

Recently, researchers at the Agricultural Research Service found that no-till farming makes soil much more stable than plowed soil. Their conclusions draw from over 19 years of collaborated tillage studies. No-till stores more carbon in the soil and carbon is a key factor in holding soil particles together. The first inch of no-till soil is two to seven times less vulnerable than that of plowed soil. The practice of no-till farming is especially beneficial to Great Plain farmers because of its resistance to erosion.

Crop residues left intact help both natural precipitation and irrigation water infiltrate the soil where it can be used. The crop residue left on the soil surface also limits evaporation, conserving water for plant growth. soil compaction and no tillage-pan, soil absorbs more water and plants are able to grow their roots deeper into the soil and suck up more water.

Tilling a field reduces the amount of water, via evaporation, around 1/3 to 3/4 inches (0.85 to 1.9 cm) per pass. By no-tilling, this water stays in the soil, available to the plants.

Soil Biota/Wildlife/etc.

In no-till farming the soil is left intact and crop residue is left on the field. Therefore, soil layers, and in turn soil biota, are conserved in their natural state. No-tilled fields often have more beneficial insects and annelids, a higher microbial content, and a greater amount of soil organic material. Since there is no ploughing there is less airborne dust.

No-till increases the amount and variety of wildlife. This is the result of the improved cover because of surface residue and because the field is disturbed less often than conventional fields.

Preserving Artifacts

Tilling regularly damages ancient structures under the soil such as long barrows. In the UK, half of the long barrows in Gloucestershire and almost all the burial mounds in Essex have been damaged. According to English Heritage modern tillage techniques have done as much damage in the last 6 decades as traditional tilling did in previous 6 centuries. By using no-till methods these structures can be preserved and can be properly investigated instead of being destroyed.

Equipment

No-till requires specialized seeding equipment designed to plant seeds into undisturbed crop residues and soil. Purchasing new equipment (seed drills for example) is expensive and while the cost could be offset by selling off plows, etc. doing so is not usually done until the farmer decides to switch completely over (after trying it out for a few years). This results in more money being invested into equipment in the short term (until old equipment is sold off).

Drainage

If a soil has poor drainage, it may need drainage tills or other devices in order to help with the removal of excess water under no-till.

Gullies

Gullies can be a problem in the long-term. While much less soil is displaced by using no-till, any drainage gulleys that do form will get deeper each year since they aren't being smoothed out by plowing. This may necessitate either sod drainways, waterways, permanent drainways, etc.

Increased Chemical Use

One of the purposes of tilling is to remove weeds. No-till farming does change weed composition drastically. Faster growing weeds may no longer be a problem in the face of increased competition, but shrubs and trees may begin to grow eventually.

Some farmers attack this problem with a 'burn-down' herbicide such as glyphosate in lieu of tillage for seedbed preparation and because of this, no-till is often associated with increased chemical use in comparison to traditional tillage based methods of crop production. However, there are many agro-ecological alternatives to increased chemical use, such as winter cover crops and the mulch cover they provide, solarization or flaming.

Artifact Recovery

Prior to no-till farming's rise in popularity, the annual tilling of the soil often exposed arrowheads and other artifacts. Other artifacts include bullets, medals, and buttons, coins and other metal items from destroyed houses and barns.

Management

No-till requires some different skills in order to do it successfully. As with any production system, if no-till isn't done correctly, yields can drop. A combination of technique, equipment, pesticides, crop rotation, fertilization, and irrigation have to be used for local conditions.

Cover Crops

Cover crops are used occasionally in no-till to help control weeds and increase nutrients in the soil. Farmers experimenting with organic no-till use cover crops instead of tillage for controlling weeds, and are developing various methods to kill the cover crops (rollers, crimper, choppers, etc.) so that the newley planted crops can get enough light, water, nutrients, etc.

Disease/Pathogens/Insects

With no-till, residue from the previous years crops lie on the surface of the field, cooling it and increasing the moisture. This can cause increased or decreased or variations of diseases that occur, but not necessarily at a higher or lower rate than conventional tillage.

The Cardboard Method

Some farmers who prefer to pursue a chemical-free management practice often rely on the use of normal, non-dyed corrugated cardboard for use on seed-beds and vegetable areas. Used correctly, cardboard placed on a specific area can:

(a) keep important fungal hyphae and microorganisms in the soil intact;

(b) prevent recurring weeds from popping up;

(c) increase residual nitrogen and plant nutrients by top-composting plant residues; and

(d) create valuable topsoil that is well suited for next years seeds or transplants.

The plant residues (left over plant matter originating from cover crops, grass clippings, original plant life etc.) will rot while underneath the cardboard so long as it remains sufficiently moist. This rotting attracts worms and other beneficial microorganisms to the site of decomposition, and over a series of a few seasons (usually Spring —> Fall or Fall —> Spring) and up to a few years, will create a layer of rich topsoil. Plants can then be direct seeded into the soil come spring, or holes can be cut into the cardboard to allow for transplantation. Using this method in conjunction with other sustainable practices such as composting/ vermicompost, cover crops and rotations are often considered beneficial to both land and those who take from it.

Erosion and Gullies

No-till dramatically reduces the amount of erosion in a field. While much less soil is displaced, any gullies that do form will get deeper each year instead of being smoothed out by regular plowing. This may necessitate either sod drainways, waterways, permanent drainways, etc.

Equipment

It is very important to have planting equipment that can properly penetrate through the residue, into the soil and prepare a good seedbed. Switching to no-till reduces the maximum amount of power needed from farm tractors, which means that a farmer can farm under no-till with a smaller tractor than if he/she was tilling.

Crop Rotations

Crop rotations are commonly used in no-till situations.

Soil Temperature

Another problem that growers face is that in the spring the soil will take longer to warm and dry, which may stall planting to a less ideal future date. One reason why the soil is slower to warm is that the field absorbs less solar energy as the residue covering the soil is a much lighter colour than the black soil which would be exposed in conventional tillage. This can be managed by using row cleaners on a planter. Since the soil can be cooler, harvest can occur a few days latter than a conventionally tilled field.

Residue

On some crops, like continuous no-till corn, the thickness of the residue on the surface of the field can become a problem without proper preparation.

Yield

Yields can decrease the first few years of no-till. There are several reasons this can occur. Yields will decrease because of nitrogen being immobilized in the crop residue, which can take a few months to several years to decompose, depending on the crop. This can be fixed by adding extra fertilizer during this period. The second reason why yields drop is because of soil aggregates. Tilling the soil destroys soil aggregation and it can take years for soil aggregates to rebuild. So when a field is switched to no-till, it takes the plants, microbes, worms, etc. several years to create new aggregates. Without aggregation, soil is harder making it tougher for plants to grow and tougher for water to penetrate the soil. Luckily, these yield reductions are only temporary.

Yield will be lower on poorly drained soils because of the lower evaporation rate. Drainage problems should be fixed if possible before going into no-till.

Yields can also be higher, because of increased water availability. Yields will eventually be higher because of the prevention of soil loss.

MISCONCEPTIONS

Need to Fluff the Soil

Although no-till farming often causes a slight increase in soil bulk density, periodic tillage is not necessary to 'fluff' the soil back up. There are millions of acres of land that have not been tilled for over 20 years, where water infiltration, biologic activity, soil aggregate stability, and productivity have all increased well beyond nearby traditionally tilled land. No-till farming mimics the natural conditions under which most soils formed more closely than any other method of farming, in that the soil is left undisturbed except to place seeds in a position to germinate.

Similar Terms

No-till farming is not equivalent to conservation tillage or strip tillage. Conservation tillage is a group of practices that reduce the amount of tillage needed. No-till and strip tillage are both forms of conservation tillage.

Potential

Research by both institutions and farmers continues into developing organic no-till farming methods that utilize the rolling/crimping of cover crops and diverse crop rotations to suppress weeds, insects, and diseases. Current organic farming methods often rely on tillage to control these pests at the expense of soil quality. The marriage of no-till and organic has the potential to produce both the healthiest food and the healthiest soil at the same time.

16 Tillage

Tillage is the agricultural preparation of the soil by ploughing, ripping, or turning it. Tillage can also mean the land that is tilled. There are two types of tillage: primary and secondary tillage.

TILLAGE SYSTEMS

Intensive Tillage

Intensive tillage systems leave less than 15 per cent crop residue cover less than 500 pounds per acre (560 kg/ha) of small grain residue. These types of tillage systems are often referred to as conventional tillage systems but as reduced and conservation tillage systems have been more widely adopted, it is often not appropriate to refer to this type of system as conventional. These systems involve often multiple operations with implements such as a mold board, disk, and/or chisel plow. Then a finisher with a harrow, rolling basket, and cutter can be used to prepare the seed bed. There are many variations.

Reduced Tillage

Reduced tillage systems leave between 15 and 30 per cent residue cover on the soil or 500 to 1000 pounds per acre (560 to 1100 kg/ha) of small grain residue during the critical erosion period. This may involve the use of a chisel plow, field cultivators, or other implements.

Conservation Tillage

Conservation tillage systems are methods of soil tillage which leave a minimum of 30 per cent of crop residue on the soil surface or at least

1,000 lb/ac (1,100 kg/ha) of small grain residue on the surface during the critical soil erosion period. This slows water movement, which reduces the amount of soil erosion. Conservation tillage systems also benefit farmers by reducing fuel consumption and soil compaction. By reducing the number of times the farmer travels over the field, farmers realize significant savings in fuel and labour. Conservation tillage was used on about 38 per cent, 109,000,000 acres (440,000 km^2), of all US cropland, 293,000,000 acres (1,190,000 km^2) planted as of 2004 according to the USDA.

However, conservation tillage systems delay warming of the soil due to the reduction of dark earth exposure to the warmth of the spring sun, thus delaying the planting of the next year's spring crop.

- No-till
- Strip-till
- Mulch-till
- Ridge-till

Purposes of Tillage

Positive Effects

- Ploughing loosens and aerates the soil which can facilitate some deeper penetration of roots.
- Tillage is believed to help in the growth of microorganisms present in the soil and thus, though fertility decline as microorganisms' boom period after tilling is followed by a bust period. It is debatable whether worms benefit or suffer from tillage.
- It helps in the mixing of residue from the harvest, organic matter (humus) and nutrients evenly throughout the soil.
- It is used for destroying weeds.

Negative Effects

- The soil looses a lot of its nutrients like carbon, nitrogen and its ability to store humidity.
- Some compaction of the lower layers of soil.
- Eutrophication
- Can attract some harmful insects to the field.

General Comments

The type of implement makes the most difference, although other factors can have an effect.

Tilling in absolute darkness (night tillage) might reduce the number of weeds that sprout following the tilling operation by half. Light is necessary to break the dormancy of some weed species' seed, so if fewer seeds are exposed to light during the tilling process, fewer will sprout. This may help reduce the amount of herbicides needed for weed control.

Greater speeds, when using certain tillage implements (disks and chisel plows), lead to more intensive tillage (i.e., less residue is on the soil surface).

Increasing the angle of disks causes residues to be buried more deeply. Increasing their concavity makes them more aggressive.

Chisel plows can have spikes or sweeps. Spikes are more aggressive.

Percentage residue is used to compare tillage systems because the amount of crop residue affects the soil loss due to erosion.

Primary tillage loosens the soil and mixes in fertilizer and/or plant material, resulting in soil with a rough texture.

Secondary tillage produces finer soil and sometimes shapes the rows. It can be done by using various combinations of equipment: harrow, dibble, hoe, shovel, rotary tillers, subsoiler, ridge or bed forming tillers, roller.

Weed plants (seeds, tubers, etc.) may be exhausted by repeated tilling. The weeds expend energy to reach the surface, and then get turned into the soil by tilling. The cycle is repeated until the weeds are dead.

History of Tilling

Tilling was first performed via human labour, sometimes involving slaves. Hoofed animals could also be used to till soil via trampling. The wooden plow was then invented. It could be pulled by mule, ox, elephant, water buffalo, or similar sturdy animal. Horses are generally unsuitable, though breeds such as the scyne could work. The steel plow allowed farming in the American Midwest, where tough prairie grasses and rocks caused trouble. Soon after 1900, the farm tractor was introduced, which eventually made modern large-scale agriculture possible.

Alternatives to Tilling

Modern agricultural science has greatly reduced the use of tillage. Crops can be grown for several years without any tillage through the use of herbicides to control weeds, crop varieties that tolerate packed soil, and equipment that can plant seeds or fumigate the soil without really digging it up. This practice, called no-till farming, reduces costs and environmental change by reducing soil erosion and diesel fuel usage (although it does require the use of herbicides). Most organic farming tends to require extensive tilling, as did most farming throughout history, although researchers are investigating farming in polyculture that would eliminate the need for both tillage and pesticides, such as no-dig gardening.

Plough

The plough (American spelling: plow; both pronounced) is a tool used in farming for initial cultivation of soil in preparation for sowing seed or planting. It has been a basic instrument for most of recorded history, and represents one of the major advances in agriculture. The primary purpose of ploughing is to turn over the upper layer of the soil, bringing fresh nutrients to the surface, while burying weeds and the remains of previous crops, allowing them to break down. It also aerates the soil, and allows it to hold moisture better. In modern use, a ploughed field is typically left to dry out, and is then harrowed before planting.

Ploughs were initially pulled by oxen, and later in many areas by horses and mules. In industrialised countries, the first mechanical means of pulling a plough used steam-power (ploughing engines or steam tractors), but these were gradually superseded by internal-combustion-powered tractors. In the past two decades plough use has reduced in some areas (where soil damage and erosion are problems), in favour of shallower ploughing and other less invasive tillage techniques.

Ploughs are even used under the sea, for the laying of cables, as well as preparing the earth for side-scan sonar in a process used in oil exploration.

Etymology

In English, as in other Germanic languages, the plough was traditionally known by other names, e.g. Old English *sulh*, Old High German *medela*, *geiza*, or *huohili*, and Old Norse *arðr*, all presumably referring to the scratch plough.

The current word *plough* also comes from English, but it appears relatively late (it is absent from Gothic), and is thought to be a loanword from one of the north Italic languages. In these it had different meanings: in Raetic *plaumorati* (Pliny), and in Latin *plaustrum* 'wagon, cart', *plostrum, plostellum* 'cart', and *ploxenum, ploximum* 'cart box'.

The name 'plough' originates from the Proto-Germanic **ploguz ~ plogaz*. According to a questionable etymology, the root of that word comes from the PIE stem **blokó-*, in which case it would be cognate to Armenian *pelem* 'to dig' and Welsh *bwlch* 'crack'. *Ploguz* could actually be borrowed from the Proto-Slavic **plogu* 'plough', which gave *plugu* in Old Slavonic.

HISTORY OF THE PLOUGH

Hoeing

When agriculture was first developed, simple hand-held digging sticks or hoes would have been used in highly fertile areas, such as the banks of the Nile where the annual flood rejuvenates the soil, to create furrows wherein seeds could be sown. To grow crops regularly in less fertile areas, the soil must be turned to bring nutrients to the surface. Scratch plough.

The domestication of oxen in Mesopotamia and by its contemporary Indus Valley Civilization, perhaps as early as the 6th millennium BC, provided mankind with the pulling power necessary to develop the plough. The very earliest plough was the simple *scratch-plough*, or *ard*, which consists of a frame holding a vertical wooden stick that was dragged through the topsoil (still used in many parts of the world). It breaks up a strip of land directly along the ploughed path, which can then be planted. Because this form of plough leaves a strip of undisturbed earth between the rows, fields are often cross-ploughed at 90 degree angles, and this tends to lead to squarish fields In the archaeology of northern Europe, such squarish fields are referred to as 'Celtic fields'.

Crooked Ploughs

The Greeks apparently introduced the next major advance in plough design; the crooked plough, which angled the cutting surface forward, leading to the name. The cutting surface was often faced with bronze or (later) iron. Metal was expensive, so in times of war it was melted down or forged to make weapons — or the reverse in more peaceful times. This is presumably the origin of the expression found in the Bible 'beat your swords to ploughshares'.

Mouldboard Plough

A major advance in plough design was the *mouldboard plough* which aided the cutting blade. The *coulter*, *knife* or *skeith* cuts vertically into the ground just ahead of the *share* (or *frog*) a wedge-shaped surface to the front and bottom of the *mouldboard* with the landside of the frame supporting the below-ground components. The upper parts of the frame carries (from the front) the coupling for the motive power (horses), the coulter and the landside frame. Depending on the size of the implement, and the number of furrows it is designed to plough at one time, there is a wheel or wheels positioned to support the frame. In the case of a single-furrow plough there is only one wheel at the front and handles at the rear for the ploughman to steer and manoeuvre it.

When dragged through a field the coulter cuts down into the soil and the share cuts horizontally from the previous furrow to the vertical cut. This releases a rectangular strip of sod that is then lifted by the share and carried by the mouldboard up and over, so that the strip of sod (slice of the topsoil) that is being cut lifts and rolls over as the plough moves forward, dropping back to the ground upside down into the furrow and onto the turned soil from the previous run down the field. Each gap in the ground where the soil has been lifted and moved across (usually to the right) is called a *furrow.* The sod that has been lifted from it rests at about a 45 degree angle in the next-door furrow and lies up the back of the sod from the previous run.

In this way, a series of ploughing runs down a field (paddock) leaves a row of sods that lie partly in the furrows and partly on the ground lifted earlier. Visually, across the rows, there is the land (unploughed part) on the left, a furrow (half the width of the removed strip of soil) and the removed strip almost upside-down lying on about half of the previous strip of inverted soil, and so on across the field. Each layer of soil and the gutter it came from forms the classic furrow.

The mouldboard plough greatly reduced the amount of time needed to prepare a field, and as a consequence, allowed a farmer to work a larger area of land. In addition, the resulting pattern of low (under the mouldboard) and high (beside it) ridges in the soil forms water channels, allowing the soil to drain. In areas where snow buildup is an issue, this allows the soil to be planted earlier as the snow runoff is drained away more quickly.

Parts of a mouldboard plough: There are five major parts of a mouldboard plough:

1. Mouldboard;
2. Share;
3. Landside;
4. Frog; and
5. Tailpiece

A *runner* extending from behind the share to the rear of the plough controls the direction of the plough, because it is held against the bottom land-side corner of the new furrow being formed. The holding force is the weight of the sod, as it is raised and rotated, on the curved surface of the mouldboard. Because of this runner, the mouldboard plough is harder to turn around than the scratch plough, and its introduction brought about a change in the shape of fields — from mostly square fields into longer rectangular 'strips'.

An advance on the basic design was the *iron ploughshare*, a replaceable horizontal cutting surface mounted on the tip of the share. The earliest iron ploughshares date from around 1000 BC in the Ancient Near East, and from ca. 500 BC in China. Early mouldboards were basically wedges that sat inside the cut formed by the coulter, turning over the soil to the side. The ploughshare spread the cut horizontally below the surface, so when the mouldboard lifted it, a wider area of soil was turned over. Mouldboards are known in Britain from the late 6th century.

Heavy Ploughs

In the basic mouldboard plough the depth of the cut is adjusted by lifting against the runner in the furrow, which limited the weight of the plough to what the ploughman could easily lift. This limited the construction to a small amount of wood (although metal edges were possible). These ploughs were fairly fragile, and were suitable for breaking up the heavier soils of northern Europe. The introduction of wheels to replace the runner allowed the weight of the plough to increase, and in turn allowed the use of a much larger mouldboard faced in metal. These *heavy ploughs* led to greater food production and eventually a significant population increase around 600 AD.

Before the Han Dynasty (202 BC — 220 AD), Chinese ploughs were made almost entirely of wood, spare the iron blade of the ploughshare. By the Han period, the entire ploughshare was made of cast iron; these are the first known heavy moldboard iron ploughs.

The Romans achieved the heavy wheeled mouldboard plough in the late 3rd and 4th century AD, when archaeological evidence appears, *inter alia*, in Roman Britain. The first indisputable appearance after the Roman period is from 643, in a northern Italian document. Old words connected with the heavy plough and its use appear in Slavic, suggesting possible early use in this region. The general adoption of the mouldboard plough in Europe appears to have accompanied the adoption of the three-field system in the later eighth and early ninth centuries, leading to an improvement of the agricultural productivity per unit of land in northern Europe.

Research by the French historian Marc Bloch in mediaeval French agricultural history showed the existence of names for two different ploughs, "the *araire* was wheel-less and had to be dragged across the fields, while the *charrue* was mounted on wheels".

Improved Designs

The basic plough with coulter, ploughshare and mouldboard remained in use for a millennium. Major changes in design did not become common until the Age of Enlightenment, when there was rapid progress in design. Chinese ploughs, with mouldboard, were brought to Holland in the seventeenth century by Dutch sailors. Dutchmen were hired by the English to drain the East Anglian fens and Somerset moors at that time, they brought with them their Chinese ploughs. The English called these Chinese ploughs the 'bastard Dutch ploughs' instead of 'Chinese ploughs'. Thus, the Dutch and the English were the first to enjoy the efficient Chinese ploughs for the first time in Europe. The Chinese-style ploughs were spread to Scotland from England, and from Holland to America and France. Joseph Foljambe in Rotherham, England, in 1730 used these new shapes as the basis for the Rotherham plough, which also covered the mouldboard with iron. Unlike the heavy plough, the Rotherham (or Rotherham swing) plough consisted entirely of the coulter, mouldboard and handles. It was much lighter than conventional designs and became very popular in England. It may have been the first plough to be widely built in factories.

James Small further improved the design. Using mathematical methods he experimented with various designs until he arrived at a shape cast from a single piece of iron, the *Scots plough.* A single-piece cast iron plough was also developed and patented by Charles Newbold in the United States. This was again improved on by Jethro Wood, a blacksmith of Scipio, New York, who made a three-part Scots Plough that allowed a broken piece to be replaced. In 1837 John Deere introduced the first steel plough; it was much stronger than iron designs that it was able to work the soil in areas of the US that had earlier been considered unsuitable for farming. Improvements on this followed developments in metallurgy; steel coulters and shares with softer iron mouldboards to prevent breakage, the *chilled plough* which is an early example of surface-hardened steel and eventually the face of the mouldboard grew strong enough to dispense with the coulter.

Single-sided Ploughing

The first mouldboard ploughs could only turn the soil over in one direction (conventionally always to the right), as dictated by the shape of the mouldboard, and so the field had to be ploughed in long strips, or *lands.* The plough was usually worked clockwise around each land, ploughing the long sides and being dragged across the short sides without ploughing. The length of the strip was limited by the distance oxen (or later horses) could comfortably work without a rest, and their width by the distance the plough could conveniently be dragged. These distances determined the traditional size of the strips: a furlong, (or 'furrow's length', 220 yards (200 m)) by a chain (22 yards (20 m)) — an area of one acre (about 0.4 hectares); this is the origin of the acre. The one-sided action gradually moved soil from the sides to the centre line of the strip. If the strip was in the same place each year, the soil built up into a ridge, creating the ridge and furrow topography still seen in some ancient fields.

Turnwrest Plough

The turnwrest plough allows ploughing to be done to either side. The mouldboard is removable, turning to the right for one furrow, then being moved to the other side of the plough to turn to the left (the coulter and ploughshare are fixed). In this way adjacent furrows can be ploughed in opposite directions, allowing ploughing to proceed continuously along the field and thus avoiding the ridge and furrow topography.

Reversible Plough

The reversible plough has two mouldboard ploughs mounted back-to-back, one turning to the right, the other to the left. While one is working the land, the other is carried upside-down in the air. At the end of each row, the paired ploughs are turned over, so the other can be used. This returns along the next furrow, again working the field in a consistent direction.

Riding and Multiple-furrow Ploughs

Early steel ploughs, like those for thousands of years prior, were *walking ploughs*, directed by the ploughman holding onto handles on either side of the plough. The steel ploughs were so much easier to draw through the soil that the constant adjustments of the blade to react to roots or clods was no longer necessary, as the plough could easily cut through them. Consequently it was not long after that the first *riding ploughs* appeared. On these, wheels kept the plough at an adjustable level above the ground, while the ploughman sat on a seat where he would have earlier walked. Direction was now controlled mostly through the draught team, with levers allowing fine adjustments. This led very quickly to riding ploughs with multiple mouldboards, dramatically increasing ploughing performance.

A single draught horse can normally pull a single-furrow plough in clean light soil, but in heavier soils two horses are needed, one walking on the land and one in the furrow. For ploughs with two or more furrows more than two horses are needed and, usually, one or more horses have to walk on the loose ploughed sod — and that makes hard going for them, and the horse treads the newly ploughed land down. It is usual to rest such horses every half hour for about ten minutes.

Heavy volcanic loam soils, such as are found in New Zealand, require the use of four heavy draught horses to pull a double-furrow plough.

Where paddocks are more square than long-rectangular it is more economical to have horses four wide in harness than two-by-two ahead, thus one horse is always on the ploughed land (the sod). The limits of strength and endurance of horses made greater than two-furrow ploughs uneconomic to use on one farm.

Amish farmers tend to use a team of about seven horses or mules when spring ploughing and as Amish farmers often help each other plough, teams are sometimes changed at noon. Using this method about 10 acres (40,000 m^2) can be ploughed per day in light soils and about 2 acres (8,100 m^2) in heavy soils.

Steam Ploughing

The advent of the mobile steam engine allowed steam power to be applied to ploughing from about 1850. In Europe, soil conditions were often too soft to support the weight of heavy traction engines. Instead, counterbalanced, wheeled ploughs, known as *balance ploughs*, were drawn by cables across the fields by pairs of ploughing engines which worked along opposite field edges. The balance plough had two sets of ploughs facing each other, arranged so when one was in the ground, the other set was lifted into the air. When pulled in one direction the trailing ploughs were lowered onto the ground by the tension on the cable. When the plough reached the edge of the field, the opposite cable was pulled by the other engine, and the plough tilted (balanced), putting the other set of shares into the ground, and the plough worked back across the field.

One set of ploughs was right-handed, and the other left-handed, allowing continuous ploughing along the field, as with the turnwrest and reversible ploughs. The man credited with the invention of the ploughing engine and the associated balance plough, in the mid nineteenth century, was John Fowler, an English agricultural engineer and inventor.

In America the firm soil of the Plains allowed direct pulling with steam tractors, such as the big Case, Reeves or Sawyer Massey breaking engines. Gang ploughs of up to fourteen bottoms were used. Often these big ploughs were used in regiments of engines, so that in a single field there might be ten steam tractors each drawing a plough. In this way hundreds of acres could be turned over in a day. Only steam engines had the power to draw the big units. When internal combustion engines appeared, they had neither the strength nor the ruggedness compared to the big steam tractors. Only by reducing the number of shares could the work be completed.

Stump-jump Plough

The Stump-jump plough was an Australian invention of the 1870s, designed to cope with the breaking up of new farming land, that contains many tree stumps and rocks that would be very expensive to remove. The plough uses a moveable weight to hold the ploughshare in position. When a tree stump or other obstruction such as a rock is encountered, the ploughshare is thrown upwards, clear of the obstacle, to avoid breaking the plough's harness or linkage; ploughing can be continued when the weight is returned to the earth after the obstacle is passed.

A simpler system, developed later, uses a concave disc (or a pair of them) set at a large angle to the direction of progress, that uses the concave shape to hold the disc into the soil — unless something hard strikes the circumference of the disk, causing it to roll up and over the obstruction. As the arrangement is dragged forward, the sharp edge of the disc cuts the soil, and the concave surface of the rotating disc lifts and throws the soil to the side. It doesn't make as good a job as the mouldboard plough (but this is not considered a disadvantage, because it helps fight the wind erosion), but it does lift and break up the soil.

Modern Ploughs

Modern ploughs are usually multiple reversible ploughs, mounted on a tractor via a three-point linkage. These commonly have between two and as many as seven mouldboards — and *semi-mounted* ploughs (the lifting of which is supplemented by a wheel about half-way along their length) can have as many as eighteen mouldboards. The hydraulic system of the tractor is used to lift and reverse the implement, as well as to adjust furrow width and depth. The ploughman still has to set the draughting linkage from the tractor so that the plough is carried at the proper angle in the soil. This angle and depth can be controlled automatically by modern tractors. As a complement to the rear plough a two or three mouldboards-plough can be mounted on the front of the tractor if it is equipped with front three-point linkage.

SPECIALIST PLOUGHS

Chisel Plough

The *chisel plough* is a common tool to get deep tillage (prepared land) with limited soil disruption. The main function of this plough is to loosen and aerate the soils while leaving crop residue at the top of the soil. This plough can be used to reduce the effects of compaction and to help break up ploughpan and hardpan. Unlike many other ploughs the chisel will not invert or turn the soil. This characteristic has made it a useful addition to no-till and limited-tillage farming practices which attempt to maximise the erosion-prevention benefits of keeping organic matter and farming residues present on the soil surface through the year. Because of these attributes, the use of a chisel plough is considered by some to be more sustainable than other types of plough, such as the mouldboard plough.

The chisel plough is typically set to run up to a depth of eight to twelve inches (200 to 300 mm). However some models may run much deeper. Each of the individual ploughs, or shanks, are typically set from nine inches (229 mm) to twelve inches (305 mm) apart. Such a plough can encounter significant soil drag, consequently a tractor of sufficient power and good traction is required. When planning to plough with a chisel plough it is important to bear in mind that 10 to 15 horsepower (7 to 11 kW) per shank will be required.

Ridging Plough

A ridging plough is used for crops, such as potatoes or scallions, which are grown buried in ridges of soil using a technique called *ridging* or *hilling*. A ridging plough has two mouldboards facing away from each other, cutting a deep furrow on each pass, with high ridges either side. The same plough may be used to split the ridges to harvest the crop.

Scottish Hand Plough

A variety of ridge plough, notable in that the blade points towards the operator. This is for use solely by human effort rather than animal or machine assistance. As such it is pulled backwards by the operator, requiring great physical effort. Particularly used for second breaking of ground, and for potato planting. Found in Shetland, some western crofts and more rarely Central Scotland. The tool epitomises a small-holding too small or poor to merit use of animals.

Mole Plough

The *mole plough* or *subsoiler* allows underdrainage to be installed without trenches, or it breaks up deep impermeable soil layers which impede drainage. It is a very deep plough, with a torpedo-shaped or wedge-shaped tip, and a narrow blade connecting this to the body. When dragged through the ground, it leaves a channel deep under the ground, and this acts as a drain. Modern mole ploughs may also bury a flexible perforated plastic drain pipe as they go, making a more permanent drain — or they may be used to lay pipes for water supply or other purposes.

Advantages of the Mouldboard Plough

Mouldboard ploughing, in cold and temperate climates, no deeper than 20 cm, aerates the soil by loosening it. It incorporates crop residues, solid manures, limestone and commercial fertilizers along with some oxygen. By doing so, it reduces nitrogen losses by volatilization, accelerates mineralization and increases short-term nitrogen availability for transformation of organic matter into humus. It erases wheel tracks and ruts caused by harvesting equipment. It controls many perennial weeds and pushes back the growth of other weeds until the following spring. It accelerates soil warming and water evaporation in spring because of the lesser quantity of residues on the soil surface. It facilitates seeding with a lighter seeder. It controls many enemies of crops (slugs, crane flies, seedcorn maggots-bean seed flies, borers). It increases the number of 'soil-eating' earthworms (endogea) but is detrimental to vertical-dwelling earthworms (anecic).

Disadvantages of the Mouldboard Plough

Over-ploughing can lead to the formation of hardpan. Typically farmers break up hardpan up with a subsoiler, which acts as a long, sharp knife to slice through the hardened layer of soil deep below the surface. Soil erosion due to improper land and plough utilization is possible. Contour ploughing mitigates soil erosion by ploughing across a slope, along elevation lines. Alternatives to ploughing, such as the no-till method, have the potential to actually build soil levels and humus, and may be suitable to smaller, more intensively cultivated plots, and to farming on poor, shallow or degraded soils which will only be further damaged by ploughing.

Plough Parts

- Frame

  Three point attach:

1. Height regulator
2. Knife or coulter
3. Chisel

   Share, also called the ploughshare.

- Mouldboard

Other portions include the frog, runner, landside, shin, trashboard and handles.

On modern ploughs and some older ploughs, the mouldboard is separate from the share and runner, allowing these parts to be replaced without replacing the mouldboard. Abrasion eventually destroys all parts of a plough that contact the soil.

17 Eutrophication

Eutrophication *eutrophia* healthy, adequate nutrition, development (Greek) *eutrophe* (German) is a scientific term describing the overfertilization of lakes with nutrients and the changes that occur as a result, i.e. the primary productivity of the waterbody. In other terms, it is the 'bloom' or great increase of phytoplankton in a water body. Negative environmental effects include anoxia, or loss of oxygen in the water with severe reductions in fish and other animal populations. Other species (such as Nomura Jellyfish in Japanese waters) may experience an increase in population that negatively affects other species in the local ecosystem.

Eutrophication can be human-caused or natural. Untreated sewage effluent and agricultural run-off carrying fertilizers are examples of human-caused eutrophication. However, it also occurs naturally in situations where nutrients accumulate (e.g. depositional environments), or where they flow into systems on an ephemeral basis. Eutrophication generally promotes excessive plant growth and decay, favouring simple algae and plankton over other more complicated plants, and causes a severe reduction in water quality. Enhanced growth of aquatic vegetation or phytoplankton and algal blooms disrupts normal functioning of the ecosystem, causing a variety of problems such as a lack of oxygen needed for fish and shellfish to survive. The water becomes cloudy, typically coloured a shade of green, yellow, brown, or red. Eutrophication also decreases the value of rivers, lakes, and estuaries for recreation, fishing, hunting, and aesthetic enjoyment. Health problems can occur where eutrophic conditions interfere with drinking water treatment.

Eutrophication was recognized as a pollution problem in European and North American lakes and reservoirs in the mid-20th century. Since then, it has become more widespread. Surveys showed that 54 per cent of lakes in Asia are eutrophic; in Europe, 53 per cent; in North America, 48 per cent; in South America, 41 per cent; and in Africa, 28 per cent.

Although eutrophication is commonly caused by human activities, it can also be a natural process particularly in lakes. Eutrophy occurs in many lakes in temperate grasslands, for instance. Paleolimnologists now recognise that climate change, geology, and other external influences are critical in regulating the natural productivity of lakes. Some lakes also demonstrate the reverse process (meiotrophication), becoming less nutrient rich with time.

Eutrophication can also be a natural process in seasonally inundated tropical floodplains. In the Barotse Floodplain of the Zambezi River, the first floodwaters of the rainy season are usually hypoxic because of material such as cattle manure and previous decay of vegetation which grew during the dry season. These so-called 'red waters' kill many fish. The process can be made worse by the use of fertilizers in crops such as maize, rice, and sugarcane grown on the floodplain.

Human activities can accelerate the rate at which nutrients enter ecosystems. Runoff from agriculture and development, pollution from septic systems and sewers, and other human-related activities increase the flow of both inorganic nutrients and organic substances into ecosystems. Elevated levels of atmospheric compounds of nitrogen can increase nitrogen availability. Phosphorus is often regarded as the main culprit in cases of eutrophication in lakes subjected to 'point source' pollution from sewage pipes. The concentration of algae and the trophic state of lakes correspond well to phosphorus levels in water. Studies conducted in the Experimental Lakes Area in Ontario have shown a relationship between the addition of phosphorus and the rate of eutrophication. Humankind has increased the rate of phosphorus cycling on Earth by four times, mainly due to agricultural fertilizer production and application. Between 1950 and 1995, an estimated 600,000,000 tonnes of phosphorus were applied to Earth's surface, primarily on croplands. Policy changes to control point sources of phosphorus have resulted in rapid control of eutrophication.

Ocean Waters

Eutrophication is a common phenomenon in coastal waters. In contrast to freshwater systems, nitrogen is more commonly the key limiting nutrient of marine waters; thus, nitrogen levels have greater importance to understanding eutrophication problems in salt water. Estuaries tend to be naturally eutrophic because land-derived nutrients are concentrated where run-off enters a confined channel. Upwelling in coastal systems also promotes increased productivity by conveying deep, nutrient-rich waters to the surface, where the nutrients can be assimilated by algae.

The World Resources Institute has identified 375 hypoxic coastal zones in the world, concentrated in coastal areas in Western Europe, the Eastern and Southern coasts of the US, and East Asia, particularly Japan.

In addition to runoff from land, atmospheric fixed nitrogen can enter the open ocean. A study in 2008 found that this could account for around one third of the ocean's external (non-recycled) nitrogen supply, and up to 3 per cent of the annual new marine biological production. It has been suggested that accumulating reactive nitrogen in the environment may prove as serious as putting carbon dioxide in the atmosphere.

Terrestrial ecosystems are subject to similarly adverse impacts from eutrophication. Increased nitrates in soil are frequently undesirable for plants. Many terrestrial plant species are endangered as a result of soil eutrophication, such as the majority of orchid species in Europe. Meadows, forests, and bogs are characterized by low nutrient content and slowly growing species adapted to those levels, so they can be overgrown by faster growing and more competitive species. In meadows, tall grasses that can take advantage of higher nitrogen levels may change the area so that natural species may be lost. Species-rich fens can be overtaken by reed or reedgrass species. Forest undergrowth affected by run-off from a nearby fertilized field can be turned into a nettle and bramble thicket.

Chemical forms of nitrogen are most often of concern with regard to eutrophication, because plants have high nitrogen requirements so that additions of nitrogen compounds will stimulate plant growth. Nitrogen is not readily available in soil because N_2, a gaseous form of nitrogen, is very stable and unavailable directly to higher plants. Terrestrial ecosystems rely on microbial nitrogen fixation to convert N_2 into other forms such as nitrates. However, there is a limit to how much nitrogen can be utilized. Ecosystems receiving more nitrogen than the plants require are called nitrogen-saturated. Saturated terrestrial ecosystems then can contribute both inorganic and organic nitrogen to freshwater, coastal, and marine eutrophication, where nitrogen is also typically a limiting nutrient. This is also the case with increased levels of phosphorus. However, because phosphorus is generally much less soluble than nitrogen, it is leached from the soil at a much slower rate than nitrogen. Consequently, phosphorus is much more important as a limiting nutrient in aquatic systems.

When an ecosystem experiences an increase in nutrients, primary producers reap the benefits first. In aquatic ecosystems, species such as algae experience a population increase (called an algal bloom). Algal blooms limit the sunlight available to bottom-dwelling organisms and cause wide swings in the amount of dissolved oxygen in the water. Oxygen is required by all respiring plants and animals and it is replenished in daylight by photosynthesizing plants and algae. Under eutrophic conditions, dissolved oxygen greatly increases during the day, but is greatly reduced after dark by the respiring algae and by microorganisms that feed on the increasing mass of dead algae. When dissolved oxygen levels decline to hypoxic levels, fish and other marine animals suffocate. As a result, creatures such as fish, shrimp, and especially immobile bottom dwellers die off. In extreme cases, anaerobic conditions ensue, promoting growth of bacteria such as *Clostridium botulinum* that produces toxins deadly to birds and mammals. Zones where this occurs are known as dead zones.

New Species Invasion

Eutrophication may cause competitive release by making abundant a normally limiting nutrient. This process causes shifts in the species composition of ecosystems. For instance, an increase in nitrogen might allow new, competitive species to invade and out-compete original inhabitant species. This has been shown to occur in New England salt marshes.

Toxicity

Some algal blooms, otherwise called 'nuisance algae' or 'harmful algal blooms', are toxic to plants and animals. Toxic compounds they produce can make their way up the food chain, resulting in animal mortality. Freshwater algal blooms can pose a threat to livestock. When the algae die or are eaten, neuro — and hepatotoxins are released which can kill animals and may pose a threat to humans. An example of algal toxins working their way into humans is the case of shellfish poisoning. Biotoxins created during algal blooms are taken up by shellfish (mussels, oysters), leading to these human foods acquiring the toxicity and poisoning humans. Examples include paralytic, neurotoxic, and diarrhoetic shellfish poisoning. Other marine animals can be vectors for such toxins, as in the case of ciguatera, where it is typically a pred.

In order to gauge how to best prevent eutrophication from occurring, specific sources that contribute to nutrient loading must be identified. There are two common sources of nutrients and organic matter: point and non-point sources.

Point Sources

Point sources are directly attributable to one influence. In point sources the nutrient waste travels directly from source to water. Point sources are relatively easy to regulate.

Non-point Sources

Non-point source pollution (also known as 'diffuse' or 'runoff' pollution) is that which comes from ill-defined and diffuse sources. Non-point sources are difficult to regulate and usually vary spatially and temporally (with season, precipitation, and other irregular events).

It has been shown that nitrogen transport is correlated with various indices of human activity in watersheds, including the amount of development. Ploughing in Agriculture and development are activities that contribute most to nutrient loading. There are three reasons that non-point sources are especially troublesome.

Soil Retention

Nutrients from human activities tend to accumulate in soils and remain there for years. It has been shown that the amount of phosphorus lost to surface waters increases linearly with the amount of phosphorus in the soil. Thus much of the nutrient loading in soil eventually makes its way to water. Nitrogen, similarly, has a turnover time of decades or more.

Runoff to Surface Water and Leaching to Groundwater

Nutrients from human activities tend to travel from land to either surface or ground water. Nitrogen in particular is removed through storm drains, sewage pipes, and other forms of surface runoff. Nutrient losses in runoff and leachate are often associated with agriculture. Modern agriculture often involves the application of nutrients onto fields in order to maximise production. However, farmers frequently apply more nutrients than are taken up by crops or pastures. Regulations aimed at minimising nutrient exports from agriculture are typically far less stringent than those placed on sewage treatment plants and other point source polluters.

Atmospheric Deposition

Nitrogen is released into the air because of ammonia volatilization and nitrous oxide production. The combustion of fossil fuels is a large human-initiated contributor to atmospheric nitrogen pollution. Atmospheric deposition (e.g., in the form of acid rain) can also affect nutrient concentration in water, especially in highly industrialized regions.

Riparian Buffer Zones

Studies show that intercepting non-point pollution between the source and the water is a successful means of prevention. Riparian buffer zones are interfaces between a flowing body of water and land, and have been created near waterways in an attempt to filter pollutants; sediment and nutrients are deposited here instead of in water. Creating buffer zones near farms and roads is another possible way to prevent nutrients from travelling too far. Still, studies have shown that the effects of atmospheric nitrogen pollution can reach far past the buffer zone. This suggests that the most effective means of prevention is from the primary source.

Prevention Policy

Laws regulating the discharge and treatment of sewage have led to dramatic nutrient reductions to surrounding ecosystems, but it is generally agreed that a policy regulating agricultural use of fertilizer and animal waste must be imposed. In Japan the amount of nitrogen produced by livestock is adequate to serve the fertilizer needs for the agriculture industry. Thus, it is not unreasonable to command livestock owners to clean up animal waste — which when left stagnant will leach into ground water.

Policy concerning the prevention and reduction of eutrophication can be broken down into four sectors: Technologies, public participation, economic instruments, and cooperation. The term technology is used loosely, referring to a more widespread use of existing methods rather than an appropriation of new technologies. As mentioned before, non-point sources of pollution are the primary contributors to eutrophication, and their effects can be easily minimized through common agricultural practices. Reducing the amount of pollutants that reach a watershed can be achieved through the protection of its forest cover, reducing the amount of erosion leeching into a watershed. Also, through the efficient, controlled use of land using sustainable agricultural practices to minimize land degradation, the amount of soil runoff and nitrogen-based fertilizers reaching a watershed can be reduced. Waste disposal technology constitutes another factor in eutrophication prevention. Because a major contributor to the non-point source nutrient loading of water bodies is untreated domestic sewage, it is necessary to provide treatment facilities to highly urbanized areas, particularly those in underdeveloped nations, in which treatment of domestic waste water is a scarcity. The technology to safely and efficiently reuse waste water, both from domestic and industrial sources, should be a primary concern for policy regarding eutrophication.

The role of the public is a major factor for the effective prevention of eutrophication. In order for a policy to have any effect, the public must be aware of their contribution to the problem, and ways in which they can reduce their effects. Programmes instituted to promote participation in the recycling and elimination of wastes, as well as education on the issue of rational water use are necessary to protect water quality within urbanized areas and adjacent water bodies.

Economic instruments, "which include, among others, property rights, water markets, fiscal and financial instruments, charge systems and liability systems, are gradually becoming a substantive component of the management tool set used for pollution control and water allocation decisions." Incentives for those who practice clean, renewable, water management technologies are an effective means of encouraging pollution prevention. By internalizing the costs associated with the negative effects on the environment, governments are able to encourage a cleaner water management.

Because a body of water can have an effect on a range of people reaching far beyond that of the watershed, cooperation between different organizations is necessary to prevent the intrusion of contaminants that can lead to eutrophication. Agencies ranging from state governments to those of water resource management and non-governmental organizations, going as low as the local population, are responsible for preventing eutrophication of water bodies.

Nitrogen Testing and Modelling

Soil Nitrogen Testing (N-Testing) is a technique that helps farmers optimize the amount of fertilizer applied to crops. By testing fields with this method, farmers saw a decrease in fertilizer application costs, a decrease in nitrogen lost to surrounding sources, or both. By testing the soil and modelling the bare minimum amount of fertilizer needed, farmers reap economic benefits while the environment remains clean and pure.

18 Organic Farming

Organic farming is the form of agriculture that relies on techniques such as crop rotation, green manure, compost and biological pest control to maintain soil productivity and control pests on a farm. Organic farming excludes or strictly limits the use of manufactured fertilizers and pesticides, plant growth regulators such as hormones, livestock antibiotics, food additives, and genetically modified organisms.

Organic agricultural methods are internationally regulated and legally enforced by many nations, based in large part on the standards set by the International Federation of Organic Agriculture Movements (IFOAM), an international umbrella organization for organic farming organizations established in 1972. IFOAM defines the overarching goal of organic farming as:

> "Organic agriculture is a production system that sustains the health of soils, ecosystems and people. It relies on ecological processes, biodiversity and cycles adapted to local conditions, rather than the use of inputs with adverse effects. Organic agriculture combines tradition, innovation and science to benefit the shared environment and promote fair relationships and a good quality of life for all involved.."
>
> ***—International Federation of Organic Agriculture Movements***

Since 1990, the market for organic products has grown from nothing, reaching $46 billion in 2007. This demand has driven a similar increase in organically managed farmland. Approximately 32,200,000 hectares

(80,000,000 acres) worldwide are now farmed organically, representing approximately 0.8 per cent of total world farmland. In addition, as of 2007 organic wild products are harvested on approximately 30 million hectares.

The organic movement began in the 1930s and 1940s as a reaction to agriculture's growing reliance on synthetic fertilizers. Artificial fertilizers had been created during the 18th century, initially with superphosphates and then ammonia-based fertilizers mass-produced using the Haber-Bosch process developed during World War I. These early fertilizers were cheap, powerful, and easy to transport in bulk. Similar advances occurred in chemical pesticides in the 1940s, leading to the decade being referred to as the 'pesticide era'.

Sir Albert Howard is widely considered to be the father of organic farming. Further work was done by J.I. Rodale in the United States, Lady Eve Balfour in the United Kingdom, and many others across the world.

Organic farming has made up only a fraction of total agricultural output from its beginning until today. Increasing environmental awareness in the general population has transformed the originally supply-driven movement to a demand-driven one. Premium prices and some government subsidies attracted farmers. In the developing world, many producers farm according to traditional methods which are comparable to organic farming but are not certified. In other cases, farmers in the developing world have converted for economic reasons.

> "An organic farm, properly speaking, is not one that uses certain methods and substances and avoids others; it is a farm whose structure is formed in imitation of the structure of a natural system that has the integrity, the independence and the benign dependence of an organism"
>
> —***Wendell Berry, "The Gift of Good Land"***

Soil Management

Plants need nitrogen, phosphorus, and potassium, as well as micronutrients and symbiotic relationships with fungi and other organisms to flourish, but getting enough nitrogen, and particularly synchronization so that plants get enough nitrogen at the right time (when plants need it most), is likely the greatest challenge for organic farmers. Crop rotation and green manure ('cover crops') help to provide nitrogen through legumes (more precisely, the *Fabaceae* family) which fix nitrogen from the atmosphere through symbiosis with the bacteria rhizobia. Intercropping, which is sometimes used for insect and disease control, can also increase soil nutrients, but the competition between the legume and the crop can be problematic and wider spacing between crop rows is required. Crop residues can be ploughed back into the soil, and different plants leave different amounts of nitrogen, potentially aiding synchronization. Organic farmers also use animal manure, certain processed fertilizers such as seed meal and various mineral powders such as rock phosphate and greensand, a naturally occurring form of potash which provides potassium. Together these methods help to control erosion. In some cases pH may need to be amended. Natural pH amendments include lime and sulfur, but in the U.S. some compounds such as iron sulfate, aluminum sulfate, magnesium sulfate, and soluble boron products are allowed in organic farming.

Mixed farms with both livestock and crops can operate as ley farms, whereby the land gathers fertility through growing nitrogen-fixing forage grasses such as white clover or alfalfa and grows cash crops or cereals when fertility is established. Farms without livestock ('stockless') may find it more difficult to maintain fertility, and may rely more on external inputs such as imported manure as well as grain legumes and green manures, although grain legumes may fix limited nitrogen because they are harvested. Horticultural farms growing fruits and vegetables which operate in protected conditions are often even more reliant upon external inputs.

Biological research on soil and soil organisms has proven beneficial to organic farming. Varieties of bacteria and fungi break down chemicals, plant matter and animal waste into productive soil nutrients. In turn, they produce benefits of healthier yields and more productive soil for future crops. Fields with less or no manure display significantly lower yields, due to decreased soil microbe community, providing a healthier, more arable soil system.

Weed Management

Organic weed management promotes weed suppression, rather than weed elimination, by enhancing crop competition and phytotoxic effects on weeds. Organic farmers integrate cultural, biological, mechanical, physical and chemical tactics to manage weeds without synthetic herbicides.

Organic standards require rotation of annual crops, meaning that a single crop cannot be grown in the same location without a different, intervening crop. Organic crop rotations frequently include weed-suppressive cover crops and crops with dissimilar life cycles to discourage weeds associated with a particular crop. Organic farmers strive to increase soil organic matter content, which can support microorganisms that destroy common weed seeds.

Other cultural practices used to enhance crop competitiveness and reduce weed pressure include selection of competitive crop varieties, high-density planting, tight row spacing, and late planting into warm soil to encourage rapid crop germination.

Mechanical and physical weed control practices used on organic farms can be broadly grouped as:

- *Tillage* — Turning the soil between crops to incorporate crop residues and soil amendments; remove existing weed growth and prepare a seedbed for planting;
- *Cultivation* — Disturbing the soil after seeding;
- *Mowing and cutting* — Removing top growth of weeds;
- *Flame weeding and thermal weeding* — Using heat to kill weeds; and
- *Mulching* — Blocking weed emergence with organic materials, plastic films, or landscape fabric.

Some naturally-sourced chemicals are allowed for herbicidal use. These include certain formulations of acetic acid (concentrated vinegar), corn gluten meal, and essential oils. A few selective bioherbicides based on fungal pathogens have also been developed. At this time, however, organic herbicides and bioherbicides play a minor role in the organic weed control toolbox.

Weeds can be controlled by grazing. For example, geese have been used successfully to weed a range of organic crops including cotton, strawberries, tobacco, and corn, reviving the practice of keeping cotton patch geese, common in the southern U.S. before the 1950s. Similarly, some rice farmers introduce ducks and fish to wet paddy fields to eat both weeds and insects.

Controlling Other Organisms

Organisms aside from weeds that cause problems on organic farms include arthropods (e.g. insects, mites), nematodes, fungi and bacteria. Organic farmers use a wide range of Integrated Pest Management practices to prevent pests and diseases. These include, but are not limited to, crop rotation and nutrient management; sanitation to remove pest habitat; provision of habitat for beneficial organisms; selection of pest-resistant crops and animals; crop protection using physical barriers, such as row covers; and crop diversification through companion planting or establishment of polycultures.

Organic farmers often depend on biological pest control, the use of beneficial organisms to reduce pest populations. Examples of beneficial insects include minute pirate bugs, big-eyed bugs, and to a lesser extent ladybugs (which tend to fly away), all of which eat a wide range of pests. Lacewings are also effective, but tend to fly away. Praying mantis tend to move more slowly and eat less heavily. Parasitoid wasps tend to be effective for their selected prey, but like all small insects can be less effective outdoors because the wind controls their movement. Predatory mites are effective for controlling other mites.

When these practices are insufficient to prevent or control pests an organic farmer may apply a pesticide. With some exceptions, naturally-occurring pesticides are allowed for use on organic farms, and synthetic substances are prohibited. Pesticides with different modes of action should be rotated to minimize development of pesticide resistance.

Naturally-derived insecticides allowed for use on organic farms use include *Bacillus thuringiensis* (a bacterial toxin), pyrethrum (a chrysanthemum extract), spinosad (a bacterial metabolite), neem (a tree extract) and rotenone (a legume root extract). These are sometimes called green pesticides because they are generally, but not necessarily, safer and more environment friendly than synthetic pesticides. Rotenone and pyrethrum are particularly controversial because they work by attacking the nervous system, like most conventional insecticides. Fewer than 10 per cent of organic farmers use these pesticides regularly; one survey found that only 5.3 per cent of vegetable growers in California use rotenone while 1.7 per cent use pyrethrum.

Naturally-derived fungicides allowed for use on organic farms include the bacteria *Bacillus subtilis* and *Bacillus pumilus*; and the fungus *Trichoderma harzianum*. These are mainly effective for diseases affecting roots. Agricultural Research Service scientists have found that caprylic acid, a naturally-occurring fatty acid in milk and coconuts, as well as other natural plant extracts have antimicrobial characteristics that can help. Compost tea contains a mix of beneficial microbes, which may attack or out-compete certain plant pathogens, but variability among formulations and preparation methods may contribute to inconsistent results or even dangerous growth of toxic microbes in compost teas.

Some naturally-derived pesticides are not allowed for use on organic farms. These include nicotine sulfate, arsenic, and strychnine.

Synthetic pesticides allowed for use on organic farms include insecticidal soaps and horticultural oils for insect management; and Bordeaux mixture, copper hydroxide and sodium bicarbonate for managing fungi.

Genetic Modification

A key characteristic of organic farming is the rejection of genetically engineered plants and animals. On October 19, 1998, participants at IFOAM's 12th Scientific Conference issued the Mar del Plata Declaration, where more than 600 delegates from over 60 countries voted unanimously to exclude the use of genetically modified organisms in food production and agriculture.

Although opposition to the use of any transgenic technologies in organic farming is strong, agricultural researchers Luis Herrera-Estrella and Ariel Alvarez-Morales continue to advocate integration of transgenic technologies into organic farming as the optimal means to sustainable agriculture, particularly in the developing world. Similarly, some organic farmers question the rationale behind the ban on the use of genetically engineered seed because they see it a biological technology consistent with organic principles.

Although GMOs are excluded from organic farming, there is concern that the pollen from genetically modified crops is increasingly penetrating organic and heirloom seed stocks, making it difficult, if not impossible, to keep these genomes from entering the organic food supply. International trade restrictions limit the availability GMOs to certain countries.

The dangers that genetic modification could pose to the environment and/or individual health are hotly contested.

Standards

Standards regulate production methods and in some cases final output for organic agriculture. Standards may be voluntary or legislated. As early as the 1970s private associations certified organic producers. In the 1980s, governments began to produce organic production guidelines. In the 1990s, a trend toward legislated standards began, most notably with the 1991 EU-Eco-regulation developed for European Union, which set standards for 12 countries, and a 1993 U.K. programme. The EU's programme was followed by a Japanese programme in 2001, and in 2002 the U.S. created the National Organic Programme (NOP). As of 2007 over 60 countries regulate organic farming (IFOAM 2007:11). In 2005 IFOAM created the Principles of Organic Agriculture, an international guideline for certification criteria. Typically the agencies accredit certification groups rather than individual farms.

Organic production materials used in and foods are tested independently by the Organic Materials Review Institute.

Composting

Under USDA organic standards, manure must be subjected to proper thermophilic composting and allowed to reach a sterilizing temperature. If raw animal manure is used, 120 days must pass before the crop is harvested if the final product comes into direct contact with the soil. For products which do not come into direct contact with soil, 90 days must pass prior to harvest.

The economics of organic farming, a subfield of agricultural economics, encompasses the entire process and effects of organic farming in terms of human society, including social costs, opportunity costs, unintended consequences, information asymmetries, and economies of scale. Although the scope of economics is broad, agricultural economics tends to focus on maximizing yields and efficiency at the farm level. Economics takes an anthropocentric approach to the value of the natural world: biodiversity, for example, is considered beneficial only to the extent that it is valued by people and increases profits. Some entities such as the European Union subsidize organic farming, in large part because these countries want to account for the externalities of reduced water use, reduced water contamination, reduced soil erosion, reduced carbon emissions, increased biodiversity, and assorted other benefits that result from organic farming.

Traditional organic farming is labour and knowledge-intensive whereas conventional farming is capital-intensive, requiring more energy and manufactured inputs.

Organic farmers in California have cited marketing as their greatest obstacle.

Geographic Producer Distribution

The markets for organic products are strongest in North America and Europe, which as of 2001 are estimated to have $6 and $8 billion respectively of the $20 billion global market (Lotter 2003:6). As of 2007 Australasia has 39 per cent of the total organic farmland, including Australia's 1,180,000 hectares (2,900,000 acres) but 97 per cent of this land is sprawling rangeland (2007:35). US sales are 20x as much. (2003:7). Europe farms 23 per cent of global organic farmland (6.9 million hectares), followed by Latin America with 19 per cent (5.8 million hectares). Asia has 9.5 per cent while North America has 7.2 per cent. Africa has 3 per cent.

Besides Australia, the countries with the most organic farmland are Argentina (3.1 million hectares), China (2.3 million hectares), and the United States (1.6 million hectares). Much of Argentina's organic farmland is pasture, like that of Australia . Italy, Spain, Germany, Brazil (the world's largest agricultural exporter), Uruguay, and the UK follow the United States in the amount of organic land.

Converted organic farms have lower pre-harvest yields than their conventional counterparts in developed countries (92%) but higher than their low-intensity counterparts in developing countries (132%). This is due to relatively lower adoption of fertilizers and pesticides in the developing world compared to the intensive farming of the developed world.

Organic farms withstand severe weather conditions better than conventional farms, sometimes yielding 70-90 per cent more than conventional farms during droughts. Organic farms are more profitable in the drier states of the United States, likely due to their superior drought performance. Organic farms survive hurricane damage much better, retaining 20 to 40 per cent more topsoil and smaller economic losses at highly significant levels than their neighbours.

Contrary to widespread belief, organic farming can build up soil organic matter better than conventional no-till farming, which suggests long-term yield benefits from organic farming. An 18-year study of organic methods on nutrient-depleted soil, concluded that conventional methods were superior for soil fertility and yield in a cold-temperate climate, arguing that much of the benefits from organic farming are derived from imported materials which could not be regarded as 'self-sustaining'.

Profitability

The decreased cost of synthetic fertilizer and pesticide inputs, along with the higher prices that consumers pay for organic produce, contribute to increased profits. Organic farms have been consistently found to be as or more profitable than conventional farms. Without the price premium, profitability is mixed. Organic production was more profitable in Wisconsin, given price premiums.

Sustainability

In 2008 the UN Environmental Programme (UNEP) and UN Conference on Trade and Development (UNCTAD) stated that "organic agriculture can be more conducive to food security in Africa than most conventional production systems, and that it is more likely to be sustainable in the long-term" and that "yields had more than doubled where organic, or near-organic practices had been used" and that soil fertility and drought resistance improved.

Agriculture imposes negative externalities (uncompensated costs) upon society through land and other resource use, biodiversity loss, erosion, pesticides, nutrient runoff, water usage, subsidy payments and assorted other problems. Positive externalities include self-reliance, entrepreneurship, respect for nature, and air quality. Organic methods reduce some of these costs. In 2000 uncompensated costs for 1996 reached 2,343 million British pounds or 208 pounds per hectare. In 2005 in the USA concluded that cropland costs the economy approximately 5 to 16 billion dollars ($30 to $96 per hectare), while livestock production costs 714 million dollars. Both studies recommended reducing externalities. The 2000 review included reported pesticide poisonings but did not include speculative chronic health effects of pesticides, and the 2004 review relied on a 1992 estimate of the total impact of pesticides.

Organic agriculture can reduce the level of negative externalities from (conventional) agriculture. Whether the benefits are private or public depends upon the division of property rights.

Most organic farms use fewer pesticides than conventional farms, some pesticides damage the environment or with direct exposure, human health. The five main pesticides used in organic farming are Bt (a bacterial toxin), pyrethrum, rotenone, copper and sulphur. Fewer than 10 per cent of organic vegetable farmers acknowledge using these pesticides regularly; 5.3 per cent of vegetable growers will admit rotenone use; while 1.7 per cent admit pyrethrum use . Reduction and elimination of chemical pesticide use is technically challenging. Organic pesticides often complement other pest control strategies.

Ecological concerns primarily focus around pesticide use, as 16 per cent of the world's pesticides are used in the production of cotton.

Runoff is one of the most damaging effects of pesticide use. The USDA Natural Resources Conservation Service tracks the environmental effects of water contamination and concluded, "the Nation's pesticide policies during the last twenty six years have succeeded in reducing overall environmental risk, in spite of slight increases in area planted and weight of pesticides applied. Nevertheless, there are still areas of the country where there is no evidence of progress, and areas where risk levels for protection of drinking water, fish, algae and crustaceans remain high".

Pest resistant genetically modified (GM) crops can eliminate pesticide use. Pesticide-resistant crops can reduce the number of applications and amount of pesticide used. Genetic modification is widely opposed in the organic farming movement due to health, environmental and philosophical concerns.

Many studies have examined the relative quality and safety benefits of organic and conventional agricultural techniques. The results are diverse. Some find no significant differences. Others disagree. An example of the 'no differences' school stated:

> No evidence of a difference in content of nutrients and other substances between organically and conventionally produced crops and livestock products was detected for the majority of nutrients assessed in this review suggesting that organically and conventionally produced crops and livestock products are broadly comparable in their nutrient content... There is no good evidence that increased dietary intake, of the nutrients identified in this review to be present in larger amounts in organically than in conventionally produced crops and livestock products, would be of benefit to individuals consuming a normal varied diet, and it is therefore unlikely that these differences in nutrient content are relevant to consumer health.

However, they also found that statistically significant differences between the composition of organic and conventional food were present for a few substances.

"Organic products stand out as having higher levels of secondary plant compounds and vitamin C". The fatty acid profile of organic milk and meat is often nutritionally superior. Organic carbohydrates and minerals are not different from conventional products. Organic foods have more nutritional value. Organic produce has double the flavonoids, an important antioxidant. Organic kiwifruit had more antioxidants.

A review of potential health effects analysed eleven articles, concluding, "because of the limited and highly variable data available, and concerns over the reliability of some reported findings, there is currently no evidence of a health benefit from consuming organic compared to conventionally produced foodstuffs. It should be noted that this conclusion relates to the evidence base currently available on the nutrient content of foodstuffs, which contains limitations in the design and in the comparability of studies".

Individual studies have considered a variety of possible impacts, including pesticide residues. Pesticide residues present a second channel for health effects. Comments include, "Organic fruits and vegetables can be expected to contain fewer agrochemical residues than conventionally grown alternatives; yet, "the significance of this difference is questionable" and "It is intuitive to assume that children whose diets consist of organic food items would have a lower probability of neurologic health risks", and pesticide exposure brought an increased risk for ADHD in one study.

Nitrate concentrations may be less, but the health impact of nitrates is debated. Lack of data has limited research on the health effects of natural plant pesticides and bacterial pathogens. Consumption of organic milk was associated with a decrease in risk for eczema, although no comparable benefit was found for organic fruits, vegetables, or meat.

The higher cost of organic food (ranging from 45 to 200%) could inhibit consumption of the recommended 5 servings per day of vegetables and fruits, which improve health and reduce cancer regardless of their source.

Clothing Quality and Safety

Recently, organic clothing has become widely available. Although many consumers of organic clothing merely dislike synthetic chemicals, a significant portion of the organic clothing market comes from those suffering from Multiple Chemical Sensitivity, a chronic medical condition characterized by symptoms that the affected person says are adverse effects from exposure to low levels of chemicals.

Soil Conservation

In *Dirt: The Erosion of Civilizations*, geomorphologist David Montgomery outlines a coming crisis from soil erosion. Agriculture relies on roughly one meter of topsoil, and that is being depleted ten times faster than it is being replaced. No-till farming, which some claim depends upon pesticides, is one way to minimize erosion. However, a recent study by the USDA's Agricultural Research Service has found that manure applications in tilled organic farming are better at building up the soil than no-till.

Climate Change

Organic agriculture emphasizes closed nutrient cycles, biodiversity, and effective soil management providing the capacity to mitigate and even reverse the effects of climate change. Organic agriculture decreases fossil fuel emissions and sequesters carbon in the soil. The elimination of synthetic nitrogen in organic systems decreases fossil fuel consumption by 33 per cent and carbon sequestration takes CO_2 out of the atmosphere by putting it in the soil in the form of organic matter which is often lost in conventionally managed soils. Carbon sequestration occurs at especially high levels in organic no-till managed soil.

Agriculture has been undervalued and underestimated as a means to combat global climate change. Soil carbon data show that regenerative organic agricultural practices are among the most effective strategies for mitigating CO_2emissions.

Nutrient Leaching

Excess nutrients in lakes, rivers, and groundwater can cause algal blooms, eutrophication, and subsequent dead zones. In addition, nitrates are harmful to aquatic organisms by themselves. The main contributor to this pollution is nitrate fertilizers whose use is expected to 'double or almost triple by 2050'. Organically fertilizing fields 'significantly [reduces] harmful nitrate leaching' over conventionally fertilized fields: "annual nitrate leaching was 4.4-5.6 times higher in conventional plots than organic plots".

The large dead zone in the Gulf of Mexico is caused in large part by agricultural runoff: a combination of fertilizer and livestock manure. Over half of the nitrogen released into the Gulf comes from agriculture. This increases costs for fishermen, as they must travel far from the coast to find fish.

Nitrogen leaching into the Danube River was substantially lower among organic farms. The resulting externalities could be neutralized by charging 1 euro per kg of released nitrogen.

Agricultural runoff and algae blooms are strongly linked in California.

Biodiversity

A wide range of organisms benefit from organic farming, but it is unclear whether organic methods confer greater benefits than conventional integrated agri-environmental programmes. Nearly all non-crop, naturally occurring species observed in comparative farm land practice studies show a preference for organic farming both by abundance and diversity. An average of 30 per cent more species inhabit organic farms. Birds, butterflies, soil microbes, beetles, earthworms, spiders, vegetation, and mammals are particularly affected. Lack of herbicides and pesticides improve biodiversity fitness and population density. Many weed species attract beneficial insects that improve soil qualities and forage on weed pests. Soil-bound organisms often benefit because of increased bacteria populations due to natural fertilizer such as manure, while experiencing reduced intake of herbicides and pesticides. Increased biodiversity, especially from soil microbes such as mycorhizzae have been proposed as an explanation for the high yields experienced by some organic plots, especially in light of the differences seen in a 21-year comparison of organic and control fields.

Biodiversity from organic farming provides capital to humans. Species found in organic farms enhance sustainability by reducing human input (e.g. fertilizers, pesticides). Farmers that produce with organic methods reduce risk of poor yields by promoting biodiversity. Common game birds such as the ring-necked pheasant and the northern bobwhite often reside in agriculture landscapes, and benefit recreational hunters.

Sales and Marketing

Most sales are concentrated in developed nations. These products are what economists call credence goods in that they rely on uncertain certification. Interest in organic products dropped between 2006 and 2008, and 42 per cent of Americans polled don't trust organic produce. 69 per cent of Americans claim to occasionally buy organic products, down from 73 per cent in 2005. One theory was that consumers were substituting 'local' produce for 'organic' produce.

Distributors

In the United States, 75 per cent of organic farms are smaller than 2.5 hectares. In California 2 per cent of the farms account for over half of sales Small farms join together in cooperatives such as Organic Valley, Inc. to market their goods more effectively.

Over twenty-five, most cooperative distributors merged or were acquired by large multinationals such as General Mills, Heinz, ConAgra, Kellogg, and others. In 1982 there were 28 consumer cooperative distributors, but as of 2007 only 3 remained. This consolidation has raised concerns among consumers and journalists of potential fraud and degradation in standards. Most sell their organic products through subsidiaries, under other labels.

Farmers Markets

Price premiums are important for the profitability of small organic farmers. Farmers selling directly to consumers at farmers' markets have continued to achieve these higher returns. In the United States the number of farmers' markets tripled from 1,755 in 1994 to 5,274 in 2009.

Capacity Building

Organic agriculture can contribute to ecologically sustainable, socio-economic development, especially in poorer countries. The application of organic principles enables employment of local resources (e.g. local seed varieties, manure, etc.) and therefore cost-effectiveness. Local and international markets for organic products show tremendous growth prospects and offer creative producers and exporters excellent opportunities to improve their income and living conditions.

Organic agriculture is knowledge intensive. Globally, capacity building efforts are underway, including localized training material, to limited effect. As of 2007, the International Federation of Organic Agriculture Movements hosted more than 170 free manuals and 75 training opportunities online.

Controversy

Norman Borlaug, father of the 'green revolution', Nobel Peace Prize laureate, Prof A. Trewavas and other critics contested the notion that organic agricultural systems are more friendly to the environment and more sustainable than conventional farming systems. Borlaug asserts that organic farming practices can at most feed 4 billion people, after expanding cropland dramatically and destroying ecosystems in the process. The Danish Environmental Protection Agency estimated that phasing out all pesticides would result in an overall yield reduction of about 25 per cent. Environmental and health effects were assumed but hard to assess.

In contrast, the UN Environmental Programme concluded that organic methods greatly increase yields in Africa. A review of over two hundred crop comparisons argued that organic farming could produce enough food to sustain the current human population and that the difference in yields between organic and non-organic methods were small, with non-organic methods yielding slightly more in developed areas and organic methods yielding slightly more in developing areas.

That analysis has been criticised by Alex Avery of the Hudson Institute, who contends that the review claimed many non-organic studies to be organic, misreported organic yields, made false comparisons between yields of organic and non-organic studies which were not comparable, counted high organic yields several times by citing different papers which referenced the same data, and gave equal weight to studies from sources which were not impartial. The Centre for Disease Control repudiated a claim by Avery's father, Dennis Avery (also at Hudson) that the risk of E. coli infection was eight times higher when eating organic food. Avery had included problems stemming from non-organic unpasteurized juice in his calculations.

Urs Niggli, director of the FiBL Institute contends that there is a global campaign against organic farming that mostly derives from Avery's book 'The truth about organic farming'.

19 Organic Certification

Organic certification is a certification process for producers of organic food and other organic agricultural products. In general, any business directly involved in food production can be certified, including seed suppliers, farmers, food processors, retailers and restaurants. Requirements vary from country to country, and generally involve a set of production standards for growing, storage, processing, packaging and shipping that include:

- avoidance of most synthetic chemical inputs (e.g. fertilizer, pesticides, antibiotics, food additives, etc), genetically modified organisms, irradiation, and the use of sewage sludge;
- use of farmland that has been free from synthetic chemicals for a number of years (often, three or more);
- keeping detailed written production and sales records (audit trail);
- maintaining strict physical separation of organic products from non-certified products; and
- undergoing periodic on-site inspections.

In some countries, certification is overseen by the government, and commercial use of the term *organic* is legally restricted. Certified organic producers are also subject to the same agricultural, food safety and other government regulations that apply to non-certified producers.

Organic certification addresses a growing worldwide demand for organic food. It is intended to assure quality and prevent fraud, and to promote commerce. While such certification was not necessary in the early days of the organic movement, when small farmers would sell their produce directly at farmers' markets, as organics have grown in popularity, more and more consumers are purchasing organic food through traditional channels, such as supermarkets. As such, consumers must rely on third-party regulatory certification.

For organic producers, certification identifies suppliers of products approved for use in certified operations. For consumers, 'certified organic' serves as a product assurance, similar to 'low fat', '100 per cent whole wheat', or 'no artificial preservatives'.

Certification is essentially aimed at regulating and facilitating the sale of organic products to consumers. Individual certification bodies have their own service marks, which can act as branding to consumers — a certifier may promote the high consumer recognition value of its logo as a marketing advantage to producers. Most UK certification bodies operate organic standards that meet the UK government's minimum requirements. Some certification bodies, such as the Soil Association, certify to higher standards.

Third Party Certification Process

To certify a farm, the farmer is typically required to engage in a number of new activities, in addition to normal farming operations:

- ***Study*** — the organic standards, which cover in specific detail what is and is not allowed for every aspect of farming, including storage, transport and sale
- ***Compliance*** — farm facilities and production methods must comply with the standards, which may involve modifying facilities, sourcing and changing suppliers, etc.
- ***Documentation*** — extensive paperwork is required, detailing farm history and current set-up, and usually including results of soil and water tests.
- ***Planning*** — a written annual production plan must be submitted, detailing everything from seed to sale: seed sources, field and crop locations, fertilization and pest control activities, harvest methods, storage locations, etc.
- ***Inspection*** — annual on-farm inspections are required, with a physical tour, examination of records, and an oral interview.
- ***Fee*** — an annual inspection/certification fee (currently starting at $400-$2,000/year, in the US and Canada, depending on the agency and the size of the operation).

- ***Record-keeping*** — written, day-to-day farming and marketing records, covering all activities, must be available for inspection at any time.

In addition, short-notice or surprise inspections can be made, and specific tests (e.g. soil, water, plant tissue) may be requested.

For first-time farm certification, the soil must meet basic requirements of being free from use of prohibited substances (synthetic chemicals, etc.) for a number of years. A conventional farm must adhere to organic standards for this period, often, two to three years. This is known as being in *transition*. Transitional crops are not considered fully organic.

Certification for operations other than farms is similar. The focus is on ingredients and other inputs, and processing and handling conditions. A transport company would be required to detail the use and maintenance of its vehicles, storage facilities, containers, and so forth. A restaurant would have its premises inspected and its suppliers verified as certified organic.

> Participatory Guarantee Systems are locally focussed quality assurance systems. They certify producers based on active participation of stakeholders and are built on a foundation of trust, social networks and knowledge exchange"
>
> — ***(IFOAM definition, 2008)***

Participatory Guarantee Systems (PGS) represent an alternative to third party certification, especially adapted to local markets and short supply chains. They can also complement third party certification with a private label that brings additional guarantees and transparency. PGS enable the direct participation of producers, consumers and other stakeholders in:

- the choice and definition of the standards;
- the development and implementation of certification procedures;
- the certification decisions.

Participatory Guarantee Systems are also referred to as 'participatory certification'.

In some countries, organic standards are formulated and overseen by the government. The United States, the European Union, Canada and Japan have comprehensive organic legislation, and the term 'organic' may be used only by certified producers. Being able to put the word 'organic' on a food product is a valuable marketing advantage in today's consumer market, but does not guarantee the product is legitimately organic.

Certification is intended to protect consumers from misuse of the term, and make buying organics easy. However, the organic labelling made possible by certification itself usually requires explanation. In countries without organic laws, government guidelines may or may not exist, while certification is handled by non-profit organizations and private companies.

Internationally, equivalency negotiations are underway, and some agreements are already in place, to harmonize certification between countries, facilitating international trade. There are also international certification bodies, including members of the International Federation of Organic Agriculture Movements (IFOAM) working on harmonization efforts. Where formal agreements do not exist between countries, organic product for export is often certified by agencies from the importing countries, who may establish permanent foreign offices for this purpose.

North America

In the US, federal organic legislation defines three levels of organics. Products made entirely with certified organic ingredients and methods can be labelled '100 per cent organic'. Products with at least 95 per cent organic ingredients can use the word 'organic'. Both of these categories may also display the USDA organic seal. A third category, containing a minimum of 70 per cent organic ingredients, can be labelled 'made with organic ingredients'. In addition, products may also display the logo of the certification body that approved them. Products made with less than 70 per cent organic ingredients cannot advertise this information to consumers and can only mention this fact in the product's ingredient statement. Similar percentages and labels apply in the EU.

In the US, the National Organic Programme (NOP), was enacted as federal legislation in Oct. 2002. It restricts the use of the term 'organic' to certified organic producers (excepting growers selling under $5,000 a year, who must still comply and submit to a records audit if requested, but do not have to formally apply). Certification is handled by state, non-profit and private agencies that have been approved by the US Department of Agriculture (USDA).

One of the first organizations to carry out organic certification in North America was the California Certified Organic Farmers, founded in 1973.

In Canada, certification was implemented at the federal level on June 30, 2009. Mandatory certification is required for agricultural products represented as organic in import, export and inter-provincial trade, or that bear the federal organic logo. In Quebec, provincial legislation provides government oversight of organic certification within the province, through the Quebec Accreditation Board.

The European organic food label has been mandatory throughout the EU since July 2010. Originally it was planned to replace the old national organic labels but it was finally decided to allow for a transition period where both the EU label and the national labels may be used to mark organic food. The new logo is a green rectangle that shows twelve stars (from the European flag) placed such that they form the shape of a leaf in the wind. Unlike earlier labels no words are presented on the label lifting the requirement for translations referring to organic food certification.

In the United Kingdom, organic certification is handled by a number of organizations, regulated by The Department for Environment, Food and Rural Affairs (DEFRA), of which the largest are the Soil Association and Organic Farmers and Growers.

In Sweden, organic certification is handled by the organisation with members such as farmers, processors, trade and also consumer, environmental and animal welfare interests.

In Ireland, organic certification is available from the Irish Organic Farmers and Growers Association.

In Greece, organic certification is available from eight organizations approved by EU. The major of them are BIOHELLAS and the DIO.

In France, organic certification was introduced in 1985. It has established a green-white logo of 'AB — agriculture biologique'. The certification for the AB label fulfills the EU regulations for organic food. The certification process is overseen a public institute ('Agence française pour le développement et la promotion de l'agriculture biologique' usually shortended to 'Agence bio') established in November 2001. The actual certification authorities include a number of different institutes like Aclave, Agrocert, Ecocert SA, Qualité France SA, Ulase, SGS ICS.

In Belgium, a similar process as in France is being used where certification of the 'Biogarantie' label is overseen by the public 'association sans but lucratif' (ASBL) administration. This administration does exist since 27. June 1921 and it was reformed on 2. May 2002 to take over the new responsibilities of the label certification.

In Germany the national label was introduced in September 2001 following in the footsteps of the political campaign of 'Agrarwende' (*agricultural major shift*) led by minister Renate Künast of the Greens party. This campaign was started after the mad-cow disease epidemic in 2000. The effects on farming are still challenged by other political parties. The national 'Bio'-label in its hexagon green-black-white shape has gained wide popularity — in 2007 there were 2431 companies having certified 41708 products. The popularity of the label is extending to neighbouring countries like Austria, Switzerland and France.

In the German-speaking countries there have been older non-government organizations that had issued labels for organic food long before the advent of the EU organic food regulations. Their labels are still used widely as they significantly exceed the requirements of the EU regulations. An organic food label like 'demetre' from Demeter International has been in use since 1928 and this label is still regarded as providing the highest standards for organic food in the world. Other active NGOs include Biokreis, Bioland, Biopark, Ecoland, Ecovin, Gäa e.V. and Naturland.

The farmland converted to produce certified organic food has seen a signification evolution in the EU15 rising from 1.8 per cent in 1998 to 4.1 per cent in 2005. For the current EU25 however the statistics do report an overall percentage of just 1.5 per cent as of 2005. Other than the percentage of farmland the statistics show a much larger percentage of organic food in terms of turnover reaching 10 per cent in France and 14 per cent in Germany. Vegetables, fruits, milk and eggs have reached a percentage of 21 per cent to be certified organic food in France. Numbers of 2010 show that 5.4 per cent of farmland in Germany have been converted to produced certified organic food, Switzerland reaches 10.4 per cent and Austria rises to 11.7 per cent of the farmland. Non-EU countries have widely adopted the European certification regulations for organic food, to increase export chances to EU countries.

In Other Countries

In Japan, the Japanese Agricultural Standard (JAS) was fully implemented as law in April, 2001. This was revised in November 2005 and all JAS certifiers were required to be re-accredited by the Ministry of Agriculture.

In Australia, the Australian Quarantine and Inspection Service (AQIS) is the controlling body for organic certification because there are no domestic standards for organic produce within Australia. Currently the government only becomes involved with organic certification at export, meaning AQIS is the default certification agency. Although there is no system for monitoring the labeling of organic produce sold within Australia, this primarily affects the retail public. Commercial buyers for whom this is an issue have simply taken the export system as a de facto standard and are willing to pay premium prices for produce from growers certified under the National schemes. As of 2006, there are seven AQIS-approved certifying organisations authorised to issue Organic Produce Certificates, and in 2004 there were 2345 certified operators. The largest importer of Australia's organic produce (by weight) is Japan (33.59%), followed by the UK (17.51%), France (10.51%), and New Zealand (10.21%). The largest certifier of organic products is Australian Certified Organic, which is a subsidiary of Biological Farmers Australia, the largest organic farmers' collective in the country.

In India, APEDA regulates the certification of organic products as per National Standards for Organic Production. "The NPOP standards for production and accreditation system have been recognized by European Commission and Switzerland as equivalent to their country standards. Similarly, USDA has recognized NPOP conformity assessment procedures of accreditation as equivalent to that of US. With these recognitions, Indian organic products duly certified by the accredited certification bodies of India are accepted by the importing countries."

In China, the China Green Food Development Center awards two Standards: A and AA; while the former standard does permit some use of synthetic agricultural chemicals, the latter is more stringent.

Certification Issues

Organic certification is not without its critics. Some of the staunchest opponents of chemical-based farming and factory farming practices also oppose formal certification. They see it as a way to drive independent organic farmers out of business, and to undermine the quality of organic food. Other organizations such as the Organic Trade Association work within the organic community to foster awareness of legislative and other related issues, and enable the influence and participation of organic proponents.

Obstacle to Small Independents

Originally, in the 1960s through the 1980s, the organic food industry was composed of mainly small, independent farmers, selling locally. Organic 'certification' was a matter of trust, based on a direct relationship between farmer and consumer. Critics view regulatory certification as a potential barrier to entry for small producers, by burdening them with increased costs , paperwork, and bureaucracy.

Manipulation of Regulations

Critics of formal certification also fear an erosion of organic standards. Provided with a legal framework within which to operate, lobbyists can push for amendments and exceptions favourable to large-scale production, resulting in 'legally organic' products produced in ways similar to current conventional food. Combined with the fact that organic products are now sold predominantly through high volume distribution channels such as supermarkets, the concern is that the market is evolving to favor the biggest producers, and this could result in the small organic farmer being squeezed out.

Manipulation of certification regulations as a way to mislead or outright dupe the public is a very real concern. Some examples are creating exceptions (allowing non-organic inputs to be used without loss of certification status) and creative interpretation of standards to meet the letter, but not the intention, of particular rules. For example, a complaint filed with the USDA in February 2004 against Bayliss Ranch, a food ingredient producer and its certifying agent, charged that tap water had been certified organic, and advertised for use in a variety of water-based body care and food products, in order to label them 'organic' under US law. Steam-distilled plant extracts, consisting mainly of tap water introduced during the distilling process, were certified organic, and promoted as an organic base that could then be used in a claim of organic content. The case was dismissed by the USDA, as the products had been actually used only in personal care products, over which the department at the time extended no labelling control. The company subsequently adjusted its marketing by removing reference to use of the extracts in food products. Several months later, the USDA extended its organic labeling to personal care products; this complaint has not been refiled.

In December 2005, the 2006 agricultural appropriations bill was passed with a rider allowing 38 synthetic ingredients to be used in organic foods. Among the ingredients are food colourings, starches, sausage and hot-dog casings, hops, fish oil, chipotle chili pepper, and gelatin. This allowed Anheuser-Busch in 2007 to have its Wild Hop Lager certified organic "even though [it] uses hops grown with chemical fertilizers and sprayed with pesticides".

Misrepresentation of the Term *Organic*

The word *organic* is central to the certification (and organic food marketing) process, and this is also questioned by some. Where organic laws exist, producers cannot use the term legally without certification. To bypass this legal requirement for certification, various alternative certification approaches, using currently undefined terms like 'authentic' and 'natural' instead of 'organic', are emerging. In the US, motivated by the cost and legal requirements of certification (as of Oct. 2002), the private farmer-to-farmer association, Certified Naturally Grown, offers a 'non-profit alternative eco-labelling programme for small farms that grow using USDA Organic methods but are not a part of the USDA Certified Organic programme'.

In the UK, the interests of smaller-scale growers who use 'natural' growing methods are represented by the Wholesome Food Association, which issues a symbol based largely on trust and peer-to-peer inspection.

A related concern holds that certification is replacing consumer education, and this goes against the essential, holistic nature of organic farming. By reducing complex issues and regulations to a simple, convenient *certified organic* label, consumers may more easily ignore the principles and practices behind organics, leaving the definition of organic farming and organic food open to manipulation.

20 Biological Pest Control

Biological control of pests in agriculture is a method of controlling pests (including insects, mites, weeds and plant diseases) that relies on predation, parasitism, herbivory, or other natural mechanisms. It can be an important component of integrated pest management (IPM) programmes.

Biological Control is defined as the reduction of pest populations by natural enemies and typically involves an active human role. Natural enemies of insect pests, also known as biological log control agents; and include predators, parasitoids, and pathogens. Biological control agents of plant diseases are most often referred to as antagonists. Biological control agents of weeds include herbivores and plant pathogens. Predators, such as birds, lady beetles and lacewings, are mainly free-living species that consume a large number of prey during their whole lifetime. Parasitoids are species whose immature develops on paper or within a single insect host, ultimately killing the host. Most have a very narrow host range. Many species of wasps and some flies are parasitoids. Pathogens are disease-causing organisms including bacteria, fungi, and viruses. They kill or debilitate their own host and are relatively specific. There are three basic types of biological control strategies; conservation, classical biological control, and augmentation.

The conservation of natural enemies is probably the most important and readily available biological control practice available to homeowners and gardeners. Natural enemies occur in all areas, from the private garden to the open field. They are adapted to the habitat and to the target pest, and their conservation is generally simple and cost-effective. Lacewings, lady beetles, hover fly larvae, and parasitized aphid mummies are almost always present in aphid colonies. Fungus-infected adult flies are often common following periods of high humidity. These naturally occurring biological controls are often susceptible to the same pesticides used to target their pest hosts. Preventing the accidental eradication of natural enemies is termed 'simple conservation'.

To conserve and encourage pest insect eating birds, including native plants and ornamental plants that supply berries, acorns, nuts, seeds, nectar, and other vegetative foods, and also bird nest building materials, encourages their presence, health, and new generations. These qualities can also increase the visible population to enjoy in a garden. Using companion planting and the birds' insect cuisine habits is a traditional method for biological control agent pest control in an organic garden and any landscape, and in organic farming and sustainable agriculture. Installing specified nest boxes for mosquito eating bats reduces a pest and increases endangered species conservation.

Effects on Native Biodiversity

Biological control can potentially have positive and negative effects on biodiversity. Usually a biological control is introduced to an area to protect a native species from an invasive or exotic species that has moved into its area. The control is introduced to lessen the competition between native and introduced species. However, the introduced control does not always target only the intended species. It can also target native species.

When introducing a biological control to a new area, a primary concern is the host-or prey-specificity of the control agent. Generalist feeders (control agents that are not restricted to a single species or a small range of species) often make poor biological control agents, and may become invasive species themselves. For this reason, potential biological control agents should be subject to extensive testing and quarantine before release into any new environment. If a species is introduced and attacks a native species, the biodiversity in that area can change dramatically. When one native species is removed from an area, it may have filled an essential ecological niche.

When this niche is absent it may directly affect the entire ecosystem because they tend to be generalist feeders, vertebrate animals seldom make good biological control agents, and many of the classic cases of 'biocontrol gone awry' involve vertebrates. For example, the cane toad, *Bufo marinus*, was introduced as a biological control and had significant negative impact on biodiversity. The cane toad was intentionally introduced to Australia to control the cane beetle. When introduced, the cane toad thrived very well and did not only feed on cane beetles but other insects as well. The cane toad soon spread very rapidly, thus taking over native amphibian habitat. The introduction of the cane toad also brought foreign disease to native reptiles. This drastically reduced the population of native toads and frogs. "The cane toad also exudes and can squirt poison from the parotid glands on their shoulders when threatened or handled. This toxin contains a cocktail of chemicals that can kill animals that eat it. Freshwater crocodiles, goannas, tiger snakes, dingos and northern quolls have all died after eating cane toads, as have pet dogs (Cane toad, 2003). This example shows how a small mis-introduced organism can alter the native biodiversity in a large ecosystem in a very expedient manner. A pyramid effect can take place if native species are reduced or eradicated. The domino effect keeps on going and can potentially exude on other bordering ecosystems until an equilibrium is reached.

A second example of a biological control agent that subsequently crossed over to native species is the *Rhinocyllus conicus*. The seed feeding weevil was introduced to North America to control exotic thistles (Musk and Canadian). However, the weevil did not target only the exotic thistles, it also targeted native thistles that are essential to various native insects. The native insects rely solely on native thistles and do not adapt to other plant species. Therefore, they cannot survive. Biological controls do not always have negative impacts on biodiversity.

Successful biological control reduces the density of the target species over several years, thus providing the potential for native species to re-establish. In addition, regeneration and reestablishment programmes can aid to the recovery of native species. Native species can be affected in a positive way as well. To develop or find a biological control that exerts control only on the targeted species is a very lengthy process of research and experiments. In the late 19th century, the citrus industry was in great fear when the cottony cushion scale was discovered. This organism could cause a great deal of economic loss to the industry. However, a biological control was introduced. The vedalia beetle and a parasitoid fly were introduced to control the pest. Within a few years time, the cottony cushion scale was controlled by the natural enemies and the citrus industry suffered little financial loss. Many exotic or invasive species can suppress the development of native species. The introduction of an effective biological control that reduces the population of the invasive species allows the rejuvenation of the native species. Biological controls can reduce competition for biotic and abiotic factors which can result in the re-establishment of the once over ran native species.

Invasive species are closely associated with biological controls because the environment in which they are invasive most likely does not contain their natural enemies. If invasive species are not controlled, biodiversity may be at great threat in the affected area. An example of an invasive species is the alligator weed. This plant was introduced to the United States from South America. This aquatic weed spreads rapidly and causes many problems in lakes and rivers. The weed takes root in shallow water causing major problems for navigation, irrigation, and flood control. The alligator weed flea beetle and two other biological controls were released in Florida. Because of their success, Florida banned the use of herbicides to control alligator weed three years after the controls were introduced (Cofrancesco 2007). Biological controls for invasive species also can have a negative impact on biodiversity.

The cane toad, as mentioned previously, is an example of trying to control an invasive species. The cane toad was introduced to eradicate an invasive species. It became invasive, thus altering the biodiversity. The introduction of the cane toad could have caused more of a disturbance in biodiversity than the targeted species did.

Classical Biological Control

Classical biological control is the introduction of natural enemies to a new locale where they did not originate or do not occur naturally. This is usually done by government authorities. In many instances the complex of natural enemies associated with an insect pest may be inadequate. This is especially evident when an insect pest is accidentally introduced into a new geographic area without its associated natural enemies. These introduced pests are referred to as exotic pests and comprise about 40 per cent of the insect pests in the United States. Examples of introduced vegetable pests include the European corn borer (*Ostrinia nubilalis*), one of the most destructive insects in North America. To obtain the needed natural enemies, scientists turned to classical biological control. This is the practice of importing, and releasing for establishment, natural enemies to control an introduced (exotic) pest, although it is also practiced against native insect pests. The first step in the process is to determine the origin of the introduced pest and then collect appropriate natural enemies associated with the pest or closely related species. The natural enemy is then passed through a rigorous quarantine process, to ensure that no unwanted organisms (such as hyperparasitoids) are introduced, then they are mass produced, and released. Follow-up studies are conducted to determine if the natural enemy becomes successfully established at the site of release, and to assess the long-term benefit of its presence.

There are many examples of successful classical biological control programmes.

Joseph Needham noted a Chinese text dating from 304AD, *Records of the Plants and Trees of the Southern Regions*, by Hsi Han, which describes mandarin oranges protected by biological pest control techniques that are still in use today.

One of the earliest successes in the west was in controlling *Icerya purchasi*, the cottony cushion scale, a pest that was devastating the California citrus industry in the late 19th century. A predatory insect *Rodolia cardinalis* (the Vedalia Beetle), and a parasitoid fly were introduced from Australia by Charles Valentine Riley. Within a few years the cottony cushion scale was completely controlled by these introduced natural enemies. Damage from *Hypera postica* Gyllenhal, the alfalfa weevil, a serious introduced pest of forage, was substantially reduced by the introduction of several natural enemies. 20 years after their introduction the population of weevils in the alfalfa area treated for alfalfa weevil in the Northeastern United States was reduced by 75 per cent. A small wasp, *Trichogramma ostriniae*, was introduced from China to help control the European corn borer making it a recent example of a long history of classical biological control efforts for this major pest. Many classical biological control programmes for insect pests and weeds are under way across the United States and Canada. The population of *Levuana irridescens* (the Levuana moth), a serious coconut pest in Fiji, was brought under control by a classical biological control programme in the 1920s.

Classical biological control is long lasting and inexpensive. Other than the initial costs of collection, importation, and rearing, little expense is incurred. When a natural enemy is successfully established it rarely requires additional input and it continues to kill the pest with no direct help from humans and at no cost. Classical biological control does not always work. It is usually most effective against exotic pests and less so against native insect pests. The reasons for failure are not often known but may include the release of too few individuals, poor adaptation of the natural enemy to environmental conditions at the release location, and lack of synchrony between the life cycle of the natural enemy and host pest.

Augmentation

This third type of biological control involves the supplemental release of natural enemies. Relatively few natural enemies may be released at a critical time of the season (inoculative release) or literally millions may be released (inundative release). Additionally, the cropping system may be modified to favour or augment the natural enemies. This latter practice is frequently referred to as habitat manipulation. An example of inoculative release occurs in greenhouse production of several crops. Periodic releases of the parasitoid, *Encarsia formosa*, are used to control greenhouse whitefly, and the predaceous mite, *Phytoseiulus persimilis*, is used for control of the two-spotted spider mite.

Lady beetles, lacewings, or parasitoids such as those from the genus *Trichogramma* are frequently released in large numbers. Recommended release rates for Trichogramma in vegetable or field crops range from 5,000 to 200,000 per acre (1 to 50 per square metre) per week depending on level of pest infestation. Similarly, entomopathogenic nematodes are released at rates of millions and even billions per acre for control of certain soil-dwelling insect pests.

The spraying of octopamine analogues (such as 3-FMC) has been suggested as a way to boost the effectiveness of augmentation. Octopamine, regarded as the invertebrate counterpart of dopamine plays a role in activating the insects' flight-or-fight response. The idea behind using octopamine analogues to augment biological control is that natural enemies will be more effective in their eradication of the pest, since the pest will be behaving in an unnatural way because its flight-or-fight mechanism has been activated. Octopamine analogues are purported to have two desirable characteristics for this type of application:

1. they affect insects at very low dosages; and
2. they do not have a physiological effect in humans (or other vertebrates).

Habitat or environmental manipulation is another form of augmentation. This tactic involves altering the cropping system to augment or enhance the effectiveness of a natural enemy. Many adult parasitoids and predators benefit from sources of nectar and the protection provided by refuges such as hedgerows, cover crops, and weedy borders. Also, the provisioning of natural shelters in the form of wooden caskets, boxes or (turnaround) flowerpots is a form of this. For example, the stimulation of the natural predator *Dermaptera* is done in gardens by hanging up turnaround flowerpots with straw or wood wool.

Mixed plantings and the provision of flowering borders can increase the diversity of habitats and provide shelter and alternative food sources. They are easily incorporated into home gardens and even small-scale commercial plantings, but are more difficult to accommodate in large-scale crop production. There may also be some conflict with pest control for the large producer because of the difficulty of targeting the pest species and the use of refuges by the pest insects as well as natural enemies.

Examples of habitat manipulation include growing flowering plants (pollen and nectar sources) such as Buckwheat near crops to attract and maintain populations of natural enemies. For example, hover fly adults can be attracted to umbelliferous plants in bloom.

Biological control experts in California have demonstrated that planting prune trees in grape vineyards provides an improved overwintering habitat or refuge for a key grape pest parasitoid. The prune trees harbour an alternate host for the parasitoid, which could previously overwinter only at great distances from most vineyards. Caution should be used with this tactic because some plants attractive to natural enemies may also be hosts for certain plant diseases, especially plant viruses that could be vectored by insect pests to the crop. Although the tactic appears to hold much promise, only a few examples have been adequately researched and developed.

Examples of Predators

Ladybugs, and in particular their larvae which are active between May and July in the northern hemisphere, are voracious predators of aphids such as greenfly and blackfly, and will also consume mites, scale insects and small caterpillars. The ladybug is a very familiar beetle with various coloured markings, whilst its larvae are initially small and spidery, growing up to 17 mm long. The larvae have a tapering segmented grey/black body with orange/yellow markings and ferocious mouthparts. They can be encouraged by cultivating a patch of nettles in the garden and by leaving hollow stems and some plant debris over winter so that they can hibernate.

Hoverflies resemble slightly darker bees or wasps and they have characteristic hovering, darting flight patterns. There are over 100 species of hoverfly whose larvae principally feed upon greenfly, one larva devouring up to fifty a day, or 1000 in its lifetime. They also eat fruit tree spider mites and small caterpillars. Adults feed on nectar and pollen, which they require for egg production. Eggs are minute (1 mm), pale yellow white and laid singly near greenfly colonies. Larvae are 8-17 mm long, disguised to resemble bird droppings, they are legless and have no distinct head. Semi-transparent in a range of colours from green, white, brown and black.

Hoverflies can be encouraged by growing attractant flowers such as the poached egg plant *(Limnanthes douglasii)*, marigolds or phacelia throughout the growing season.

Dragonflies are important predators of mosquitoes, both in the water, where the dragonfly naiads eat mosquito larvae, and in the air, where adult dragonflies capture and eat adult mosquitoes. Community-wide mosquito control programmes that spray adult mosquitoes also kill dragonflies, thus removing an important biocontrol agent, and can actually increase mosquito populations in the long term.

Other useful garden predators include lacewings, pirate bugs, rove and ground beetles, aphid midge, centipedes, spiders, predatory mites, as well as larger fauna such as frogs, toads, lizards, hedgehogs, slow-worms and birds. Cats and rat terriers kill field mice, rats, June bugs, and birds. Dogs chase away many types of pest animals. Dachshunds are bred specifically to fit inside tunnels underground to kill badgers.

More examples:

- *Phytoseiulus persimilis* (against spider mites)
- *Amblyseius californicus* (against spider mites)
- *Amblyseius cucumeris* (against spider mites)
- *Typhlodromips swirskii* (against spider mites, thrips, and white flies)
- *Feltiella acarisuga* (against spider mites)
- *Stethorus punctillum* (against spider mites)
- *Macrolophus caluginosus* (against spider mites)

Parasitoid Insects

Most insect parasitoids are wasps or flies. Parasitoids comprise a diverse range of insects that lay their egg on or in the body of an insect host, which is then used as a food for developing larvae. Parasitic wasps take much longer than predators to consume their victims, for if the larvae were to eat too fast they would run out of food before they became adults. Such parasites are very useful in the organic garden, for they are very efficient hunters, always at work searching for pest invaders. As adults they require high energy fuel as they fly from place to place, and feed upon nectar, pollen and sap, thereby pollinating plenty of flowering plants, particularly buckwheat, umbellifers, and composites will encourage their presence.

Four of the most important groups are:

1. *Ichneumonid wasps:* (5-10 mm). Prey mainly on caterpillars of butterflies and moths.
2. *Braconid wasps:* Tiny wasps (up to 5 mm) attack caterpillars and a wide range of other insects including greenfly. A common parasite of the cabbage white caterpillar- seen as clusters of sulphur yellow cocoons bursting from collapsed caterpillar skin.

3. *Chalcid wasps:* Among the smallest of insects (<3 mm). Parasitize eggs/ larvae of greenfly, whitefly, cabbage caterpillars, scale insects and Strawberry Tortrix Moth (*Acleris comariana*).

4. *Tachinid flies:* Parasitize a wide range of insects including caterpillars, adult and larval beetles, true bugs, and others.

   Examples of parasitoids:

- *Encarsia formosa* (against white flies)
- *Eretmocerus* spp. (against white flies)
- *Aphidius colemani* (against aphids)

Biological Control with Micro-organisms

Various microbial insect diseases occur naturally, but may also be used as biological pesticides. When naturally occurring, these outbreaks are density dependent in that they generally only occur as insect populations become denser.

Bacteria and Biological Control

Bacteria used for biological control infect insects via their digestive tracts, so insects with sucking mouth parts like aphids and scale insects are difficult to control with bacterial biological control. *Bacillus thuringiensis* is the most widely applied species of bacteria used for biological control, with at least four sub-species used to control Lepidopteran (moth, butterfly), Coleopteran (beetle) and Dipteran (true flies) insect pests.

Fungi and Biological Control

Fungi that cause disease in insects are known as entomopathogenic fungi, including at least fourteen species of entomophthoraceous fungi attack aphids. Species in the genus *Trichoderma* are used to manage some soilborne plant pathogens. *Beauveria bassiana* is used to manage different types of pest such whiteflies, thrips, aphids and weevils.

Examples of entomopathogenic fungi:

- *Beauveria bassiana* (against white flies, thrips, aphids and weevils)
- *Paecilomyces fumosoroseus* (against white flies, thrips and aphids)
- *Metarhizium* spp. (against beetles, locusts, Hemiptera, spider mites and other pests)
- *Lecanicillium lecanii* (against white flies, thrips and aphids)
- *Cordyceps* species (sometines teleomorphs of the above: that infect a wide spectrum of arthropods)

Plants to Regulate Insect Pests

Choosing a diverse range of plants for the garden can help to regulate pests in a variety of ways, including:

- Masking the crop plants from pests, depending on the proximity of the companion or intercrop.
- Producing olfactory inhibitors, odors that confuse and deter pests.
- Acting as trap plants by providing an alluring food that entices pests away from crops.
- Serving as nursery plants, providing breeding grounds for beneficial insects.
- Providing an alternative habitat, usually in a form of a shelterbelt, hedgerow, or beetle bank where beneficial insects can live and reproduce. Nectar-rich plants that bloom for long periods are especially good, as many beneficials are nectivorous during the adult stage, but parasitic or predatory as larvae. A good example of this is the soldier beetle which is frequently found on flowers as an adult, but whose larvae eat aphids, caterpillars, grasshopper eggs, and other beetles.
- Some plants have chemical defences in order to regulate pests. The geranium has developed such a defence against Japanese beetles, one of the most damaging and expensive pests to control when it comes to ornamental and turf plants. The geranium's petals contain a chemical compound that paralyzes the beetle within 30 minutes of ingestion. The beetle will remain paralyzed for several hours and will typically regain movement within 24 hours. However, while paralyzed the beetle is very vulnerable to its predators and is usually hunted before the paralysis subsides. Agricultural Research Service (ARS) scientists are working to isolate the chemical compound in geraniums that causes the paralysis in the beetles. Scientists hope to one day use this natural pesticide to control the population of beetles. In addition to this research ARS scientists are studying ways to help geranium leaves better hold on to pesticide chemicals that are sprayed on them, that way less pesticides will have to be applied to the leaves.

Most of the biological controls listed above depend on providing incentives in order to 'naturally' attract beneficial insects to the garden. However there are occasions when biological controls can be directly introduced. Common biocontrol agents include parasitoids, predators, pathogens or weed feeders. This is particularly appropriate in situations such as the greenhouse, a largely artificial environment, and are usually purchased by mail order.

Some biocontrol agents that can be introduced include;

- *Encarsia formosa*. This is a small predatory chalcid wasp which is parasitical on whitefly, a sap-feeding insect which can cause wilting and black sooty moulds. It is most effective when dealing with low level infestations, giving protection over a long period of time. The wasp lays its eggs in young whitefly 'scales', turning them black as the parasite larvae pupates. It should be introduced as soon as possible after the first adult whitefly are seen. Should be used in conjunction with insecticidal soap.
- Red spider mite, another pest found in the greenhouse, can be controlled with the predatory mite *Phytoseilus persimilis*. This is slightly larger than its prey and has an orange body. It develops from egg to adult twice as fast as the red spider mite and once established quickly overcomes infestation.
- A fairly recent development in the control of slugs is the introduction of 'Nemaslug', a microscopic nematode (*Phasmarhabditis hermaphrodita*) which will seek out and parasitize slugs, reproducing inside them and killing them. The nematode is applied by watering onto moist soil, and gives protection for up to six weeks in optimum conditions, Nemaslug nematodes are mainly effective with small and young slugs under the soil surface.
- A bacterial biological control which can be introduced in order to control butterfly caterpillars is *Bacillus thuringiensis*. This available in sachets of dried spores which are mixed with water and sprayed onto vulnerable plants such as brassicas and fruit trees. The bacterial disease will kill the caterpillars, but leave other insects unharmed. There are strains of *Bt* that are effective against other insect larvae. *Bt israelensis* is effective against mosquito larvae and some midges.
- A viral biological control which can be introduced in order to control the overpopulation of European rabbit in Australia is the rabbit haemorrhagic disease virus that causes the rabbit haemorrhagic disease.
- A biological control being developed for use in the treatment of plant disease is the fungus *Trichoderma viride*. This has been used against Dutch Elm disease, and to treat the spread of fungal and bacterial growth on tree wounds. It may also have potential as a means of combating silver leaf disease.
- Several species of dung beetle were introduced to Australia from South Africa and Europe during the Australian Dung Beetle Project (1965-1985) led by Dr. George Bornemissza of the Commonwealth Scientific

and Industrial Research Organisation in order to biologically control the population of pestilent bush flies and parasitic worms.

- The parasitoid *Gonatocerus ashmeadi* (Hymenoptera: Mymaridae) has been introduced to control the glassy-winged sharpshooter *Homalodisca vitripennis* (Hemipterae: Cicadellidae) in French Polynesia and has successfully controlled ~95 per cent of the pest density.

In some cases, biological pest control can have unforeseen negative results that could outweigh all benefits. For example, when the mongoose was introduced to Hawaii in order to control the rat population, it preyed on the endemic birds of Hawaii, especially their eggs, more often than it ate the rats. However, that the introduction of the mongoose was not undertaken based on scientific — or perhaps any — understanding of the consequences of such an action. The introduction of a generalist mammal for biocontrol of anything would be unthinkable by any reasonable standards today.

Cane toads (*Bufo marinus*) were introduced to Australia in the 1930s in a failed attempt to control the cane beetle, a pest of sugarcane crops. 102 toads were obtained from Hawaii and bred in captivity to increase their numbers until they were released into the sugarcane fields of the tropic north in 1935. It was later discovered that the toads can't jump very high so they did not eat the cane beetles which stayed up on the upper stalks of the cane plants. The toads soon became very numerous and out-competed native species and became very harmful to the Australian environment, including being very toxic to would-be predators such as native snakes.

Living organisms evolve and increase their resistance to biological, chemical, physical or any other form of control. Unless the target population is completely exterminated or is rendered incapable of reproduction, the surviving population will inevitably acquire a tolerance of whatever pressures are brought to bear — this results in an evolutionary arms race.

21 Crop Rotation

Crop rotation is the practice of growing a series of dissimilar types of crops in the same area in sequential seasons for various benefits such as to avoid the build up of pathogens and pests that often occurs when one species is continuously cropped. Crop rotation also seeks to balance the fertility demands of various crops to avoid excessive depletion of soil nutrients. A traditional element of crop rotation is the replenishment of nitrogen through the use of green manure in sequence with cereals and other crops. It is one component of polyculture. Crop rotation can also improve soil structure and fertility by alternating deep-rooted and shallow-rooted plants.

Crop rotation avoids a decrease in soil fertility, as growing the same crop in the same place for many years in a row disproportionately depletes the soil of certain nutrients. With rotation, a crop that leaches the soil of one kind of nutrient is followed during the next growing season by a dissimilar crop that returns that nutrient to the soil or draws a different ratio of nutrients, for example, rice followed by cotton. By crop rotation farmers can keep their fields under continuous production, without the need to let them lie fallow, and reducing the need for artificial fertilizers, both of which can be expensive. Rotating crops adds nutrients to the soil. Legumes, plants of the family Fabaceae, for instance, have nodules on their roots which contain nitrogen-fixing bacteria. It therefore makes good sense agriculturally to alternate them with cereals (family Poaceae) and other plants that require nitrates. An extremely common modern crop rotation is alternating soybeans and maize (corn). In subsistence farming, it also makes good nutritional sense to grow beans and grain at the same time in different fields.

Crop rotation is a type of cultural control that is also used to control pests and diseases that can become established in the soil over time. The changing of crops in a sequence tends to decrease the population level of pests. Plants within the same taxonomic family tend to have similar pests and pathogens. By regularly changing the planting location, the pest cycles can be broken or limited. For example, root-knot nematode is a serious problem for some plants in warm climates and sandy soils, where it slowly builds up to high levels in the soil, and can severely damage plant productivity by cutting off circulation from the plant roots. Growing a crop that is not a host for root-knot nematode for one season greatly reduces the level of the nematode in the soil, thus making it possible to grow a susceptible crop the following season without needing soil fumigation.

It is also difficult to control weeds similar to the crop which may contaminate the final produce. For instance, ergot in weed grasses is difficult to separate from harvested grain. A different crop allows the weeds to be eliminated, breaking the ergot cycle.

This principle is of particular use in organic farming, where pest control may be achieved without synthetic pesticides.

A general effect of crop rotation is that there is a geographic mixing of crops, which can slow the spread of pests and diseases during the growing season. The different crops can also reduce the effects of adverse weather for the individual farmer and, by requiring planting and harvest at different times, allow more land to be farmed with the same amount of machinery and labour.

The choice and sequence of rotation crops depends on the nature of the soil, the climate, and precipitation which together determine the type of plants that may be cultivated. Other important aspects of farming such as crop marketing and economic variables must also be considered when choosing a crop rotation.

Historic crop rotation methods are mentioned in Roman literature, and referred to by several civilizations in Asia and on three major elements: sophisticated systems of crop rotation, highly developed irrigation techniques and the introduction of a large variety of crops which were studied and catalogued according to the season, type of land and amount of water they require. Numerous farming encyclopaedias were produced.

In Europe, since the times Charlemagne, there was a transition from a two-field crop rotation to a three-field crop rotation. Under a two-field rotation, half the land was planted in a year while the other half lay fallow. Then, in the next year, the two fields were reversed. Under three-field rotation, the land was divided into three parts. One section was planted in the Fall with winter wheat or rye. The next Spring, the second field was planted with other crops such as peas, lentils, or beans and the third field was left fallow. The three fields were rotated in this manner so that every three years, a field would rest and be unplanted. Under the two field system, if one has a total of 600 fertile acres of land, one would only plant 300 acres. Under the new three-field rotation system, one would plant (and thereby harvest) 400 acres. But, the additional crops had a more significant effect than mere productivity. Since the Spring crops were mostly legumes, they increased the overall nutrition of the people of Northern Europe.

From the end of the Middle Ages until the 20th century, the three-year rotation was practised by farmers in Europe with a rotation of rye or winter wheat, followed by spring oats or barley, then letting the soil rest (leaving it fallow) during the third stage. The fact that suitable rotations made it possible to restore or to maintain a productive soil has long been recognized by planting spring crops for livestock in place of grains for human consumption.

A four-field rotation was pioneered by farmers, namely in the region Waasland in the early 16th century and popularised by the British agriculturist Charles Townshend in the 18th century. The system (wheat, turnips, barley and clover), opened up a fodder crop and grazing crop allowing livestock to be bred year-round. The four-field crop rotation was a key development in the British Agricultural Revolution. George Washington Carver pioneered crop rotation methods in the United States by teaching southern farmers to rotate soil depleting crops like cotton with soil enriching crops like peanuts and peas.

In the Green revolution, the traditional practice of crop rotation gave way in some parts of the world to the practice of supplementing the chemical inputs to the soil through top dressing with fertilizers, e.g., adding ammonium nitrate or urea and restoring soil pH with lime in the search for increased yields, preparing soil for specialist crops, and seeking to reduce waste and inefficiency by simplifying planting and harvesting. Some disadvantages of this type of monoculture have since become apparent, notably from the perspective of sustainable agriculture and the risk of catastrophic crop failure.

Effects on Soil Erosion

Crop rotation can greatly affect the amount of soil lost from erosion by water. In areas that are highly susceptible to erosion, farm management practices such as zero and reduced tillage can be supplemented with specific crop rotation methods to reduce raindrop impact, sediment detachment, sediment transport, surface runoff, and soil loss.

Protection against soil loss is maximized with rotation methods that leave the greatest mass of crop stubble (plant residue left after harvest) on top of the soil. Stubble cover in contact with the soil minimizes erosion from water by reducing overland flow velocity, stream power, and thus the ability of the water to detach and transport sediment Soil Erosion and Cill prevent the disruption and detachment of soil aggregates that cause macrospores to block, infiltration to decline, and runoff to increase. This significantly improves the resilience of soils when subjected to periods of erosion and stress.

The effect of crop rotation on erosion control varies by climate. In regions under relatively consistent climate conditions, where annual rainfall and temperature levels are assumed, rigid crop rotations can produce sufficient plant growth and soil cover. In regions where climate conditions are less predictable, and unexpected periods of rain and drought may occur, a more flexible approach for soil cover by crop rotation is necessary. An opportunity cropping system promotes adequate soil cover under these erratic climate conditions. In an opportunity cropping system, crops are grown when soil water is adequate and there is a reliable sowing window. This form of cropping system is likely to produce better soil cover than a rigid crop rotation because crops are only sown under optimal conditions, whereas rigid systems are sown in the best conditions available.

Crop rotations also affect the timing and length of when a field is subject to fallow. This is very important because depending on a particular region's climate, a field could be the most vulnerable to erosion when it is under fallow. Efficient fallow management is an essential part of reducing erosion in a crop rotation system. Zero tillage is a fundamental management practice that promotes crop stubble retention under longer unplanned fallows when crops cannot be planted. Such management practices that succeed in retaining suitable soil cover in areas under fallow will ultimately reduce soil loss.

22 Dryland Farming

Dryland farming is an agricultural technique for non-irrigated cultivation of land which receives little natural rainfall.

Dryland farming is used in the Great Plains, the Palouse plateau of Eastern Washington, and other arid regions of North America, the Middle East and in other grain growing regions such as the steppes of Eurasia and Argentina. Dryland farming was introduced to the southern Russian Empire by Russian Mennonites under the influence of Johann Cornies, making the region the breadbasket of Russia. It is widely practised in all states of Australia (but not the Northern Territory).

Crops

Winter wheat is the typical crop although skilled dryland farmers sometimes grow corn, beans or even watermelons. Successful dryland farming is possible with as little as 9 inches (230 mm) of precipitation a year, higher rainfall increases the variety of crops. Native American tribes in the arid Southwest subsisted for hundreds of years on dryland farming in areas with less than 10 inches (250 mm) of rain. The choice of crop is influenced by the timing of the predominant rainfall in relation to the seasons. For example, winter wheat is more suited to regions with higher winter rainfall while areas with summer wet seasons may be more suited to summer growing crops such as sorghum, sunflowers or cotton.

Process

Dryland farming has evolved as a set of techniques and management practices used by farmers to continually adapt to the presence or lack of moisture in a given crop cycle. In marginal regions, a farmer should be financially able to survive occasional crop failures, perhaps for several years in succession. Survival as a dryland farmer requires careful husbandry of the moisture available for the crop and aggressive management of expenses to minimize losses in poor years.

System

Dryland farming is uniquely dependent on natural rainfall, which can leave the ground vulnerable to dust storms, particularly if poor farming techniques are used or if the storms strike at a particularly vulnerable time. The fact that a fallow period must be included in the crop rotation means that fields cannot always be protected by a cover crop, which might otherwise offer strong protection against erosion.

Key Elements

Capturing and Conservation of Moisture: In regions such as Eastern Washington state, the average annual precipitation available to a dryland farm may be as little as 8.5 inches (220 mm). Consequently moisture must be captured until the crop can utilize it. Techniques include summer fallow rotation (in which one crop is grown on two seasons' precipitation, leaving standing stubble and crop residue to trap snow, and preventing runoff by terracing fields.

'*Terracing*' is also practised by farmers on a smaller scale by laying out the direction of furrows to slow water runoff downhill, a practice known as contour plowing. Moisture can be conserved by eliminating weeds and leaving crop residue to shade the soil.

Effective Use of Available Moisture: Once moisture is available for the crop to use, it must be used as effectively as possible. Seed planting depth and timing are carefully considered to place the seed at a depth at which sufficient moisture exists, or where it will exist when seasonal precipitation falls. Farmers tend to use crop varieties which are drought and heat-stress tolerant, (even lower-yielding varieties). Thus the likelihood of a successful crop is hedged if seasonal precipitation fails.

Soil Conservation: The nature of dryland farming makes it particularly susceptible to erosion, especially wind erosion. Some techniques for conserving soil moisture (such as frequent tillage to kill weeds) are at odds with techniques for conserving topsoil. Since healthy topsoil is critical to sustainable dryland agriculture, its preservation is generally considered the most important long-term goal of a dryland farming operation. Erosion control techniques such as windbreaks, reduced tillage or no-till, spreading straw (or other mulch on particularly susceptible ground), and strip farming are used to minimize topsoil loss.

Control of Input Costs: Dryland farming is practised in regions inherently marginal for non-irrigated agriculture. Because of this, there is an increased risk of crop failure and poor yields which may occur in a dry year (regardless of money or effort expended). Dryland farmers must evaluate the potential yield of a crop constantly throughout the growing season and be prepared to decrease inputs to the crop such as fertilizer and weed control if it appears that it is likely to have a poor yield due to insufficient moisture. Conversely, in years when moisture is abundant, farmers may increase their input efforts and budget to maximize yields and to offset poor harvests.

Companion Planting

Companion planting is the planting of different crops in proximity (in gardening and agriculture), on the theory that they assist each other in nutrient uptake, pest control, pollination, and other factors necessary to increasing crop productivity.

Companion planting is used by farmers and gardeners in both industrialized and developing countries for many reasons. Many of the modern principles of companion planting were present many centuries ago in cottage gardens in England and Home gardens in Asia.

For farmers using an integrated pest management system, increased yield and/or reduction of pesticides is the goal.

For gardeners, the combinations of plants also make for a more varied, attractive vegetable garden, as well as allowing more productive use of space.

Companion planting is considered to be a form of polyculture.

In China, the mosquito fern has been used for at least one thousand years, as a companion plant for rice crops. It hosts a special cyanobacteria that fixes nitrogen from the atmosphere, and also blocks out light from getting to any competing plants, aside from the rice, which is planted when tall enough to stick out of the water above the azolla layer.

Companion planting was practised in various forms by Native Americans prior to the arrival of Europeans. One common system was the planting of corn (maize) and pole beans together. The cornstalk would serve as a trellis for the beans to climb while the beans would fix nitrogen for the corn. The inclusion of squash with these two plants completes the Three Sisters technique, pioneered by Native American peoples.

Companion planting was widely touted in the 1970s as part of the organic gardening movement. It was encouraged for pragmatic reasons, such as natural trellising, but mainly with the idea that different species of plant may thrive more when close together. It is also a technique frequently used in permaculture, together with mulching, polyculture, and changing of crops.

Examples of Companion Plants

Nasturtium are well-known to attract caterpillars, therefore, planting them around vegetables such as lettuce or cabbage protects them from damage, as egg-laying insects will tend to prefer the nasturtium. This practice is called trap cropping.

Marigolds assist crops suffering from aphids (greenfly among others) through their smell being deterrent to aphids and attractant to hoverflies (a predator of aphids).

Versions

There are a number of systems and ideas using companion planting.

Square foot gardening, for example, attempts to protect plants from many normal gardening problems by packing them as closely together as possible, which is facilitated by using companion plants, which can be closer together than normal.

Another system using companion planting is the forest garden, where companion plants are intermingled to create an actual ecosystem, emulating the interaction of up to seven levels of plants in a forest or woodland.

Organic gardening often depends on companion planting for its best performance, since so many synthetic means of fertilizing, weed reduction, pest control, and other garden needs are forbidden.

Good Weeds

There are many beneficial weeds, which can be allowed to grow alongside plants, imparting the same kinds of benefits as mixing cultivated crops.

Host-finding Disruption

Recent studies on host-plant finding have shown that flying pests are far less successful if their host-plants are surrounded by any other plant or even 'decoy-plants' made of green plastic, cardboard, or any other green material.

The host-plant finding process occurs in phases:

- The first phase is stimulation by odours characteristic to the host-plant. This induces the insect to try to land on the plant it seeks. But insects avoid landing on brown (bare) soil. So if only the host-plant is present, the insects will quasi-systematically find it by simply landing on the only green thing around. This is called (from the point of view of the insect) 'appropriate landing'. When it does an 'inappropriate landing', it flies off to any other nearby patch of green. It eventually leaves the area if there are too many 'inappropriate' landings.

- The second phase of host-plant finding is for the insect to make short flights from leaf to leaf to assess the plant's overall suitability. The number of leaf-to-leaf flights varies according to the insect species and to the host-plant stimulus received from each leaf. The insect must accumulate sufficient stimuli from the host-plant to lay eggs; so it must make a certain number of consecutive 'appropriate' landings. Hence if it makes an 'inappropriate landing', the assessment of that plant is negative, and the insect must start the process anew.

Thus it was shown that clover used as a ground cover had the same disruptive effect on eight pest species from four different insect orders. An experiment showed that 36 per cent of cabbage root flies laid eggs beside cabbages growing in bare soil (which resulted in no crop), compared to only 7 per cent beside cabbages growing in clover (which allowed a good crop). Simple decoys made of green cardboard also disrupted appropriate landings just as well as did the live ground cover.

Companion Plant Categories

Companion plants can benefit each other in a number of different ways, including:

- *Flavour enhancement* — some plants, especially herbs, seem to subtly change the flavor of other plants around them.
- *Hedged investment* — multiple plants in the same space increase the odds of some yield being given, even if one category encounters catastrophic issues.
- *Increased level interaction* — plants that grow on different levels in the same space, perhaps providing ground cover or working as a trellis for another plant.
- *Nitrogen fixation* — plants that fix nitrogen in the ground, making it available to other plants.
- *Pest suppression* — repelling pest insects, weeds, nematodes, or pathogenic fungi, through chemical means.
- *Pollinator and predator recruitment* — The use of plants that produce copious nectar and protein-rich pollen in a vegetable garden (insectary plants) is a good way to recruit higher populations of beneficial insects

that control pests. Some insects in the adult form are nectar or pollen feeders, while in the larval form they are voracious predators of pest insects.

- *Positive hosting* — attracts or is inhabited by beneficial insects or other organisms which benefit plants, as with ladybugs or some 'good nematodes'.
- *Protective shelter* — one type of plant may serve as a wind break or shade for another.
- *Trap cropping* — plants that attract pests away from others.
- *Pattern disruption* — in a monoculture, pest spread from one plant to the next, is interrupted by companion plants.

23 Integrated Pest Management

Integrated pest management (IPM) is an integrated approach of crop management to solve ecological problems when applied in agriculture.

These methods are performed in three stages: *prevention, observation,* and *intervention.* It is an ecological approach with a main goal of significantly reducing or eliminating the use of pesticides while at the same time managing pest populations at an acceptable level.

For their leadership in developing and spreading IPM worldwide, Dr. Perry Adkisson and Dr. Ray F. Smith received the 1997 World Food Prize.

Shortly after World War II, when synthetic insecticides became widely available, entomologists in California developed the concept of 'supervised insect control'. Around the same time, entomologists in cotton-belt states such as Arkansas were advocating a similar approach. Under this scheme, insect control was 'supervised' by qualified entomologists, and insecticide applications were based on conclusions reached from periodic monitoring of pest and natural-enemy populations. This was viewed as an alternative to calendar-based insecticide programmes. Supervised control was based on a sound knowledge of the ecology and analysis of projected trends in pest and natural-enemy populations.

Supervised control formed much of the conceptual basis for the 'integrated control' that University of California entomologists articulated in the 1950s. Integrated control sought to identify the best mix of chemical and biological controls for a given insect pest. Chemical insecticides were to be used in manner least disruptive to biological control. The term 'integrated' was thus synonymous with "compatible." Chemical controls were to be applied only after regular monitoring indicated that a pest population had reached a level (the economic threshold) that required treatment to prevent the population from reaching a level at which economic losses would exceed the cost of the artificial control measures.

IPM extended the concept of integrated control to all classes of pests and was expanded to include tactics other than just chemical and biological controls. Artificial controls such as pesticides were to be applied as in integrated control, but these now had to be compatible with control tactics for all classes of pests. Other tactics, such as host-plant resistance and cultural manipulations, became part of the IPM arsenal. IPM added the multidisciplinary element, involving entomologists, plant pathologists, nematologists, and weed scientists.

In the United States, IPM was formulated into national policy in February 1972 when President Nixon directed federal agencies to take steps to advance the concept and application of IPM in all relevant sectors. In 1979, President Carter established an interagency IPM Coordinating Committee to ensure development and implementation of IPM practices.

Principles

An IPM system is designed around six basic components: The US Environmental Protection Agency has a useful set of IPM principles.

Acceptable pest levels: The emphasis is on *control*, not *eradication*. IPM holds that wiping out an entire pest population is often impossible, and the attempt can be more costly, environmentally unsafe, and frequently unachievable. IPM programmes first work to establish acceptable pest levels, called action thresholds, and apply controls if those thresholds are crossed. These thresholds are pest and site specific, meaning that it may be acceptable at one site to have a weed such as white clover, but at another site it may not be acceptable. This stops the pest gaining resistance to chemicals produced by the plant or applied to the crops. If many of the pests are killed then any that have resistance to the chemical will rapidly reproduce forming a resistant population. By not killing all the pests there are some un-resistant pests left that will dilute any resistant genes that appear.

Preventive cultural practices: Selecting varieties best for local growing conditions, and maintaining healthy crops, is the first line of defence, together with plant quarantine and 'cultural techniques' such as crop sanitation (*e.g.* removal of diseased plants to prevent spread of infection).

Monitoring: Regular observation is the cornerstone of IPM. Observation is broken into two steps, first; inspection and second; identification. Visual inspection, insect and spore traps, and other measurement methods and monitoring tools are used to monitor pest levels. Accurate pest identification is critical to a successful IPM programme. Record-keeping is essential, as is a thorough knowledge of the behaviour and reproductive cycles of target pests. Since insects are cold-blooded, their physical development is dependent on the temperature of their environment. Many insects have had their development cycles modelled in terms of degree days. Monitor the degree days of an environment to determine when is the optimal time for a specific insect's outbreak.

Mechanical controls: Should a pest reach an unacceptable level, mechanical methods are the first options to consider. They include simple hand-picking, erecting insect barriers, using traps, vacuuming, and tillage to disrupt breeding.

Biological controls: Natural biological processes and materials can provide control, with minimal environmental impact, and often at low cost. The main focus here is on promoting beneficial insects that eat target pests. Biological insecticides, derived from naturally occurring microorganisms (*e.g.*: *Bt*, entomopathogenic fungi and entomopathogenic nematodes), also fit in this category.

Chemical controls: Synthetic pesticides are generally only used as required and often only at specific times in a pests life cycle. Many of the newer pesticide groups are derived from plants or naturally occurring substances (*e.g.*: nicotine, pyrethrum and insect juvenile hormone analogues), and further 'biology-based' or 'ecological' techniques are under evaluation.

An IPM regime can be quite simple or sophisticated. Historically, the main focus of IPM programmes was on agricultural insect pests. Although originally developed for agricultural pest management, IPM programmes are now developed to encompass diseases, weeds, and other pests that interfere with the management objectives of sites such as residential and commercial structures, lawn and turf areas, and home and community gardens.

IPM is applicable to all types of agriculture and sites such as residential and commercial structures, lawn and turf areas, and home and community gardens. Reliance on knowledge, experience, observation, and integration of multiple techniques makes IPM a perfect fit for organic farming (sans artificial pesticide application). For large-scale, chemical-based farms, IPM can reduce human and environmental exposure to hazardous chemicals, and potentially lower overall costs of pesticide application material and labour.

1. *Proper identification of pest* — What is it? Cases of mistaken identity may result in ineffective actions. If plant damage due to over-watering are mistaken for fungal infection, spray costs can be incurred, and the plant is no better off.

2. *Learn pest and host life cycle and biology* — At the time you see a pest, it may be too late to do much about it except maybe spray with a pesticide . Often, there is another stage of the life cycle that is susceptible to preventative actions. For example, weeds reproducing from last year's seed can be prevented with mulches. Also, learning what a pest needs to survive allows you to remove these.

3. *Monitor or sample environment for pest population* — How many are here? Preventative actions must be taken at the correct time if they are to be effective. For this reason, once the pest is correctly identified, monitoring must begin *before* it becomes a problem. For example, in school cafeterias where roaches may be expected to appear, sticky traps are set out before school starts. Traps are checked at regular intervals so populations can be monitored and controlled before they get out of hand. Some factors to consider and monitor include: Is the pest present/absent? What is the distribution — all over or only in certain spots? Is the pest population increasing or decreasing?

4. *Establish action threshold* (*economic, health or aesthetic*) — How many are too many? In some cases, a certain number of pests can be tolerated. Soybeans are quite tolerant of defoliation, so if there are a few caterpillars in the field and their population is not increasing dramatically, there is not necessarily any action necessary. Conversely, there is a point at which action *must* be taken to control cost. For the farmer, that point is the one at which the cost of damage by the pest is *more* than the cost of control. This is an economic threshold. Tolerance of pests varies also by whether or not they are a health hazard (low tolerance) or merely a cosmetic damage (high tolerance in a non-commercial situation).

   Different sites may also have varying requirements based on specific areas. White clover may be perfectly acceptable on the sides of a tee box on a golf course, but unacceptable in the fairway where it could cause confusion in the field of play.

5. *Choose an appropriate combination of management tactics* — For any pest situation, there will be several options to consider. Options include, mechanical or physical control, cultural controls, biological controls and chemical controls. Mechanical or physical controls include picking pests off plants, or using netting or other material to exclude pests

such as birds from grapes or rodents from structures. Cultural controls include keeping an area free of conducive conditions by removing or storing waste properly, removing diseased areas of plants properly. Biological controls can be support either through conservation of natural predators or augmentation of natural predators.

Augmentative control includes the introduction of naturally occurring predators at either an inundative or inoculative level. An inundative release would be one that seeks to inundate a site with a pest's predator to impact the pest population. An inoculative release would be a smaller number of pest predators to supplement the natural population and provide ongoing control. Chemical controls would include horticultural oils or the application of pesticides such as insecticides and herbicides. A Green Pest Management IPM programme would use pesticides derived from plants, such as botanicals, or other naturally occurring materials.

6. *Evaluate results* — How did it work? Evaluation is often one of the most important steps. This is the process to review an IPM programme and the results it generated. Asking the following questions is useful: Did actions have the desired effect? Was the pest prevented or managed to farmer satisfaction? Was the method itself satisfactory? Were there any unintended side effects? What can be done in the future for this pest situation? Understanding the effectiveness of the IPM programme allows the site manager to make modifications to the IPM plan prior to pests reaching the action threshold and requiring action again.

24 Biodynamic Agriculture

Biodynamic agriculture is a method of organic farming that treats farms as unified and individual organisms, emphasizing balancing the holistic development and interrelationship of the soil, plants, animals as a self-nourishing system without external inputs insofar as this is possible given the loss of nutrients due to the export of food.

Regarded by some as the first modern ecological farming system and one of the most sustainable, biodynamic farming has much in common with other organic approaches, such as emphasizing the use of manures and composts and excluding of the use of artificial chemicals on soil and plants. Methods unique to the biodynamic approach include the use of fermented herbal and mineral preparations as compost additives and field sprays and the use of an astronomical sowing and planting calendar. Biodynamics originated out of the work of Rudolf Steiner, the founder of the spiritual philosophy anthroposophy.

The development of biodynamic agriculture began in 1924 with a series of eight lectures on agriculture given by Rudolf Steiner at Schloss Koberwitz in what was then Silesia, Germany, (now in Poland east of Wroclaw). The course was held in response to a request by farmers who noticed degraded soil conditions and a deterioration in the health and quality of crops and livestock resulting from the use of chemical fertilizers. An agricultural research group was subsequently formed to test the effects of biodynamic methods on the life and health of soil, plants and animals.

Today biodynamics is practised in more than 50 countries worldwide. Demeter International is the primary certification agency for farms and gardens using the methods.

Biodynamic Method of Farming

Biodynamic agriculturalists conceive of the farm as an organically self-contained entity with its own individuality, within which organisms are interdependent. "Emphasis is placed on the integration of crops and livestock, recycling of nutrients, maintenance of soil, and the health and well being of crops and animals; the farmer too is part of the whole." Cover crops, green manures and crop rotations are used extensively and the farms foster bio-diversity.

Biodynamic farms often have a cultural component and encourage local community. Some biodynamic farms use the Community Supported Agriculture model, which has connections with social three-folding.

Biodynamic Preparations

Steiner prescribed nine different preparations to aid fertilization which are the cornerstone of biodynamic agriculture, and described how these were to be prepared. Steiner believed that these preparations transferred supernatural terrestrial and cosmic 'forces' into the soil. The prepared substances are numbered 500 through 508, where the first two are used for preparing fields whereas the latter seven are used for making compost. A long term trial (DOK experiment) evaluating the biodynamic farming system in comparison with organic and conventional farming systems, found that preparations have influence on soil structure and micro-organisms enhancing soil fertility and increasing biodiversity. Regarding compost development beyond accelerating the initial phase of composting, some positive effects have been noted:

- The field sprays contain substances that stimulate plant growth include cytokinins.

  Some improvement in nutrient content of compost.

Field Preparations

Field preparations, for stimulating humus formation:

- **500**: (horn-manure) a humus mixture prepared by filling the horn of a cow with cow manure and burying it in the ground (40-60 cm below the surface) in the autumn. It is left to decompose during the winter and recovered for use the following spring.
- **501**: Crushed powdered quartz prepared by stuffing it into a horn of a cow and buried into the ground in spring and taken out in autumn. It can be mixed with 500 but usually prepared on its own (mixture of 1 tablespoon of quartz powder to 250 litres of water) The mixture

is sprayed under very low pressure over the crop during the wet season, in an attempt to prevent fungal diseases. It should be sprayed on an overcast day or early in the morning to prevent burning of the leaves.

Both 500 and 501 are used on fields by stirring about one teaspoon of the contents of a horn in 40-60 litres of water for an hour and whirling it in different directions every second minute. Although some biodynamic beliefs refer to buried quartz "fermenting", a 2004 review commented that it is unclear what this actually means, as rock does not ferment.

Compost Preparations

Compost preparations, used for preparing compost, employ herbs which are frequently used in medicinal remedies:

- **502**: Yarrow blossoms (*Achillea millefolium*) are stuffed into urinary bladders from Red Deer (*Cervus elaphus*), placed in the sun during summer, buried in earth during winter and retrieved in the spring.
- **503**: Chamomile blossoms (*Matricaria recutita*) are stuffed into small intestines from cattle buried in humus-rich earth in the autumn and retrieved in the spring.
- **504**: Stinging nettle (*Urtica dioica*) plants in full bloom are stuffed together underground surrounded on all sides by peat for a year.
- **505**: Oak bark (*Quercus robur*) is chopped in small pieces, placed inside the skull of a domesticated animal, surrounded by peat and buried in earth in a place where lots of rain water runs past.
- **506**: Dandelion flowers (*Taraxacum officinale*) is stuffed into the peritoneum of cattle and buried in earth during winter and retrieved in the spring.
- **507**: Valerian flowers (*Valeriana officinalis*) are extracted into water.
- **508**: Horsetail (*Equisetum*).

One to three grams (a teaspoon) of each preparation is added to a dung heap by digging 50 cm deep holes with a distance of 2 meters from each other, except for the 507 preparation, which is stirred into 5 liters of water and sprayed over the entire compost surface. All preparations are thus used in homoeopathic quantities. Each compost preparation is designed to guide a particular decomposition process in the composting mass.

One study found that the oak bark preparation improved disease resistance in zucchini.

Astronomical Planting Calendar

The approach considers that there are astronomical influences on soil and plant development, specifying, for example, what phase of the moon is most appropriate for planting, cultivating or harvesting various kinds of crops. This aspect of biodynamics has been termed 'astrological' in nature.

Treatment of Pests and Weeds

Biodynamic agriculture sees the basis of pest and disease control arising from a strong healthy balanced farm organism. Where this is not yet achieved it uses techniques analogous to fertilization for pest control and weed control. Most of these techniques include using the ashes of a pest or weed that has been trapped or picked from the fields and burnt. A biodynamic farmer perceives weeds and plant vulnerability to pests as a result of imbalances in the soil.

Pests such as insects or field mice (*Apodemus*) have more complex processes associated with them, depending on what pest is to be targeted. For example field mice are to be countered by deploying ashes prepared from field mice skin when Venus is in the Scorpius constellation.

Weeds are combated (besides the usual mechanical methods) by collecting seeds from the weeds and burning them above a wooden flame that was kindled by the weeds. The ashes from the seeds are then spread on the fields, then lightly sprayed with the clear urine of a sterile cow (the urine should be exposed to the full moon for six hours), this is intended to block the influence from the full moon on the particular weed and make it infertile.

Seed Production

Biodynamic agriculture has focussed on open pollination of seeds (permitting farmers to grow their own seed) and the development of locally adapted varieties. The seed stock is not controlled by large, multinational seed companies.

Trademark Protection of term Biodynamic

The term *Biodynamic* is a trademark held by the Demeter association of biodynamic farmers for the purpose of maintaining production standards used both in farming and processing foodstuffs.(This is not a trademark held privately in New Zealand) The trademark is intended to protect both the consumer and the producers of biodynamic produce. Demeter International is an organization of member countries; each country has its own Demeter organization which is required to meet international production standards (but can also exceed them). The original Demeter organization was founded in 1928; the U.S. Demeter Association was formed in the 1980s and certified its first farm in 1982. In France, Biodivin certifies biodynamic wine. In Egypt, SEKEM has created the Egyptian Biodynamic Association (EBDA), an association that provides training for farmers to become certified.

Studies of Efficacy

Studies have compared biodynamic farming methods to both other organic methods and to conventional methods. Most studies have found that biodynamic farms have soil quality significantly better than conventionally farmed soils but comparable to the soil quality achieved by other organic methods; the decisive factor is likely to be the use of compost. Studies of yields differ in their conclusions.

A 1993 study compared soil quality and financial performance of Biodynamic and conventional farms in New Zealand. The study reported that, "The Biodynamic farms proved in most enterprises to have soils of higher biological and physical quality: significantly greater in organic matter, content and microbial activity, more earthworms, better soil structure, lower bulk density, easier penetrability, and thicker topsoil." The biodynamic farms were just as financially viable on a per hectare basis. The study compared biodynamic farms with adjacent conventional farms, but didn't attempt to compare farms of similar size, or with similar crops.

A further study investigated whether biodynamic preparations had any effect on the yield and growth of lentil and wheat crops, weed populations and soil fertility in the short term. The study found that "in general, soils and crops treated with biodynamic preparations showed few differences from those not treated". Plots tended with biodynamically treated compost produced results for yield, crop quality and soil fertility that were similar to those tended with non-biodynamic composts and NPK fertilizers. Some alteration was observed in the nitrogenous chemistry of the soil and grain where biodynamic field sprays were applied, however the study did not ascribe or discern any biological significance to the difference. Among the variables considered by the study, some measured outcomes correlated with biodynamic field spray usage, including a higher per-unit biomass yield ratio for lentils and a lowering of carbon and crude protein contents in wheat grains. The study's conclusion remarked that "any additional short-term benefits from biodynamic preparations remain questionable".

A long-term study conducted at a commercial vineyard in California compared vineyard blocks treated with biodynamic preparations alongside those tended with general organic farming methods, to examine effects upon soil and crop quality. "No differences were found in soil quality" during the first six years of the study, and analyses of other indicators including the yield per vine, clusters per vine, cluster and berry weight also showed there were no differences. The study did find a statistically significant (p-value < 0.05) difference in the yield-to-pruning weight ratio, indicating an "ideal vine balance for producing high-quality wine grapes" for the biodynamically treated crop, but noted the control vines had been 'slightly overcropped'. In one particular year of the study the biodynamically treated wine grapes had significantly higher Brix and notably higher total phenols and anthocyanins. In conclusion, the study found that biodynamic preparations 'may affect' the vine canopy and chemistry, but showed no effects on the soil and tissue nutrient parameters measured in the study.

A 21-year study by the FiBL Institute in Switzerland compared the agronomic and ecological performance of biodynamic, organic and two conventional systems. The study found that nutrient input in the biodynamic and organic systems was 34 to 51 per cent lower than in the conventional systems but crop yield was only 20 per cent lower on average, indicating more efficient production. The total energy (for fuel, production of mineral fertilizer and pesticides, etc.) to produce a dry-matter unit of crop was 20 to 56 per cent lower for the biodynamic and organic systems, and pesticide input was reduced by 97 per cent (by 100% for the biodynamic system). In regard to soil aggregate stability, soil pH, humus formation, soil calcium, microbial biomass, and faunal biomass (earthworms and arthropods), the biodynamic system was superior even to the organic system, which in turn had superior results over the conventional systems. With the significant increase in microbial diversity in the biodynamic and organic systems, there was a significant associated decrease in metabolic quotient, indicating a greater ability to use organic material for plant growth.

25 Compost

Compost is plant matter that has been decomposed and recycled as a fertilizer and soil amendment. Compost is a key ingredient in organic farming. At its most essential, the process of composting requires simply piling up waste outdoors and waiting a year or more. Modern, methodical composting is a multi-step, closely monitored process with measured inputs of water, air and carbon-and nitrogen-rich materials. The decomposition process is aided by shredding the plant matter, adding water and ensuring proper aeration by regularly turning the mixture. Worms and fungi further break up the material. Aerobic bacteria manage the chemical process by converting the inputs into heat, carbon dioxide and ammonium. The ammonium is further refined by bacteria into plant-nourishing nitrites and nitrates.

Compost can be rich in nutrients. It is used in gardens, landscaping, horticulture, and agriculture. The compost itself is beneficial for the land in many ways, including as a soil conditioner, a fertilizer, addition of vital humus or humic acids, and as a natural pesticide for soil. In ecosystems, compost is useful for erosion control, land and stream reclamation, wetland construction, and as landfill cover.

Composting as a recognized practice dates to at least the early Roman era since Pliny the Elder (AD 23-79) who refers to compost in his writings. Traditionally, composting was to pile organic materials and let them stand for about a year, or until the next planting season, at which time the materials would be ready for soil application. The main advantage of this method is that little working time or effort is required from the composter and it fits in naturally with agricultural practices in temperate climates. Disadvantages (from the modern perspective) are that space is used for a whole year, some nutrients might be leached due to exposure to rainfall, and disease producing organisms, some weed, weed seeds and insects may not be adequately controlled.

Composting was somewhat modernized beginning in the 1920 in Europe as a tool for organic farming. The first industrial station for the transformation of urban organic materials into compost was set up in Wels/ Austria in the year 1921. The early personages most cited for propounding composting within farming are for the German-speaking world Rudolf Steiner, founder of a farming method called biodynamics, and Annie Francé-Harrar, who was appointed on behalf of the government in Mexico and supported the country 1950-1958 to set up a large humus organization in the fight against erosion and soil degradation. In the English-speaking world it was Sir Albert Howard who worked extensively in India on sustainable practices and Lady Eve Balfour who was a huge proponent of composting. Composting was imported to America by various followers of these early European movements in the form of persons such as J.I. Rodale (founder of Rodale Organic Gardening), E.E. Pfeiffer (who developed scientific practices in biodynamic farming), Paul Keene (founder of Walnut Acres in Pennsylvania), and Scott and Helen Nearing (who inspired the back-to-land movement of the 1960s). Coincidentally, some of these personages met briefly in India — all were quite influential in the U.S. from the 1960s into the 1980s.

There are many modern proponents of rapid composting which attempt to correct some of the perceived problems associated with traditional, slow composting. Many advocate that compost can be made in 2 to 3 weeks. Many such short processes involve a few changes to traditional methods, including smaller, more homogenized pieces in the compost, controlling carbon to nitrogen (CN) ratio at 30 to 1 or less, and monitoring the moisture level more carefully. However, none of these parameters differ significantly from early writings of Howard and Balfour, suggesting that in fact modern composting has not made significant advances over the traditional methods which take a few months to work. For this reason and others, many modern scientists who deal with carbon transformations are sceptical that there is a 'super-charged' way to get nature to make compost rapidly. They also point to the fact that it is the structure of the natural molecules — such as carbohydrates, proteins, and cellulose — that really dictate the rate at which microbial-mediated transformations are possible.

Ingredients

Home compost barrel in the Escuela Barreales, Chile.

Composting organisms require four equally important things to work effectively:

- *Carbon* — for energy; the microbial oxidation of carbon produces the heat.
- High carbon materials tend to be brown and dry.
- *Nitrogen* — to grow and reproduce more organisms to oxidize the carbon.
- High nitrogen materials tend to be green (or colourful, such as fruits and vegetables) and wet.
- *Oxygen* – for oxidizing the carbon, the decomposition process.
- *Water* — in the right amounts to maintain activity without causing anaerobic conditions.

Certain ratios of these materials will provide beneficial bacteria with the nutrients to work at a rate that will heat up the pile. In that process much water will be released as [evaporation | vapour] ('steam'), and the oxygen will be quickly depleted, explaining the need to actively manage the pile. The hotter the pile gets, the more often added air and water is necessary; the air/water balance is critical to maintaining high temperatures until the materials are broken down. At the same time, too much air or water also slows the process, as does too much carbon (or too little nitrogen).

The most efficient composting occurs with a carbon:nitrogen mix of about 30 to 1. Nearly all plant and animal materials have both carbon and nitrogen, but amounts vary widely, with characteristics noted above (dry/wet, brown/green). Fresh grass clippings have an average ratio of about 15 to 1 and dry autumn leaves about 50 to 1 depending on species. Mixing equal parts by volume approximates the ideal C:N range. Few individual situations will provide the ideal mix of materials at any point in time - in this respect, home composting is like horseshoes, perfect is great, but close still works. Observation of amounts, and consideration of different materials as a pile is built over time, can quickly achieve a workable technique for the individual situation.

Urine

People excrete far more of certain water-soluble plant nutrients (nitrogen, phosphorus, potassium) in urine than in feces. Human urine can be used directly as fertilizer or it can be put onto compost. Adding a healthy person's urine to compost usually will increase temperatures and therefore increase its ability to destroy pathogens and unwanted seeds.

Urine from a person with no obvious symptoms of infection, is generally much more sanitary than fresh feces. Unlike feces, urine doesn't attract disease-spreading flies (such as house flies or blow flies), and it doesn't harbour the most hardy of pathogens, such as parasitic worm eggs. Urine usually does not stink for long, particularly when it is fresh, diluted, or put on sorbents.

Urine is primarily composed of water and urea. Although metabolites of urea are nitrogen fertilizers, it is easy to over-fertilize with urine creating too much ammonia for plants to absorb, acidic conditions, or other phytotoxicity.

Micro-organisms

With the proper mixture of water, oxygen, carbon, and nitrogen, micro-organisms are allowed to break down organic matter to produce compost. The composting process is dependant on micro-organisms to break down organic matter into compost. There are many types of microorganisms found in active compost of which the most common are:

- *Bacteria* — The most numerous of all the microorganisms found in compost.
- *Actinomycetes* — Necessary for breaking down paper products such as newspaper, bark, etc.
- *Fungi* — Molds and yeast help break down materials that bacteria cannot, especially lignin in woody material.
- *Protozoa* — Help consume bacteria, fungi and micro organic particulates.
- *Rotifers* — Rotifers help control populations of bacteria and small protozoans.

In addition, earthworms not only ingest partly composted material, but also continually re-create aeration and drainage tunnels as they move through the compost.

A lack of a healthy micro-organisms community is the main reason why composting processes are slow in landfills with environmental factors such as lack of oxygen, nutrients or water being the cause of the depleted biological community.

Uses

Compost is generally recommended as an additive to soil, or other matrices such as coir and peat, as a tilth improver, supplying humus and nutrients. It provides a rich *growing medium*, or a porous, absorbent material that holds moisture and soluble minerals, providing the support and nutrients in which plants can flourish, although it is rarely used alone, being primarily mixed with soil, sand, grit, bark chips, vermiculite, perlite, or clay granules to produce loam.

Generally, direct seeding into a compost is not recommended due to the speed with which it may dry and the possible presence of phytotoxins which may inhibit germination, and the possible tie up of nitrogen by incompletely decomposed lignin. It is very common to see blends of 20-30 per cent compost used for transplanting seedlings at cotyledon stage or later.

Destroying Pathogens, Seeds, or Unwanted Plants

Composting can destroy pathogens or unwanted seeds. Unwanted living plants (or weeds) can be destroyed by covering with mulch/compost.

The "microbial pesticides" in compost may include thermophiles and mesophiles, however certain composting detritivores such as black soldier fly larvae and redworms, also reduce many pathogens. Thermophilic (high-temperature) composting is well known to destroy many seeds and nearly all types of pathogens (exceptions may include prions). However, thermophilic composting requires a fair amount of material, around a cubic meter.

The sanitizing qualities of (thermophilic) composting are desirable where there is a high likelihood of pathogens, such as with manure. Applications include humanure composting or the deep litter technique.

TYPES

Compost Tea

Compost tea is a liquid solution or suspension made by steeping compost in water. It is used as both a fertilizer and in attempts to prevent plant diseases. The liquid is applied as a spray to non-edible plant parts, or as a soil-drench (root dip), such as seedlings, or as a surface spray to reduce incidence of harmful phytopathogenic fungi in the phyllosphere.

Vermicompost

Vermicompost is the product of composting utilizing various species of worms, usually red wigglers, white worms, and earthworms to create a heterogeneous mixture of decomposing vegetable or food waste, bedding materials, and vermicast. Vermicast, also known as worm castings, worm humus or worm manure, is the end-product of the breakdown of organic matter by species of earthworm.

The earthworm species (or composting worms) most often used are Red Wigglers (*Eisenia foetida* or *Eisenia andrei*), though European nightcrawlers (*Eisenia hortensis*) could also be used. Users refer to European nightcrawlers by a variety of other names, including *dendrobaenas*, *dendras*, and Belgian nightcrawlers.

Containing water-soluble nutrients, vermicompost is a nutrient-rich organic fertilizer and soil conditioner.

Bokashi Composting

Bokashi is a method of intensive composting. It can use an aerobic or anaerobic inoculation to produce the compost. Once a starter culture is made, it can be used to extend the culture indefinitely, like yogurt culture. Since the popular introduction of effective microorganisms (EM), Bokashi is commonly made with only molasses, water, EM, and wheat bran.

In home composting applications, kitchen waste is placed into a container which can be sealed with an air tight lid. These scraps are then inoculated with a Bokashi EM mix. This usually takes the form of a carrier, such as rice hulls, wheat bran or saw dust, that has been inoculated with composting micro-organisms. The EM are natural lactic acid bacteria, yeast, and phototrophic bacteria that act as a microbe community within the kitchen scraps, fermenting and accelerating breakdown of the organic matter. The user would place alternating layers of food scraps and Bokashi mix until the container is full.

Hugelkultur

The practice of making raised beds filled with rotting wood. It is in effect creating a Nurse log though covered with dirt. The buried decomposing wood will give off heat, as all compost does, for several years. This effect has been used by Sepp Holzer for one to allow fruit trees to survive at otherwise inhospitable temperatures and altitudes.

Alternative to Landfilling

As concern about landfill space increases, worldwide interest in recycling by means of composting is growing, since composting is a process for converting decomposable organic materials into useful stable products. Industrial scale composting in the form of in-vessel composting, aerated static pile composting, and anaerobic digestion takes place in most Western countries now, and in many areas is mandated by law. There are process and product guidelines in Europe that date to the early 1980s (Germany, Holland, Switzerland) and only more recently in the UK and the US. In both these countries, private trade associations within the industry have established loose standards, some say as a stop-gap measure to discourage independent government agencies from establishing tougher consumer-friendly standards. The USA is the only Western country that does not distinguish sludge-source compost from green-composts, and by default in the USA 50 per cent of states expect composts to comply in some manner with the federal EPA 503 rule promulgated in 1984 for sludge products. Compost is regulated in Canada and Australia as well.

Industrial Systems

Industrial composting systems are increasingly being installed as a waste management alternative to landfills, along with other advanced waste processing systems. Mechanical sorting of mixed waste streams combined with anaerobic digestion or in-vessel composting, is called mechanical biological treatment, increasingly used in developed countries due to regulations controlling the amount of organic matter allowed in landfills. Treating biodegradable waste before it enters a landfill reduces global warming from fugitive methane; untreated waste breaks down anaerobically in a landfill, producing landfill gas that contains methane, a potent greenhouse gas.

Large-scale composting systems are used by many urban centres around the world. Co-composting is a technique which combines solid waste with de-watered biosolids, although difficulties controlling inert and plastic contamination from municipal solid waste makes this approach less attractive. The world's largest MSW co-composter is the Edmonton Composting Facility in Edmonton, Alberta, Canada, which turns 220,000 tonnes of residential solid waste and 22,500 dry tonnes of biosolids per year into 80,000 tonnes of compost.

Uses of Compost

Compost is a versatile product resulting from composting — the biodegradation of organic waste, industrially, commercially or domestically produced. The basic use is conditioning and fertilizing soil by the addition of humus, nutrients and beneficial soil bacteria, with a wide range of specific applications.

Open ground: For growing wheat, corn, soybeans, and similar crops, compost theoretically can be broadcast across the top of the soil using spreader trucks or spreaders pulled behind a tractor. It is expected that the spread layer is very thin (approximately 6 mm (0.25 in.)) and worked into the soil prior to planting. However, application rates of 25 mm (one in.) or more are not unusual when trying to rebuild poor soils or control erosion. Due to the extremely high cost of compost per unit of nutrients in the western world (such as USA) on-farm use is relatively rare since rates over 4 tons/acre can not be afforded. This is unfortunate and results from over-emphasis on 'recycling organic matter' than on 'sustainable nutrients'. In other countries such as Germany, where compost distribution and spreading are partially subsidized in the original waste fees, compost is used more frequently on open ground, but only on the premise of nutrient 'sustainability'.

Plasticulture: Strawberries, tomatoes, peppers, melons, and other fruits and vegetables are often grown under plastic to control temperature, retain moisture and control weeds. Compost may be banded (applied in strips along rows) and worked into the soil prior to bedding and planting, be applied at the same time the beds are constructed and plastic laid down, or used as a 'top dressing'.

Transplant mix: Many crops are not seeded directly in the field but are started in seed trays in a greenhouse. When the seedlings reach a certain stage of growth, they are transplanted in the field. Compost can be used as an ingredient in the mix used to grow the seedlings, but is not normally used as the only planting substrate. The crop to be grown and the seeds' sensitivity to nutrients, salts, etc. dictates the ratio of the blend, and maturity is important to insure that oxygen deprivation will not occur or that no lingering phyto-toxins remain.

Horticulture

Bedding mixes: Compost can be mixed with sand, clay, aged sawdust, and other materials to create an enriched mix for landscape beds or raised-bed gardens. Compost should be no more than 30 per cent of the total mix. Use a high quality mature compost to avoid nutrient and oxygen competition with plants.

Container mixes: Like bedding mixes, compost may be a beneficial ingredient in potting media, used up to 30 per cent of the total mix, depending on salinity and maturity. It is considered a partial substitute for peat moss, but generally lacks the porosity and water-holding capacity of peat so must be used in limited percentages. The nutrient content of compost can also reduce the need for supplement chemical fertilizers, although this has to be determined in each situation.

Foundation plantings: Excavated areas around the foundation of new buildings are backfilled when construction is complete, but these planting zones may contain rubble, residues of toxic chemicals, and other undesirable substances. Removing the backfill and replacing it with a soil/compost mix will improve soil structure and give foundation plantings a healthier start.

Mulch/weed control: Two or more inches of compost can be used alone or in conjunction with conventional mulch products to keep root zones cool, conserve moisture, and act as a slow-release fertilizer, provided the product is course textured and mature. For a weed barrier, double or triple the depth of compost can be used, placed on top of a thick layer of newspapers, to replace geomembrane weed barriers. This is obviously only true if the compost is weed free; many are not.

Trees and shrubs: Mix *well aged* compost with the native soil and use as backfill when planting trees and shrubs. Immature composts may cause settling and young root disturbance due to oxygen deprivation. Seasonally, top dress with compost to the drip line and rake into the soil.

Turf and pasture management: To establish new turf areas (lawns, recreation fields, golf courses), apply compost prior to seeding or sodding and work into the soil. Seasonally, top dress with compost and rake into the soil. Some turf farms also use compost, growing grass in a couple of inches of the material to prevent topsoil loss.

Erosion Control

Topsoil loss is a serious planetary issue. The use of compost to control sediment run-off and fight erosion is a relatively new technology, now being adopted by local authorities, developers, farmers, and other major disturbers of soil as another tool to reduce topsoil loss.

Compost blankets: A layer of compost spread over a disturbed area of soil is called a compost blanket. With a high water-holding capacity, compost is not tilled into the soil but remains on the surface to temper the impact of rainfall. Even small amounts can help, but typical recommendations call for a 5 cm (2 in.) layer to insure adequate surface coverage. The blanket can also be directly planted into.

Compost berms and filter socks: Compost berms and socks are used alone or in conjunction with compost blankets to mitigate the impact of high volume water discharges and flows. Compost berms are more aesthetically pleasing than silt fences and eliminate the need to remove the berm when the project is complete. Over time, a compost berm simply biodegrades and returns to the earth. As the name implies, a compost sock is a mesh tube stuffed with compost. Socks stand up better to heavy equipment, can be anchored in place, and are easily removed/reused. If a biodegradable fibre is used for the sock, it can also be left in place to biodegrade. This is rarely if ever practiced, however, since it defeats the idea of the sock.

Special Uses

Constructed wetlands: Compost is used as a planting media for constructed or artificial wetlands.

Landfill cover: When a landfill cell is closed, compost can be added to the soil used to cap the cell to encourage vegetation and reduce erosion.

Streambank restoration: Erosion along streambanks threatens trees and property, but the use of compost can not only restore functionality and beauty to riparian zones, but also mitigate future damage.

Regulation and Voluntary Standards

EPA Class A and B guidelines in the U.S.A. were developed solely to manage the processing and beneficial reuse of sludge, also now called biosolids, following the US EPA ban of ocean dumping. About 26 American states now require composts to be processed according to these federal protocols for pathogen and vector control, even though the application to non-sludge materials has not been scientifically tested. For example green waste composts are used at much higher rates than sludge composts were ever anticipated to be applied at. U.K guidelines also exist regarding compost quality, as well as Canadian, Australian, and the various European states.

In the USA some compost manufacturers participate in a testing programme offered the U.S. Composting Council, a private lobbying organization for the industry. The USCC was originally established to promote composting of disposable diapers, but ultimately the idea was aboned. The current quality guidelines of the USCC called 'Seal of Testing Assurance' ('STA') programme, and for a fee, the applicant may display the USCC logo, agreeing to volunteer to customers a current laboratory analysis that includes parameters established by the private consultant-run group on certain nutrients, respiration rate, salt content, pH, and other indicators . However, the STA programme is not ISO approved, and is a financially beneficial activity for the USCC. By approving all products that pay the fee, and being monitored by consultants to the industry, it is not likely to be recognized as a bona-fide quality standard.

Index